Reclaiming Iraq

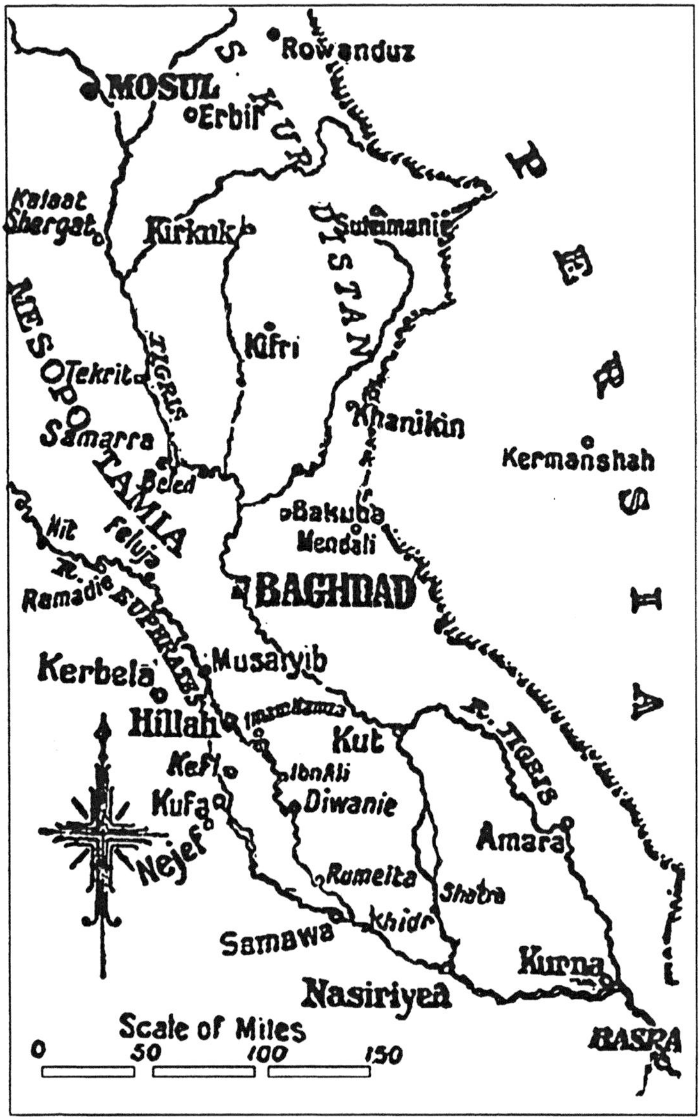

MAP 1.1. *Iraq in 1920.* Times *(London), 3 September 1920.*

Reclaiming Iraq

THE 1920 REVOLUTION AND THE FOUNDING OF THE MODERN STATE

By Abbas Kadhim

University of Texas Press *Austin*

Printed in the United States of America
First edition, 2012

♾ The paper used in this book meets the minimum requirements of ANSI/NISO Z39.48-1992 (R1997) (Permanence of Paper).

LIBRARY OF CONGRESS CATALOGING-IN-PUBLICATION DATA
Kadhim, Abbas K.
Reclaiming Iraq : the 1920 revolution and the founding of the modern state / by Abbas K. Kadhim. — 1st ed.
p. cm.
Includes bibliographical references and index.
ISBN 978-0-292-75689-2
1. Iraq—History—Revolt, 1920. 2. Iraq—History—Autonomy and independence movements. I. Title.
DS79.K34 2012
956.704'1—dc23
First paperback edition, 2013 2012016104

To Bushra, Ali, Huda, and Hussein

Contents

Acknowledgments

IN WRITING THIS BOOK, I FELL IN DEBT TO MANY people who made my undertaking fruitful. Dr. Muhammad Abu Ṭabīkh and the late Dr. Ali Abu Ṭabīkh, sons of Sayyid Muḥsin Abu Ṭabīkh, kindly provided me with much-needed access to personal information about their father's struggle during the 1920s and 1930s, including many previously untold stories. Our many telephone interviews were often taxing, and they generously accepted the burden. I also owe special gratitude to Dr. Jamil Abu Ṭabīkh, who made available many documents, including a copy of the unedited version of his father's memoirs, and provided much help during my September 2006 research trip to London.

Many thanks are owed also to all the authors whose previous works on the history of Iraq and the era covered by this book were tremendously helpful for me, for both the insight they provided and the approaches they used in examining the events leading to and accompanying the revolution.

Professor Robert Gregg of Stanford University facilitated my access to materials held there. Also, I owe a great debt of gratitude to my colleague Professor Robert Looney, who read and commented on earlier versions of the manuscript or parts of it. My lifelong friend Dr. Hassan Nadhem was with me throughout the research and writing and provided tremendous help and advice.

The Center for Middle Eastern Studies at the University of California, Berkeley, and the Center for Comparative Studies in Race and

Ethnicity at Stanford University sponsored lectures in November 2006 and June 2007 at which I presented my ongoing research results.

Zooey Lober, Irma Fink, and Daryle Carlson at the library of the Naval Postgraduate School, in Monterey, California, worked tirelessly to bring me many books from faraway places and made my research possible. I cannot thank them enough.

The two anonymous reviewers were the best experts any author could hope to have. Their notes, questions, and suggestions enriched the manuscript and gave me invaluable insight. Falah Raheem, a prominent Iraqi critic, read the final manuscript and provided important feedback on many theoretical aspects. At the University of Texas Press, Jim Burr took an early interest in the manuscript and sponsored it with grace and efficiency; Lynne Chapman directed the production of the book; Nancy Bryan worked tirelessly with me in the final stages of production; and Kip Keller copyedited the text. Also, Kaila Wyllys and Regina Fuentes devoted great effort during the production phase.

Finally, my wife, Bushra, and my children, Ali, Huda, and Hussein, have sacrificed a great deal for the past five years while I was on research trips, in the library, or at my desk.

INTRODUCTION

State-sponsored history writing and cultural production complement the state's use of violence.

ERIC DAVIS, *MEMORIES OF STATE*

THE 1920 REVOLUTION FOUGHT BY IRAQIS AGAINST British occupation was a seminal event in the history of modern Iraq. Anti-British fighters, predominantly tribal Shīʿa in the Middle Euphrates region, engaged the thinly stretched occupation forces in a series of battles between June and November 1920, costing the British thousands of casualties and more than £40 million. This often-cited figure is the direct cost of the revolution. In its total cost, direct and indirect, the revolution "demanded the employment of 65,000 troops to quell it and the expenditure of £100,000,000 by the Imperial Exchequer."[1] This Middle Euphrates revolution came after a number of violent episodes that occurred immediately after the British invaded southern Iraq, then part of the Ottoman Empire, in 1914, during an early campaign of World War I. But none of these episodes of resistance can be compared to the 1920 Revolution in their intensity, impact, and scale of popular participation.

When the British invasion of southern Iraq became imminent, a group of Baṣra residents sent a message on 9 November 1914 to the clergy in the holy cities, asking them to "help by ordering the tribes to defend" the city.[2] By 16 December, the leading *mujtahid* in Iraq, Sayyid Kadhim al-Yazdi, spoke from the podium of the Imam Ali shrine in Najaf, ordering the people "to defend the Islamic territories and mandating that those unable to participate in fighting provide money to contribute financially for enabling those who are physically able to participate."[3] Similar measures were taken by the Shīʿa mujtahids in Karbalāʾ, Baghdad, and Sāmarrāʾ—some of them even joined the tribal fighters and assumed leading or support positions. This effort resulted in the first successful battle against the British forces, fought at Rōṭa, east of the Tigris, on 18 January 1915. The tribal and Ottoman forces, led by General Sulayman ʿAskari and the mujtahid Sayyid Mahdi al-Ḥaydari, managed to stop a British assault and force the attacking units to retreat.[4] The next engagement against the British took place four months later at the celebrated battle of Shaʿaiba, near Baṣra, and involved 6,000 Ottoman troops and approximately 20,000 tribal fighters. Ignoring the advice of tribal leaders to put the British under siege, Sulayman ʿAskari ordered an attack on the British forces, and on the third day of fighting, just as the British were getting ready to withdraw, he ordered his troops to stop the attack; the Iraqis ended up losing the battle.[5]

While the tribal fighters and the mujtahids stood firm in their support of the Ottomans, the latter continued their centuries-long oppression of the Shīʿa cities. In November 1916, a force led by ʿĀkif Bey attacked Ḥilla, burning many houses and killing more than 1,500 people. The Ottomans also transferred a number of townspeople, including women and children to Anatolia, resulting in the deaths of many during the journey. Before leaving the devastated city, ʿĀkif Bey ordered the hanging of 126 men.[6] This atrocity caused a great deal of disillusion among the Iraqis. On 11 December 1916, Shaykh ʿAbd al-Ḥusayn Maṭar sent a letter from the battlefield to Sayyid Kadhim al-Yazdi in Najaf, asking him to issue a fatwa concerning the Ḥilla atrocity and informing him about the confusion it caused among the tribes.[7]

At the time, the city of Najaf was autonomously governed by a council of its local leaders.[8] Its fight against the Ottomans began on 22 May 1915, when the Najafis engaged the city's Ottoman unit for three days and forced its members to surrender. This defiance of the Ottoman authority spread among other cities in the Middle Euphrates: Karbalāʾ, Ḥilla, Samāwa, Ṭwairīj, Kūfa, and Shāmiyya.[9] But unlike the other cities, where local rule did not last very long, Najaf remained under the collective management of its local leaders until July 1917, when the British appointed Captain Balfour as political officer for Shāmiyya and Najaf. Balfour moved his residence out of the holy city, and his Muslim deputy, Ḥamīd Khan, represented the British inside Najaf.

The relation between the Najafis and the British remained nonconfrontational until October 1917, when a large caravan came to the city with a letter to Ḥamīd Khan, asking him to facilitate the purchase of a large amount of grain to be taken to Ramadi. The news caused prices to rise significantly. The followers of ʿAṭayya Abu Gilal, the leader of the ʿImara section of Najaf, attacked the caravan, killing a few camels and looting some goods and rifles. As relations between the two groups deteriorated, the British felt the need to bring forces to the city, in violation of their previous promises to ʿAṭayya Abu Gilal and the Najaf mujtahids. After several confrontations between Najafis and British troops, a man named Najm al-Baqqāl formed a group of fighters who took matters into their own hands; on 18 March 1918, they assassinated Captain Marshal, the political officer who had replaced Ḥamīd Khan on 1 February 1918.

This act and several ensuing incidents constituted a citywide uprising in Najaf. The British put the city under siege for more than forty days, denying the residents access to food and water. When all attempts to lift the siege failed, including persistent letters from the leading mujtahid, Sayyid Kadhim al-Yazdi, to the British commanders, the Najafis tried to seek help from the tribes, but their messenger was caught crossing British lines, and executed. Unable to endure the siege, the city agreed to British demands. More than a hundred Najafis surrendered and were taken to Kūfa for temporary detention. After a short time, sixty-five of them were sent into exile in India, while the others had to face a military tribunal. Eleven of the detainees were sentenced to death, and the others received prison terms ranging from six years to life. The hangings took place on 30 May 1918, and Najaf came back under British control.

These uprisings were local, short-lived, and limited in their consequences. But the Iraqis had learned a critical lesson: no successful uprising could be achieved without the involvement of the tribes. In addition to the tribes' long history of fighting the Ottomans and their intertribal violence, they enjoyed an advantage the cities did not possess: they could not be placed under siege. Their region was vast; they had abundant water and food supplies; and they could engage the British in a fierce fight for a long time. This was exactly what took place between June and November 1920, and it was the main reason why the revolution became the most important anti-British resistance movement in Iraq.

Furthermore, the condition of Iraq during the 1920 Revolution was different from that of any previous period in its modern history. The population, except for a minority of the affluent, was united against a domineering British occupation that had replaced the equally exploitative four-century-long Ottoman occupation. The Ottomans had become the self-appointed protectors of Sunni Islam after the forced conversion of Iran to Shīʿism by the Safavids, who in turn became the self-appointed protectors of the world's Shīʿa in the sixteenth century. The Shīʿa of Iraq were put in a precarious position as their country became a battlefield between those two empires. Selim I (ruled 1512–1520) retaliated against the Safavid persecution of Iranian Sunnis by instituting an inquisition of his own.[10] He managed to extract from his clergy a fatwa that declared the Shīʿa unbelievers, and as a result, he killed approximately 40,000 of them.[11] These massacres continued throughout the Ottoman era. The final Ottoman conquest of Iraq was supremely sectarian. Murad IV (ruled 1623–1640) is said to have killed 50,000 Shīʿa. Dāūd Pasha, a Mamluk ruler, put the city of Karbalāʾ under siege for five years (1825–1830); ten years later, Karbalāʾ again came under assault when Najīb Pasha sacked the holy city and massacred more than 20,000 of its residents.[12]

Whatever the Ottomans did not commit with their own hands, they allowed to be committed on their watch. The Saudi-Wahhabi atrocity of 1802 in Karbalāʾ is a case in point. The Ottomans' failure (perhaps unwillingness) to defend the city facilitated its sacking, proudly described by a Saudi historian:

> The Muslims [i.e., the Wahhabis] scaled the walls, entered the city by force and killed the majority of its people in the markets and in their homes. Then they destroyed the dome placed over the grave of al-Ḥusayn by those who believe in such things . . . They took everything they found in town: different

> types of property, weapons, clothing, carpets, gold, silver, precious copies of the Qur'an, as well as much else — more than can be enumerated.[13]

The Sunnis of Iraq were not in a better situation. The Ottomans mistreated them on the account of their ethnicity and generally neglected their needs and aspirations. This injurious history is perhaps the reason for the initial tolerance of the British invasion, which promised the Iraqis prosperity and self-determination.

When these promises proved to be illusory, both Sunni and Shīʿa Iraqis, who had engaged each other in periodic violence since the seventh century, found a common foe that united them, albeit temporarily, in the hope for autonomy and freedom. By the end of World War I, British promises of liberation and self-determination had evaporated, and Iraqis began to encounter a foreign administration that was there to stay. At Versailles, Britain advanced the imperial argument that the former Mesopotamian provinces of the Ottoman Empire were as yet incapable of managing their own affairs; the British Empire was eventually awarded the League of Nations' mandate for the region.[14] These conditions united Iraqis of all backgrounds against both the British and a small number of Iraqis whose economic interests or political ambitions led them to support the British administration.

In response to the British occupation, Shīʿa and Sunnis set aside their sectarian differences and attended prayers in the same mosques and participated in each other's rituals — Sunnis participated in commemorating the martyrdom of Imam Ḥusayn (d. AD 681), and the Shīʿa attended the Sunni chanting rituals at the Prophet's birthday (*mawālid*). Sunnis also participated in the service gatherings after the death of the leading mujtahid, Sayyid Kadhim al-Yazdi, in the summer of 1919.

There was also a significant involvement of other minorities in these activities. Muslims from both sects participated in Christian celebrations, and Christians offered greetings during the Muslim religious celebrations on 18 June 1920. A high-profile delegation of Jewish leaders visited their Muslim counterparts in an "unprecedented scenario" of multiconfessional solidarity.[15] This national rapprochement continued throughout 1920, notwithstanding the positions taken by some pro-British Iraqis in the major cities.

This book contends that the 1920 Revolution was essentially an uprising carried out by tribal forces, but still takes into account the noncombatant involvement of the urban areas. Intellectuals in Baghdad and other major cities contributed to the ideological framing of the revolution and provided the tribes with valuable awareness and a sense of nationalist direction. But none of the major cities joined in the fighting. The British did not feel any true security threats at all in Baghdad, Baṣra, or Ḥilla. The cities of Karbalāʾ, Najaf, Kūfa, and Dīwāniyya, which ultimately became part of the revolution, did not take part in it because their residents decided to take up arms against the British; instead they were besieged, attacked, and finally captured by the tribes after the British unilaterally decided to evacuate their positions. Those cities where the tribal attacks were not successful, such as Ḥilla, remained under British control. Similarly, when the tribes were being subjected to overwhelming British bombardment, the cities were the first to surrender and to accept all the British conditions, while the tribes remained fighting until the end of the revolution. As soon as the tribes lost the city of Ṭwairīj—between Ḥilla and Karbalāʾ—on 12 October 1920, notables in Karbalāʾ, led by Shaykh Fakhri Kammūna, began to form a committee to negotiate a surrender with the British. The city opened its gates a week later. The same happened to Najaf after the capture of Kūfa. The British captured Kūfa on 17 October 1920, and Najaf surrendered the next day.[16] The early collapse of the cities was a reminder of the lessons learned earlier from the Najaf revolution of 1918: no effective revolution could happen, or persist, without the support and active participation of the tribes.

When the revolution ended and, consequently, the framework of a national government was being contemplated, the bases of alliances shifted from mainly economic and ideological grounds to sectarian ones. The Shīʿa allies of yesteryear were cast aside by the emerging Sunni political elite, merely because the Shīʿa fell on the other side of the sectarian line of division. The British institutionalized this political exclusion, in keeping with their often-expressed anti-Shīʿa sentiment. And in the aftermath of the revolution, its fervent supporters retained nothing but their wounds while its cynical detractors collected the spoils.

SOME TERMS DEFINED

The historiography of the 1920 Revolution has been another example of history written by the victors, the officials of the British administration and the successive Iraqi governments. Without discounting the importance of those sources, this book is an attempt to incorporate the narratives of the vanquished, those who lost the battle but ultimately won the war for Iraq's independence, which was achieved in 1932.

The title *Reclaiming Iraq* refers to the main goal of the revolution: to reclaim Iraq from six and a half centuries of uninterrupted foreign rule (1258–1920). This book is written with the awareness of the argument commonly made by many scholars that there was no "Iraq" before 1921. While acknowledging the technical merits of this argument, we should also note that what is meant by "Iraq" here is not the nation-state that was defined by the League of Nations and granted independence in 1932 following a decade of British tutelage. "Iraq," for the purpose of this book, is the historic territory that carried this name for more than fourteen centuries and was never identified by another name throughout that period.

In his encyclopedia of cities and regions, *Muʿjam al-Buldan,* Yaqūt al-Ḥamawi (d. AD 1225) reserved a lengthy entry titled "al-ʿIraq" and cross-referenced Iraq with another entry titled "al-Sawād." In the latter entry, he situated Iraq from Mosul to Baṣra and from east of the Tigris to west of the Euphrates.[17] A review of Arabic literature and history leads to the firm conclusion that "Iraq" was not invented by the British in the way they invented some of the political entities in the New World. Rather, it has existed for fourteen hundred years as a well-defined place whose people were always called "*Ahl al-ʿIraq*" (the people of Iraq).[18] The Greek word "Mesopotamia," which was common in British sources, was not used by the Arabs before the arrival of the British or during the occupation.

Practically, the British understood the Arabic term "Iraq" differently from the Greek term "Mesopotamia." The former was taken to mean anything below latitude 34° north, while the latter was taken to mean, more or less, the land "lying between the mountains of Kurdistan and the Persian Gulf."[19] This appears to have been one of the main points of dispute between the British and the notables of the Middle

Euphrates during a meeting held in Najaf on 11 January 1918 to prepare for a plebiscite. Muhammad Riḍā al-Shabībi, a Najafi intellectual who spoke on behalf of the Iraqi attendees and who came to play a major role in the 1920 Revolution, and stated the Iraqis' conception of their own territory: "The Iraqi people consider Mosul to be an integral part of Iraq that cannot be carved out." He went on to emphasize what his people expected from the election: "The Iraqis also consider it a right to form a completely independent and national government (*ḥukūma waṭaniyya*). None among us desires to choose a foreign ruler."[20] We notice from this quotation, which is representative of many, that in the mind of the Iraqis, well before 1921, "Iraq" was clearly defined as Yaqūt al-Ḥamawi described it in the thirteenth century AD. Al-Shabībi spoke about Iraq, the Iraqi people (*al-shaʿb al-ʿIraqi*), and the Iraqis (*al-ʿIraqiyyūn*), indicating that Iraqis who revolted against the British did inhabit an Iraq before 1921 and that, in their minds, it was a territory extending from Mosul to Baṣra. The stated purpose of their revolution was to reclaim Iraq from any form of foreign control, not to replace one master with another.

Similarly, when the Iraqi officers reestablished the ʿAhd Association in Damascus, in 1919, their stated goal, articulated in the first point of the association's charter, was "the independence of Iraq . . . within its natural borders which are . . . from the line of the Euphrates north of Dayr al-Zōr and the Tigris River Bank near northern Diyār Bakr to the Gulf of Baṣra. It also includes the banks of the Tigris and the Euphrates east and west, as confined by the natural barriers."[21]

The subtitle of the book refers to the 1920 Revolution, that is, the events that targeted the British occupation in Iraq from June to November 1920. While these events did not follow the patterns of "major revolutions" such as the French Revolution or the Russian Revolution, the definition of revolution used in this book does not rely on the magnitude of the events or the success or failure of their results. Rather, the interest here concerns the levels of public participation, the social and political networks involved in the events, the motives and goals of the participants, and the methods employed to reach those goals.

The historical literature refers to the aforementioned events of 1920 in many ways, ranging from official British pejorative terms of the time, such as "rebellion," "insurrection," and "insurgency," to the more sympathetic "rising," "uprising," and "revolt," which are used by the leading scholars in Iraqi studies. Among the writings of British colonial officials, we encounter the term "revolution" only in Thomas Lyell's book, *The Ins and Outs of Mesopotamia*.[22] The word used in all major Iraqi sources is "*thawra*," which is reserved for "revolution," as opposed to *wathba* and *intifāḍa*, which are used mostly for limited popular uprisings;[23] although the word *thawra* was emptied of its original revolutionary meaning when it began to be officially used for military coups d'état and palace coups that enjoy limited or no popular support. For elderly Iraqis, especially those who use terms that predate Iraq's "republican" era, political change that occurs at the top without popular support or participation is called *ḥaraka* or *inqilāb*.[24] The one important exception in this regard is Mujtahid Hibat al-Dīn al-Shahrastāni, whose participation in the 1920 Revolution cannot be overstated. He rejected the term *thawra*. In praising a book on the revolution by Farīq Mizhir al-Farʿōn and acknowledging the contribution of the author's tribe, al-Shahrastāni says, "I shared with them the work in all of the uprisings (*nahḍāt*) . . . especially our greatest uprising (*nahḍatunā al-kubrā*) in 1920, which the enemies called a revolution."[25] Defending his choice to call it a revolution, Farʿōn inserts the following footnote: "The enemies called this *nahḍa* a revolution (*thawra*), meaning it was a revolution against the occupying government, but I wanted to call it a revolution against oppression and colonization." Farʿōn's explanation was unhelpful, of course, because it implies that a revolution against an "occupying government" is a vice.

Historians writing in English use different terms. Phebe Marr uses the term "revolt," which is the one most frequently used in the literature. It is also used by Charles Tripp, Yitzhak Nakash, and Gareth Stansfield. Peter Sluglett uses the terms "revolt" and "rising" interchangeably, while Hanna Batatu uses "revolt" and "uprising" interchangeably. Eric Davis is the only leading scholar that used the term "revolution."[26] Ghassan Atiyyah, an Iraqi who wrote his dissertation in English and whose father was an important participant in the revolution, describes it as the "1920 rising or revolution, as nationalists prefer to call it." He does not elaborate on his choice, but goes on to drop the term "revolution" in favor of "rising."[27]

The 1920 Revolution was a political revolution, a category of revolutions that "transform state structures but not social structures, and they are not necessarily accomplished through class conflict."[28] Political revolutions can be distinguished from social revolutions, which are, according to one definition, "rapid, basic transformations of a society's state and class structures . . . accompanied and in part carried through by class-based revolts from below."[29] That it was a political revolution is evidenced by the changes it imposed on the existing political structure in Iraq and the reversal of British policy. As Marr accurately describes the impact of the events of June–October 1920:

> Although the British have often claimed that the revolt did not change British policy, the claim is not entirely borne out by the evidence . . . Although the revolt did not achieve Iraqi independence or turn real authority over to the Iraqis, it did succeed in discrediting the India Office policy thoroughly, and it assured a much larger measure of participation by the Iraqis in their first national government.[30]

This statement echoes Philip Ireland's assessment in 1937 that "to Iraqis, the insurrection, although suppressed, has been a National War of Independence, directly responsible for forcing the British Government to set up an Arab Government and, eventually, to grant independence."[31] This opinion, he notes, was endorsed by Arnold Toynbee and Quincy Wright. Among the significant changes in policy was the creation of the modern state of Iraq as we know it today, instead of one based on the War Cabinet plan. Had the revolution not taken place, here is how the British would have organized the country, in accordance with the policy adopted by the War Cabinet after the capture of Baghdad (March 1917):

> Baṣra with Nasiriyeh, Shatt al-Hai, Kut, and Bedrai as its western and northern limits to remain permanently under British Administration . . . Baghdad to be an Arab State with local ruler or government under British protectorate in everything but name . . . Shiah holy places to form separate enclave not under direct British control, care being taken not to include any important irrigated or irrigable areas in it.[32]

The policy to shape Iraq into its current geographic structure, however, was the result of outrage concerning the cost of the revolution, which Sir Percy Cox, the high commissioner in Iraq, and the British government encountered while Cox was in London during the revolution. It was a compromise intended to appease the prevailing official and popular demands for the British to evacuate Iraq. In the words of Cox, establishing a national government was "the only alternative to the withdrawal" from Iraq.[33] This mission to establish an Iraqi national government represented another political consequence of the revolution, "the termination of the existing military administration as Chief British Representative in Mesopotamia."[34] Arnold T. Wilson, who headed the military administration and pursued a governance style mainly informed by the India Office policy outlined above, was replaced by Cox; as civil commissioner he was given the task of forming a national government. Although not the kind hoped for by the revolution, the national government more nearly fulfilled the revolutionary aims than the objectives set by the India Office.

REPOSITIONING THE 1920 REVOLUTION

Historians refer to 1921 as the first year in the modern history of Iraq, mainly because it marks the start of the nation-building project under the British mandate. Likewise, they consider King Fayṣal I (ruled 1921–1932) to be the first Arab head of the Iraqi state after six and a half centuries of foreign rule, from the Mongol invasion in 1258 to the 1918 collapse of the Ottomans and the subsequent British occupation.[35] This book seeks to offer an alternative narrative about the dawn of the Iraqi state: namely, that the modern Iraqi state came into being before the coronation of Fayṣal. After the Najaf uprising in 1915, there was a series of limited local attempts at self-rule. But a true measure of widespread independence came only with the 1920 Revolution, when the Iraqis established an independent government to oversee the areas they liberated from the British. They appointed Sayyid Muḥsin Abu Ṭabīkh as the first Iraqi chief executive, albeit over only a limited part of the country. Significantly, his jurisdiction extended beyond a single city, and the leaders intended to add to it all the Iraqi territories after their liberation from foreign control. The administration was set up temporarily in Karbalā᾽ and enjoyed the full authority to administer justice, collect taxes, keep the peace, and perform all of the functions of an independent government. Its jurisdiction was automatically extended to every territory the tribes captured from the British.

The purpose of emphasizing this first attempt at an Iraqi state is not to minimize the role of Fayṣal I in the founding of modern Iraq, but to tell a story that remains untold in the current literature. As this book demonstrates, the idea of an independent Iraq was not a part of British plans before 1920. The British appointment of Fayṣal was merely a modification of the original Iraqi plan for independence, a move to secure British interests by installing a government more friendly to the empire than the one established by the leaders of the revolution the previous year.

The aim of this book is to examine the 1920 Revolution and its aftermath through the lens of the memoirs of Muḥsin Abu Ṭabīkh, one of the most influential leaders of the revolution and a key power broker in the period that accompanied the establishment of the Iraqi state, as well as the memoirs of other participants in the revolution. These memoirs reveal, inter alia, the mind-set, assumptions, and goals of the men who played leading roles in the revolution. The memoirs also shed light on the collision between the entrenched customs and beliefs predominant in the Middle Euphrates region and an imported model of government that served British interests without providing the conditions for a transition to independence. This coercive process sparked the 1920 Revolution.

The book also examines documents and correspondence from the revolutionary era. These documents shed light on many aspects of the revolution that have not been carefully studied before. They include correspondence between the revolution's leaders, between them and the mujtahids, and between the mujtahids themselves. There are fatwas and other opinions that show the extent of support the revolution enjoyed at the time as a commendable effort to win full independence from any foreign influence.

The main questions this book raises are the following: How can we restore the distorted history of the revolution after many decades of historical examination that have relied mainly on hostile narratives or ones tampered with for various purposes, but seldom on the narratives of the actors themselves? What narrative best describes the events, the motives for them, and their ramifications? And equally importantly, how can we situate the founding events of modern Iraq within the country's historical framework, the beginning of which is currently set a year after the revolution? There are no easy answers to these difficult questions. One of the main contributions of this book is to include, in addition to the British and official Iraqi accounts, a third narrative, one that has thus far been missing or inadequately employed. While this firsthand narrative of the revolutionaries has its own bias as well, adding this element of the revolution supplies some missing parts of the puzzle.

For the last question, it may be argued that by convincingly establishing an earlier date for the founding of the state, we can situate the revolution in its proper place in history and perhaps generate more studies and further analyses of an era that remained too long in the shadow of Iraq's "official" nation building. It is true that the Iraqi state that was declared in Karbalā᾽, headed by Sayyid Muḥsin Abu Ṭabīkh, might not have been truly representative of all Iraqis, but it should not be disregarded in favor of either the one in Baghdad, under ʿAbd al-Raḥmān al-Naqīb, which was handpicked by the British administration and included no representation of the Shīʿa—more than half of Iraqis at the time—among its portfolio ministries,[36] or the throne of Fayṣal, which was established by elaborate British plots and an admittedly rigged referendum.[37] The three models should rather be considered successive stages toward the establishment of a state with increasingly representative government, a quest that is yet to be satisfied. More importantly, this book argues that all of these stages resulted directly from the 1920 Revolution.

This book includes primary sources that were neglected or downplayed in the past. Some of these primary sources were not accessible to previous authors, and so their inclusion here marks an important addition to the existing literature. And although it should go without saying, these firsthand accounts by the history makers themselves and other eyewitnesses were subjected to the same scrutiny as the other primary sources, namely, the British and Iraqi official sources. It was assumed that the revolutionaries and other participants had a stake in the nature of the historical narrative that would prevail about a hotly disputed era. Indeed, these sources themselves talked to, and against, one another. Some of the primary narratives were composed in response to others and for the sole purpose of refuting certain claims by other participants. All this was taken into careful consideration whenever a conclusion relied on these sources.

There are also many points of agreement and substantiation among these sources, and conclusions derived from them were made with confidence. Similarly, there were cases when corroboration took place among primary sources across lines of interest; for example, a revolutionary claim being corroborated by a British source, or vice versa. In other words, every effort was made to search for instances in which independent, unconnected sources supported the same version of events, thereby undercutting any sort of "conspiracy" that might attempt to falsify a claim or a story. An example: the discussion of the British attack on the village of Abu Ḥassān and the atrocities committed there was taken as a fact as narrated in the memoirs of Muḥsin Abu Ṭabīkh, having been fully substantiated by the commander of the British forces, Lieutenant General Haldane. It is not hard for the historian to understand the discrepancy between Abu Ṭabīkh's description of the act as a gratuitous atrocity and Haldane's description of it as an act based on a "rather rash advice."[38]

British sources were also treated open-mindedly. Unlike the common Iraqi view of the British sources, which contends that they all are tainted imperialist accounts written to justify the invasion and occupation of Iraq, this study takes a more nuanced view of these sources. First, it is true that many opinions expressed by British military and civilian officials about Iraq, the Iraqis, and the events of the revolution were made with utter prejudice and were often plagued with ignorance. Examples of this are omnipresent in the writings of Thomas Lyell, James S. Mann, Sir Aylmer Haldane, and even Gertrude Bell and Arnold T. Wilson. Seeing through this bias is not difficult for any historian decently familiar with the culture and social characteristics of the Iraqi people.

Another important aspect of the primary British sources is that they are often written with a sense of undisguised personal vendetta. There is the military-civilian feud, the natural amour propre manifested in the tendency to assign the blame for failure to others, as well as in the many cases of highlighting one's accomplishments when some credit is there to be claimed. Examples of this are found in Haldane's blaming Arnold T. Wilson's administration for failing to do its part in keeping Iraqis quiet and, in response, Wilson's accusing Haldane of incompetence; and on at least one occasion, Wilson described a military decision taken by Haldane as "disgraceful."[39] While Haldane tried to show sympathy with Wilson by declaring that "the bitter criticism to which he has been subjected was undeserved," he made this statement only after saying that the results of his performance "fell short of what was expected."[40] On another occasion, and without naming Wilson, Haldane made a stinging remark about his performance in the attempt to arrest the leading nationalists in Baghdad on 12 August 1920:

> The attempt to arrest several of the agitators . . . proved a failure, and probably did more harm than good. I have been told that the intentions of the civil police were known not only to those whose liberty was threatened, but to many others in Baghdad. In consequence the police met with opposition and there were a few casualties among the populace; and under cover of the disturbance those who were "wanted" made good their escape, and afterwards were constantly heard of in different parts of Iraq doing their best to keep the fires of insurrection burning.[41]

According to Haldane's account, Wilson, although he was a lieutenant colonel, was the last person who should have been criticizing his (Haldane's) war performance, having failed to carry out a simple police operation in Baghdad to arrest a few unarmed political activists. The fact that Haldane mentions this "failure" while talking about his operation in Baʿqūba is important, because that was the very operation that Wilson described as "disgraceful."[42]

Similar instances of internal resentment in the British administration are found in the writings of Gertrude Bell. She considered General Stanley Maude someone who was completely oblivious of what was needed in Iraq, ending one of her letters by crudely stating, "No one ever chose a more fortunate moment for dying than he."[43] Bell also at times resented the acting high commissioner, Wilson, whom she blamed for the revolution because of his failure, or refusal, to establish native institutions. She stated in a letter on 10 January

1921: "If we had begun establishing native institutions two years ago! by now we should have got Arab govt. and an Arab army going; we should have had no tribal revolt; all the money and lives wasted this year would have been saved. Damn A. T. Wilson." It is telling that she expressed similar frustration, to the point of using a curse word, only on 3 October 1920: "I hear that the Young Arabs of Baghdad are now running down Abdullah on the ground that he's a savage and Faysal seems to be barred by French susceptibilities, so that the prospect in that direction doesn't seem very hopeful. Damn the French."

Another level of discrepancies is found between the writings of high-ranking British officials and those at the local level, especially the assistant political officers. Frustrated by the challenge of trying to reconcile the overarching British policies with the requirements of their day-to-day tasks, they often voiced anger at the policies. In Captain James Mann's words: "I don't see what we can do about these broken promises; no one but fools or politicians would ever had made them, but as they were made they are in a way binding . . . The politician must prevaricate in order to live, and thus make things intolerable for an Administration like ours!"[44]

In writing about the revolution, it is important to understand the context of its events, a task made easier by examining the social and human terrain of the Middle Euphrates. This book provides many details about the region and its tribal associations and the networks of authority and social bonds. The revolution was not an organized militia undertaking, nor was it led by military units or civilian parties. The combat actions were entirely conducted in the classic pattern of tribal warfare. Therefore, it is essential to shed light on the tribes and their leaders in order to understand their goals and motivations.

The focus on some biographical aspects of leaders such as Sayyid Muḥsin Abu Ṭabīkh, Shaykh ʿAbd al-Wāḥid Āl Sikar, and others is not meant to present a family history of these figures, but to present the human side of the revolution. In many sources, the actions of Iraqis in 1920 are presented as a movement against law and order or as an example of people who acted against their self-interest—or who were manipulated by urban intellectuals to act the way they did. Presenting the biographical background of the leaders of the revolution is perhaps the best way to demonstrate that the leaders of the revolution were independent actors and not puppets of the urban intellectuals or any other external influence.

PLAN OF THE BOOK

The following six chapters examine the revolution's history, causes, events, and aftermath. The first chapter reviews historians' treatment of the revolution and Iraqis' remembrance and commemoration of it. In addition to the literature already available in English, the chapter examines in detail many sources in Arabic, including the writings of people who participated in the revolution or were eyewitnesses to its events. Furthermore, the chapter traces the representations of the revolution in Iraq's memory up to the present.

The second chapter traces the various events and intellectual trends that may have helped initiate the revolution or influence its course. The restive conditions in the region surrounding Iraq were associated with the decision to revolt, the nature of Iraqis' demands, and the course of events. But the argument here is that local causes and the occupation carried more weight than external incentives.

The third chapter sheds light on the events between June and November 1920 and the course of the revolution. While the main events took place in the Middle Euphrates, which is the predominantly Shīʿa region at the center of Iraq, the revolution extended for a brief period to some other parts of the country. This chapter highlights the main violent encounters between the Iraqis and the British forces and examines the obstacles to the expansion of the revolution to some major cities.

The fourth chapter presents an extensive discussion of the journalism during the revolution. In response to the lack of sympathetic voices on the existing papers, which were generally pro-British, some leading intellectuals associated with the revolution decided to establish two papers that became, in the short period of their circulation, the revolution's voice and stood among its most important historical records. This chapter represents one of the main contributions of this volume.

The fifth chapter provides a sociopolitical context by highlighting the social and economic conditions of the Middle Euphrates and the tribal networks in the region. The historical treatment of the revolution is enriched by focusing on the lives and characters of some leading participants in the revolution and their roles during and after the course of its events.

Finally, if the 1920 Revolution is, in essence, Iraq's war of independence, then it is important to shed light on the aftermath of the revolution and assess the points of its success and failure in light of Iraq's journey toward independence. The sixth chapter provides a comparison between the revolution's aspirations and the reality that was imposed by the British as an alternative to their failed colonization.

CHAPTER ONE

The 1920 Revolution in History

Although the revolt did not achieve Iraqi independence or turn real authority over to the Iraqis, it did succeed in discrediting the India Office policy thoroughly, and it assured a much larger measure of participation by the Iraqis in their first national government.

PHEBE MARR, *THE MODERN HISTORY OF IRAQ*

What a botched revolution;
We did the farming and others harvested!

AḤMAD AL-ṢĀFI AL-NAJAFI, IRAQI POET

CREDIBLE HISTORIES OF THE 1920 REVOLUTION have traditionally relied on two sources: first, the official British narrative, based on intelligence and administrative reports written by colonial officials in Mesopotamia for their superiors in India or London; second, the memoirs of those Iraqis who worked for or collaborated with the British.

British officials saw the Arabs as backward and uncivilized, in great need of, but resistant to, the benefits of British tutelage. The words of Stephen Longrigg from 1953 clearly illustrate this mind-set:

> The disorders which broke out among ʿIraq tribes in the mid-summer of 1920 were immediately caused by elements partly long familiar in ʿIraq—tribal recalcitrance, love of freedom and loot, self-interested Mujtahid promptings, local shaykhly ambitions or rancours, dislike of taxation, grievances against government as such—and partly by vigorous and well-financed nationalist propaganda and devotion to that cause. They were facilitated by the dispersal, paucity, and static preoccupations of the British forces, and by a military command sometimes clumsily or tardily exercised, sometimes, rightly or wrongly, unsympathetic to the needs or pleas of the Administration.[1]

This particular point of view, omnipresent in the works of British colonial officials and historians of the time, would have us believe that neither the oppressive conduct of British colonial officers nor the people's natural aversion to occupation played a significant role in instigating the revolution. Rather, all the blame was due to the "uncivilized" nature of the Iraqis, who detested "government as such." Even the Iraqis' "love of freedom" is presented as a vice. All the blame, according to Longrigg, fell on the chiefs of the tribes and the mujtahids (the senior religious clergy). If the British were to blame for anything, he argued, it was for their lack of resolve in deterring the Iraqis with more brutality than was meted out to them, which is the actual meaning of the euphemistic expression "the needs or pleas of the Administration."

Britain's Iraqi collaborators concurred that the Iraqis who took up arms in 1920 were little more than a mob of medieval-minded troublemakers, accusing those who took part in the revolution of being agents of foreign countries (Turkey, Iran, or even the Bolsheviks in Russia), thus denying the Arab identity of the revolution. This interpretation pervades Iraqi and Arab nationalist writings that generally dismiss the Shīʿa as counterfeit Arabs and disloyal Iraqis.

A third, shifting narrative is supplied by the successive Iraqi regimes that sought to manipulate the past to legitimize their claims to power. In the process, the 1920 Revolution became the discordant prologue to Iraq's real history, which can be dated from the foundation of the monarchy in 1921.[2] The monarchy glorified the role of the

Iraqi-Ottoman officers who assisted Fayṣal before, during, and after the Arab Revolt (1915–1918) and went on to serve in his short-lived kingdom in Syria in 1920. They were portrayed as the true pioneers of Iraqi independence and the "inspiration" for the 1920 Revolution, as they themselves often claimed. In this way, the fact that these officers had not actually participated in the country's founding event in no way made them ineligible for high political and military positions in Fayṣal's court.

The 1958 fall of the Hashemite monarchy precipitated a need for a more "republican" version of the past, one that relegated the role of royalist former Ottoman officers to the basement of Iraq's history. Delegitimized also were wealthy landowners, who were written out of the "revolutionary" script before being stripped of their lands by the Agrarian Reform Law of 1958.[3] Patriots who had risked their lives and treasure for the revolution in 1920 became, under the pens of regime historians, a selfish clique—which, even if true, was no reason to ignore their impact on Iraq's founding.

The blatant anti-Shīʿa stance of Baʿthist governments from 1963 until the fall of the Baʿth in 2003 required that the revolution be relocated from the Shīʿa-dominated Middle Euphrates to the Sunni heartland of the Upper Euphrates and given an entirely new cast of characters. The true leaders of the revolution, such as Shaʿlān Abu al-Chōn, Sayyid Muḥsin Abu Ṭabīkh, and Sayyid Nūr al-Yāsiri, were lost to memory and replaced by Sunnis such as Shaykh Ḍāri and others whose roles in the revolution were peripheral at best and participation subsequent. Furthermore, during the last sixty years of the twentieth century, the names of provinces, towns, and villages that had been centers of resistance to the British in 1920 went unmentioned in official history books and maps, while Sunni towns with secondary roles were given prominence. Indeed, the uninformed were hard-pressed to locate historic battlefields after the town of Rāranjiyya was renamed al-Rustumiyya, after al-Siwāriyya became al-Fayṣaliyya before being rebaptized al-Mishkhāb, after Abu Ṣkhair was renamed al-Manādhira, and after al-Ḥamza became al-Midḥatiyya, to cite only a few examples from the Middle Euphrates region.[4]

This book offers several contributions to the existing literature. Most importantly, it presents voices not yet heard, namely, those of the participants in the revolution themselves, now given a chance to explain their actions and their motives in their own words. Also, the book places the revolution in the context of the regional political changes that took place in Iran, Syria, Turkey, Egypt, Jordan, and the Arabian Peninsula. The next chapter demonstrates that Iraq was uniquely situated at the crossroads of the various events that unfolded throughout the region before, during, and after the 1920 Revolution, because Iraq was tied in a certain way to each one of these places. Simply stated, Iraq in 1920 was a former Ottoman territory with certain lingering ties to Turkey, but there was a shifting balance of influence in favor of Iran through the Shīʿa mujtahids and their tribal constituencies. In the meantime, there was an indissoluble bond with the extended Arab world beyond Iraq's boundaries, which made the events in Iraq a major concern for the Arabs and, similarly, made events in other Arab countries a source of Iraqi aspirations.

Another contribution of this book is the presentation of ample evidence of the politicization of history, not only by the British occupiers, but also by subsequent Iraqi regimes. It is critical for the historian of modern Iraq to verify the official British and Iraqi versions of the country's founding events by comparing them with the memoirs of the history makers themselves and the accounts by eyewitnesses. By doing this, the present volume provides some of the missing parts of the revolution's history.

The published memoirs of Sayyid Muḥsin Abu Ṭabīkh, Farīq Mizhir Āl Farʿōn, and Muhammad Ali Kamāl al-Dīn—all of whom participated in the revolution and witnessed its events firsthand—present a stark challenge to the dominant versions currently available. I sought information from people who had witnessed the events of the revolution or its aftermath. Interviews were conducted by telephone, via e-mail, and in person in the United States, the United Kingdom, and Iraq to clarify the complexities of certain disputes.

It is reasonable to ask the following questions: why should we trust these original sources more than the British narratives or the ever-changing official narratives presented by various Iraqi regimes? Were not the writers of these memoirs trying to present history through the lens most sympathetic to their own worldview? To be sure, these memoirs are not immune to bias, any more than those of other participants. Their writers too tend occasionally to claim more credit for themselves and their partisans than might be strictly accurate. Not surprisingly, their views are influenced by sectarianism, tribalism, and regionalism. In the words of Iraq's leading historian, Ali al-Wardi,

> Each writer would like to attribute to his faction most of the contribution to the revolution and minimize the role of others in it. Whoever reads *The Plain Facts* by Farīq Mizhir Āl Farʿōn, for example, will sense that he wanted to say that the Āl Fatla [tribe] were the backbone of the revolution and the central element in it. Others have followed his path [in maximizing their respective roles] in different degrees and forms.
>
> The most outlandish claims indeed were presented by a writer named Abbas Ali in a book he wrote entitled *The Leader of the Iraqi Revolution*. He claimed that the entire revolution was the product of the planning of one man, Sayyid Muhammad al-Ṣadr, filling his book with exaggerations and lofty praise similar to the old style of orators. Indeed, he perhaps had hurt Sayyid Muhammad more than benefiting him because exaggerations in a matter like this can generate a negative reaction.[5]

Together, these accounts represent the best firsthand sources for the views and actions of those who, until now, have been left out of Iraq's past. This book does not propose to completely replace the existing narratives with those provided by the participants in the revolution. Rather, it proposes to rescue these narratives, which have been unjustifiably underrepresented, even completely excluded, from existing analyses of the revolution, and use them to clarify and better delineate what happened in Iraq in 1920.

A BRIEF HISTORIOGRAPHY OF MODERN IRAQ

In general, the secondary literature on early Iraq cannot claim to be accurate or thorough. To reiterate, the main reason for the mistreatment of the 1920 Revolution in the literature is the focus on 1921 as the official beginning of the story of modern Iraq. The failure to place the state-building events of 1921 in the context of the 1920 Revolution has often relegated the former to the status of background anecdotes to be presented as a matter of fact and without careful examination. These shortcomings are illustrated repeatedly in the course of this volume.

There are several divergent accounts of the causes of the revolution as well as the time and place of the first spark that led to a wide revolt against the British occupation of Iraq. There are also several opposing accounts of the personalities of those involved in the fight against British forces.

Muḥsin Abu Ṭabīkh, one of the most important leaders of the revolution, made the following statement, since he found that no account of the 1920 Revolution remotely resembled the event in which he had played a major role—although he refrained from commenting for four decades:[6]

> The Iraqi Revolution, as you know, is a sacred revolution; a revolution that had deep influence on history. The best evidence of its consequences was the fruit it produced, which was the main purpose behind it; namely, the establishment of the Iraqi state, which is considered today among the best Arab states. Unfortunately, however, the political and military events of the revolution as well as its results were analyzed by some writers who were biased, hired, or ignorant . . . Biased writers inserted what has not been part of the true nature of the revolution or its goals. Hired writers, on the other hand, have attributed it to a certain faction and not to others and a certain group of people rather than others and to a few people who had nothing to do with it; while ignorant writers continued to shoot in the dark and write whatever felt good. All this caused the concealment of its truth and the loss of its sacredness, so that anyone who reads such contradictory books with what they contain, from myths to pure lies, would detest them and see no historical value in them.[7]

Abu Ṭabīkh here provides a view shared by all his companions who reflected later on their participation in the revolution. It is also supported, as will be shown, by their declarations and statements during the course of the revolution.

The consensus among the revolution's leaders contrasts with diverse analyses in the secondary literature. Philip Ireland's book *Iraq: A Study in Political Development* (1937) is one of the earliest histories of the British occupation. Although more objective than the rest of his British compatriots at the time, he pins the cause of revolution and the failure to suppress it quickly on the lack of "prompt and effectively directed action . . . with sufficient troops."[8] He attributes the delay in the spread of the revolution to the western region (the Upper Euphrates) to the "vigorous methods" of Colonel G. E. Leachman and the cooperation displayed by Shaykhs Ali al-Sulayman and Fahd al-Hadhdhāl of the Dulaym and ʿAniza tribes, respectively, "who remained loyal throughout."[9] This region, west of Baghdad, did join the revolution, but only after the killing of Colonel Leachman at the hands of Shaykh Ḍāri of the Zōbaʿ tribe and his relatives on 12 August 1920, forty-four days after the revolution had broken out in Rumaitha. The revolution in the western region did not last long; British forces reoccupied Fallūja and Ramadi on 24 and 26 September, respectively, and by 4 October, the entire Upper Euphrates region was again under British control.[10]

Ireland highlights the importance of the Shīʿa mujtahids in Iraq, who complicated the task of ending the revolution. He cites a British administrative report—which refers to two documents, one from Najaf and another from Gharrāf, northeast of Baṣra—demanding "the institution of a theocratic Government built up on one of the fundamental principles of the Shīʿa doctrine." The report concludes that these documents provided "evidence of the power and hold of the Shīʿa divines [i.e., the mujtahids] on the religious emotions of the uneducated tribes."[11]

Ireland apologized for the actions of the British and acknowledged that the financial and military consequences of the revolution had forced the change in British plans from direct rule over Iraq to implementing the mandate by treaty, "bringing Iraq into the League of Nations more quickly than H.M. Government had originally contemplated when assuming the Mandate."[12] Hence, according to Ireland, the revolution was considered by the Iraqis "a National War of Independence directly responsible for forcing the British to set up an Arab Government and, eventually, to grant independence."[13] This view was vastly different from that of the British authorities, who considered it "a revolt against authority, costing 426 British lives, 1,228 wounded and 615 missing and prisoners, as well as 8,450 casualties among the insurgents."[14]

John Glubb, who served in the British forces and witnessed both the military campaign and the political process, presents in his book *Arabian Adventures* (1978), some revealing viewpoints. He attributes the revolution to three problems. First was the "disillusionment amongst the tribesmen," who became disappointed with the performance of the British administration, whose accomplishments in enhancing Iraq's infrastructure, for instance, were minimal as compared with British development in Egypt. Second was tribal resentment of the "tyrannical rule of the Shaykhs," who had been "imposed upon them" by the British.[15] Although he stops short of mentioning the tyrannical rule of the British officers and administrators, of whom he was one important example, Glubb at least admits some fault on the part of the British, perhaps the only British official to do so. He certainly had his reasons for doing so, having been dismissed from his position in Iraq after the formation of the provisional government, which he oddly refers to as "a generous measure of self-government."[16] It is hard to follow Glubb's reasoning on this point: the tribes joined their shaykhs to fight the British, yet he argues that they were driven to fighting by their resentment against the shaykhs. The third reason for the revolution, according to Glubb, was the disappointment of the elites, especially the officers, who realized that the British were not going to keep their prewar promises.[17] Again, he distributes blame on both sides, the elites for their impatience and the British for their lack of clarity in articulating their "true" intentions. As this book shows, the problem was not the lack of clarity in articulating their true intentions, but rather their true intentions themselves.

In spite of some problematic errors and misrepresentations, Hanna Batatu's *The Old Social Classes and the Revolutionary Movements of Iraq* (1978), contains a wealth of information on twentieth-century Iraq. Batatu emphasizes the Shīʿa-Sunni unity in the time leading to the 1920 Revolution. He points out that the religious dimension of the events where this cooperation manifested itself was fictional, because the real purpose was political.[18] Batatu argues that like every other event before 1936, the 1920 Revolution "was a Shaykh's affair." As he correctly notes: "Baghdad's only contributions to it were pamphlets, demonstrations and some clandestine correspondence."[19] But he does not seem to accept the possibility of nationalist sentiment arising in the tribal milieu of the Middle Euphrates—giving the impression that nationalism was an exclusive doctrine reserved only for the educated elite. He therefore asks: "What was 'nationalist' about the 1920 revolt except the attempt of the numerically insignificant nationalists to use the tribes for nationalist ends?"[20] Like Ireland, Batatu, sees in the tribes that participated wholeheartedly in the revolution merely uneducated folks going to war for no particular cause. They were, in his opinion, manipulated and used by the "numerically insignificant nationalists." This book shows that Iraq's full independence from foreign influence as the goal of the revolution, the call for an Arab king, and the rising above sectarian and ethnic differences in favor of the higher cause of independence all gave the revolution a stronger nationalist underpinning than many scholars have conceded it.

One of the best sources on modern Iraqi history is Phebe Marr's *The Modern History of Iraq* (1985). Marr characterized the revolution as being "directed above all at the India Office policy." As to the causes, she cites the announcement of the mandate over Iraq, which was awarded to the British at the San Remo Conference in April 1920.[21]

Marr cites earlier efforts to resist the British occupation of Iraq. These claims were cited by some authors to assert that the revolution originated outside Iraq, mainly in the calls by Fayṣal's officers in 1919 for the establishment of a national government in Iraq. She also cites the unsuccessful revolt in Talʿafar, in the Mosul province. These contentions, however, run against the unanimous views expressed by participants in the 1920 Revolution, who said more than once that their revolution was not connected to, or inspired by, what was taking place in Syria or elsewhere.[22] Marr dismisses the British claim that the revolution was "a little more than a localized tribal insurgency fomented by a nationalist agitation from Syria," and instead endorses the belief that the revolution "was a genuine nationalist rebellion, the first in a series of abortive attempts to overthrow unwanted British rule."[23]

Unlike the historians who attribute the revolution solely to the heavily taxed tribes, Marr credits several groups, each of which had its own reasons but all of which "were united by the desire to be free of British rule."[24] She also disagrees with the contention, made by Ireland and others, that the revolution did not influence the direction of British policy toward Iraq. Marr is one of a few authors to state, albeit very briefly, the devastating consequences of the revolution not only for British blood and treasure, but also for the credibility of the India Office and its colonialist propensity.

Another important source of modern Iraqi history is Yitzhak Nakash's *The Shīʿis of Iraq* (1994). In keeping with the framework of his research, Nakash views the causes of the revolution as deriving from the interests and impulses of the religious scholars, the mujtahids, in the holy cities. Unlike authors who focus on the nationalist inspirations of the revolution's leaders—and so look at trends and activities in Syria, Egypt, and Ḥijaz—Nakash highlights the Iranian connections of the mujtahids and their concern for the nature of Anglo-Iranian relations. Further, the mujtahids, according to Nakash, were disturbed by the way British administrators regulated the traffic of pilgrims and corpses to the holy cities, dealing a severe blow to their main sources of revenue. The same sentiment, he argues, was formed by the Arab sayyids who lived among the tribesmen. They stood to lose their prestige among the tribes and their income from the contributions of tribesmen. Hence, Nakash views the 1920 Revolution as a joint effort by these two groups: "The Arab Sayyids and the Persian mujtahids thus had a common interest in inciting the tribes to revolt so as to preserve their own eminent position among their Shīʿa constituency in Iraq."[25] This assessment makes their motives seem purely personal rather than national or patriotic, and paints the tribes in an unflattering light.

But Nakash acknowledges, contrary to his previous assertion, that the mujtahids took their position in part under a sense of religious duty, because the British occupation was essentially a Christian occupation of Muslim territory.

Charles Tripp's *A History of Iraq* (2000) pays special attention to political organization of the Iraqi groups. He credits the awakening of nationalist sentiments, which led to the revolution, to the work of two secret political parties: al-ʿAhd al-ʿIraqi and Ḥaras al-Istiqlal; the first was mainly a Sunni group dominated by military Ottoman officers, while the second was predominantly a Shīʿa party comprised mostly of civilians.[26]

Tripp highlights the sense of humiliation felt by the elite when a mandate was declared, which gave the impression that the ability of the Iraqis to govern themselves was, at best, in doubt. Indeed, this was not just an impression, but a mantra repeated by almost every British official.

Tripp attributes the revolution to a variety of causes, including the usual issues of taxation, land disputes, tribal relations, and so on. On the motivation of the leading mujtahid, Muhammad Taqi al-Shirazi, to lead the revolution, Tripp alludes to the arrest of Shirazi's son, a member of Ḥaras al-Istiqlal and an active opponent of the British occupation.[27] Tripp correctly concludes that the participants in the revolution made the sacrifices only to watch the elite of Baghdad, who opposed the revolution, reap the benefits of the emerging new political order.[28]

In *Inventing Iraq: The Failure of Nation Building and a History Denied* (2003), Toby Dodge attributes the revolution to the "heavy-handed approach of the occupying forces"—however, he does not mention Iraqis' aspirations or their rejection of the occupation. Revolutionary leaders like Abu Ṭabīkh argue that this heavy-handedness served only to hasten the eruption of the revolution, which was going to happen anyway because the British showed no signs of granting Iraq full independence. The cost of the revolution in both lives and treasure, Dodge correctly states, "made the continued occupation of Iraq very unpopular with British public opinion."[29]

Dodge considers the belief that the revolution was "the founding act of the nation" to be part of "Iraqi political mythology."[30] He subscribes also to the opinion that the revolution was the result of "anger at the military imposition of efficient tax gathering,"[31] a point he reiterates: "The disgruntlement of the heavily taxed tribes in southern Iraq . . . exploded into a widespread revolt against the British presence in the country."[32] Scholars who espouse this view, however, never explain two facts that acutely undermine their position. First is the participation of religious scholars as the supreme leaders of the revolution, despite the imposition of taxes not being an issue for them. Likewise, the landowners who led their tribesmen in the revolution were not harmed by the British taxation system. Indeed, the present volume shows that they received tax reductions, better treatment than they had under the Ottomans, and more services. Although Dodge dismisses the role of the revolution in founding the nation, he acknowledges that its effects on the British "marked a decisive shift in the attitudes and perceptions structuring British government discussions and colonial officials' actions."[33]

More emphasis is given to the Shīʿa and Sunni roles in the revolution by Eric Davis in his outstanding book, *Memories of State: Politics, History, and Collective Identity in Modern Iraq* (2005). Contrary to conventional wisdom, Davis emphasizes the Shīʿa–Sunni cooperation in the 1920 Revolution and states that this "was not a historical aberration" in Iraq, citing earlier attempts to form political groups from both sects in order to work for Iraq's interests.[34] For Davis, the significance of the 1920 Revolution did not pertain solely to its immediate political aftermath. Rather, he convincingly argues that the revolution presented an important revelation: "It was not preordained that Iraq should be plagued by ethnic and confessional cleavages, and that Sunnis and Shīʿa should remain mutually hostile and unable to cooperate in nation building."[35]

Davis blames both the British administration and the state that was formed under its suzerainty for the failure to nurture this "spirit of cooperation," which was displayed by both sides before and during the revolution. Precisely, Davis finds fault with the Sunni elite, who "did everything possible to limit Shīʿi participation in the new administration at both the national and local levels."[36] He finds it only natural that this covetousness on the part of the Sunnis and their exclusion of the Shīʿa from political power caused the earlier spirit of cooperation to be replaced by mistrust and resentment.

THE 1920 REVOLUTION IN IRAQI MEMORY

Had Shaʿlan known
The Revolution was stolen
He would have split the ground
And emerged from the grave
The "Great Question" was at the Suwair Bridge
And the evidence is here
We are the orphans of 1920

These lines are a colloquial poem of the genre called *hōsa,* an Iraqi tribal chant often accompanied by a war dance to mobilize fighters or demonstrate a tribe's power and pride. This particular *hōsa* was composed by a Samāwa poet to protest a film commissioned in 1983 by the government of Saddam Hussein to commemorate the 1920 Revolution.[37] The motion picture was highly patronized by the government, in a country where the film industry received virtually no attention from the government. The Iraqi director of the film, Muḥammad Shukri Jamīl, was authorized to recruit well-known Western actors to play the roles of British officials. He recruited Oliver Reed and Helen Ryan to play major roles in the film and signed up a group of the best actors in Iraq.

As far as portraying the revolution's narrative, the film was a historical atrocity. The revolution was reduced only to events that took place in Fallūja, and the film's main Iraqi character was Shaykh Ḍāri, leaving out the real leaders of the revolution. The choice of starring actor, Ghāzi al-Tikrīti, was symbolic as well. Far from being the best Iraqi actor at the time to play the leading role, it appears that his last name was the most important reason for his selection.[38] The Shīʿa were banished from art just as they were from Iraqi politics.

It appears that the "dwarfing" of the Shīʿa leaders and the augmentation of Ḍāri were unrelated to history or the art of cinema, or even to the preferences of the film's director and scriptwriters. In a talk given on 22 January 2010 at the Madā Center for Art and Culture in Baghdad, the actor Yūsuf al-ʿĀni, who played the Shīʿa leader and poet Muḥammad Mahdi al-Baṣīr, revealed that two of his best scenes were excised from the film's final version in compliance with "high orders," leaving al-Baṣīr, the revolution's poet, with only brief, marginal appearances.[39]

This examination of such attempts to tamper with history is not to diminish the role of Ḍāri, an important figure in the history of Iraq. Rather, it is important to place his role in the general context of the revolution and to illustrate that more has been attributed to the man than he ever took credit for when he was alive. The reason for this augmentation was more political than historical. The capture of Ḍāri and his trial in 1928 projected an objectionable image of the new Iraqi political regime, whose subservience to the British facilitated the farcical trial of a practically dead man. He was sentenced to death on 30 January 1928. Then his sentence was commuted to life in prison, of which he served two days only, dying on 1 February 1928.

The editor of Baghdad's *Al-Istiqlāl*, ʿAbd al-Ghafūr al-Badri, was perhaps the first writer to put Ḍāri on a pedestal. Seeing that during the week after Ḍāri's death, none of his fellow patriots had stepped forward to do right by a man who was an important symbol of Iraq's struggle against British occupation, al-Badri published an exhortation, under a pseudonym, commemorating the death of Ḍāri and describing Ḍāri as "one of the symbols of the Iraqi revolution; *indeed the greatest of its symbols*."[40] Subsequent writings on the revolution, especially those of the participants, always mentioned Ḍāri and his role, but did not consider him "the greatest symbol of the revolution." This held true until the rise of the regime of the ʿĀrif brothers (1963–1968). Ḍāri was the maternal uncle of both presidents, so an orchestrated effort was made to put him on a taller pedestal. In the last year of the ʿĀrif regime, two Iraqi writers were commissioned to produce a book titled *Al-Shaykh Ḍāri al-Maḥmūd: The Chief of Zōbaʿ Tribe and the Killer of Colonel Leachman in Khan al-Nuqṭa*. Considering the status of the writers, ʿAbd al-Ḥamīd Al-ʿAlawchi and ʿAzīz Jāsim Al-Ḥajjiyya, the book is a disappointment. Almost half of the book is an unedited record of the trial. The remaining sixty pages contain generic information about Shaykh Ḍāri, presented in an oratorical style. The authors' interview with Ḍāri's son, Sulaymān, is the book's biggest missed opportunity. The four pages, exclusively devoted to Sulaymān's account of the killing of Leachman, provide no major revelations. The authors did not extract any important memories from Sulaymān, who was an eyewitness of the entire involvement of Zōbaʿ in the revolution and served as his father's companion in the revolution and afterward.

THE FARʿŌN, KHALĪLI, AND BĀZIRGĀN DISPUTE

In 1952, Farīq Mizhir Āl Farʿōn published his account of the 1920 Revolution in two volumes titled *Al-Ḥaqāʾiq al-Nāṣiʿa fi al-Thawra al-ʿIrāqiyya Sanat 1920 wa Natāʾijihā* (The Pure Truths about the Iraqi Revolution of the Year 1920 and Its Consequences). The title is fully loaded. On the one hand, it implies that previous narratives were lacking in truth, and on the other hand, it raises the expectation of presenting to readers and historians the "pure truths."

Whatever has been said about this book, which will be discussed here, it has been one of the most important sources of information on the revolution because the author was a witness to its events, a shaykh of the Fatla tribe, and a cousin of Shaykh ʿAbd al-Wāḥid Āl Sikar, one of the three undisputed leaders of the revolution in the Middle Euphrates. Āl Farʿōn presents 600 pages of thorough narratives and many documents. Judith Yaphe describes his work best: "It should be noted that these accounts are more than histories; they are memoirs of events both observed and participated in by the writers. They become more than historical summations as they include faithful reproductions of documents and articles of correspondence unobtainable elsewhere."[41]

The introduction sets the stage for a battle that existed for the three decades between the Middle Euphrates and Baghdad, a battle between the ones who fought the war of independence in 1920 and the ones who founded the state on completely different principles than those of the revolution; a battle between the seekers of full independence and the pragmatists who settled for a mandate-cum-puppet monarchy. Furthermore, it was a battle between Iraqi nationalists and Arab nationalists. Āl Farʿōn laments the state of the country, whose children study the French Revolution in detail but have sketchy knowledge of the Iraqi Revolution. He also deplores, perhaps rightfully, a government that builds monuments to Gertrude Bell and Sir Stanley Maude, but none to Gāṭiʿ al-ʿAwwādi and Hādi Mgōṭir, among other symbols of the 1920 Revolution. He questions why there is a square in Baghdad named after the battle of El Alamein, which was won by the British against the Germans in North Africa, but no square named after Rāranjiyya, the main victory in 1920. Actually, had Āl Farʿōn been a little more attentive, he would not have found this strange, because the pro-British politicians not only failed to name a square after Rāranjiyya, but also wiped its name off the Iraqi map, as they did with many other towns associated with battles. Additionally, and here is the real divergence, he was frustrated with the Iraqi politicians who wanted to raise a generation that would "liberate Palestine and North Africa and enter the history books . . . forgetting that this generation talks about the politicians' neglect of the heroes who liberated Iraq from the British occupation."[42]

Āl Farʿōn clearly indicates that the people of Baghdad "played no role in [the 1920 Revolution]" and that "some men in Baghdad had indeed held it in contempt." He goes on to cite Muzaḥim al-Pāchachi's notorious speech wherein he praised the "noble British commitments" toward Iraq and condemned the revolution as a "non-Arab movement."[43] Āl Farʿōn alludes to the depiction of Baghdad's demonstrations and activities in the months leading up to the revolution as the revolution's root, whereas actions in the Middle Euphrates were a mere branch, and considers this "the worst error in the distorted narratives."[44]

In response to Āl Farʿōn's book, several people expressed varying levels of dismay. This was perhaps the worthiest contribution of his book, enticing many of the surviving participants and eyewitnesses to break their silence, search their memories, and present what each of them deemed to be the real story. Muḥsin Abu Ṭabīkh, for example, showed clear disproval of Āl Farʿōn's assigning disproportionate credit to his tribe and his family, noting that the book should have been called *Al-Ḥaqāʾiq al-Ḍāʾiʿa* (The Lost Truths).[45] Similarly, Āl Farʿōn managed to excite the wrath of ʿAbd al-Shahīd al-Yāsiri by claiming that al-Yāsiri's father, Sayyid Nūr, was hired as a mayor of Najaf, which would have made him a subordinate of Sayyid Muḥsin Abu Ṭabīkh. It seems that Āl Farʿōn made up this story, which was refuted by Abu Ṭabīkh and others.[46] However, Jaʿfar al-Khalīli, in the first extensive response to Āl Farʿōn, confirmed the appointment of Sayyid Nūr, saying that "he held the position for one day only, for reasons in need of a long explanation."[47]

Al-Khalīli presented his book as a recommended supplement "for those who bought Āl Farʿōn's book."[48] In the most concise terms, al-Khalīli accuses Āl Farʿōn of three kinds of atrocious tampering with the history of the revolution—some of these accusations were echoed by other critics. First, Āl Farʿōn overemphasized the contribution of his own tribe, the Fatla, and his own immediate family, while not giving due credit to others. It is true that ʿAbd al-Wāḥid Āl Sikar, the shaykh of Fatla, is correctly considered one of the most prominent leaders of the revolution in the Middle Euphrates, but others led and sacrificed also and therefore deserve proper credit. Al-Khalīli points out Āl Farʿōn's exaggeration of his cousin's credentials, which essentially turned into defamation of others: "Most of the revolutionaries compromised, while the vanguard of the resolute was ʿAbd al-Wāḥid; the hearts of some of them were lured by the gold, except for ʿAbd al-Wāḥid." In response, al-Khalīli presents a list of more than thirty leaders and asks Āl Farʿōn to select those among them, whose hearts were "lured by the gold."[49]

The second accusation against Āl Farʿōn was that he wrote under the influence of emotions and vendetta. As an example, al-Khalīli highlights the way Āl Farʿōn treated the history of the shaykhs of Banu Ḥasan, ʿAlwān, and ʿUmrān Āl Ḥāj Saʿdūn. Because of the generations-long animosity between the Fatla tribe and the Banu Ḥasan, mainly caused by the blood shed over land disputes, Āl Farʿōn "inherited the hatred for Banu Ḥasan . . . therefore he understated their contributions to the revolution and overstated any suspect behavior on their part, which was the opposite of his treatment of his, Fatla, tribe."[50] One example of the preferential treatment handed out by Āl Farʿōn was the account given of his father, Shaykh Mizhir, whose participation in the revolution was nominal. Āl Farʿōn makes several excuses for his father, whereas others are criticized for their lack of, or only halfhearted, participation.[51] The only exception to this rule was the treatment of a prominent shaykh from the Fatla, Āl Farʿōn's own brother, ʿAbd al-ʿAbbas, who participated in the revolution with valor, but is not given credit in Āl Farʿōn's book. The reason, according to al-Khalīli, was the author's indifference toward ʿAbd al-ʿAbbas, because he was a brother from a different mother, as opposed to his full brother, Sertīb, whom he credits with several fabricated achievements.[52]

The fabrication of stories, events, and statements constitute the third accusation against Āl Farʿōn's book. For instance, the author claims that his aforementioned brother, Sertīb, was the addressee of a letter from the mujtahid Shaykh al-Sharīʿa, asking him to take care of British prisoners and ensure that their needs were met. Āl Farʿōn attributed this important task to his brother because the addressee's name was not specified. The actual addressee, according to al-Khalīli, was Muḥsin Shlāsh.[53] The identity of the addressee was confirmed by Muḥammad Bāqir al-Shabībi, who quoted the letter in his famous response to Arnold T. Wilson.[54] He told ʿAbd al-Shahīd al-Yāsiri that the letter was sent to Muḥsin Shlāsh.[55]

Other fabrications were alleged, including the use of photos unrelated to the revolution but claimed to be authentic. The worst of these fabricated photos was one supposedly of a certain Kraizi, who is identified as "the first martyr in Abu Ṣkhair," implying that he is from the Fatla tribe. Al-Khalīli published the original photo and stated that this was a picture of a man from Najaf named Mṭashshar, who was killed in the Battle of Shaʿaiba, five years before the revolution.[56]

Another expression of serious disappointment with Āl Farʿōn came from a fellow participant in the revolution, Ali al-Bāzirgān. He wrote a book with an equally promising title, *Al-Waqāʾiʿ al-Ḥaqīqiyya fi al-Thawra al-ʿIrāqiyya* (The True Events of the Iraqi Revolution). The subtitle describes the book in the following terms: "A treatise consisting of discussion and analysis of the events of Iraqi Revolution on 30 June 1920 and refutation of any fabrications that have been affixed to it and correction of the errors about it."

In addition to some important firsthand observations and valuable memoirs, the book, unfortunately, descends often to the level of petty polemic and, occasionally, takes on an obvious tone of sectarian and class-based prejudice. To make matters worse, the book was republished in 1991 with numerous footnotes and editorial additions written by the author's son, Ḥassān al-Bāzirgān, whose sectarian attitudes took the book to horrendous levels of prejudice and distortion.[57] Not only the Shīʿa were attacked, but the wrath of the Bāzirgāns came down on the Jews as well—first from the father and then from the son. In his recollections of his role in establishing the first school in Baghdad, Ali al-Bāzirgān presents an interesting tale. In 1908, the merchant Ḥāj Salmān Abu al-Timman imported some exotic samovars, which flew off the shelves. Abu al-Timman asked his clerk, who was a Jew named Shamīl Sōmekh, to order more samovars. After a month, the exotic samovars hit the market, but not through Ḥāj Salmān's store. The new wholesale merchant was a Baghdadi Jew; the story does not name him. Here, Ali al-Bāzirgān enters the story with the million-dollar question to Ḥāj Salmān: "Had your clerk been a Muslim, would he have cheated you?" "What is to be done?" asked the bewildered Ḥāj Salmān. "You must start your own schools to teach your [Muslim] young men foreign languages."[58]

This one Jew, who may have taken advantage of mercantile competition to make his "commission," if the story is true to begin with, became the representative of all Jews in al-Bāzirgān's mind. Similarly, Ḥassān al-Bāzirgān accuses Mīr Baṣri, an Iraqi Jew whose works are invaluable, of distorting the history of Iraq, and claims that the alternative account Mīr Baṣri narrated on the authority of Jaʿfar Abu al-Timman about the establishment of the school was motivated by Ali al-Bāzirgān's story about the Jewish clerk.[59] Ḥassān al-Bāzirgān goes on to ask Iraq's historians to particularly scrutinize everything Mīr Baṣri wrote, because all of it is "a Zionist distortion."[60]

It is worth noting that the second edition of al-Bāzirgān's book begins with an extravagant tribute to Saddam Hussein, who apparently ordered that al-Bāzirgān's picture be included in the museum of the revolution. Ḥassān al-Bāzirgān wrote the following in a letter to the Iraqi dictator: "Before the justice of the Leader, may Allah protect him, I cannot but present pure thanks to our Inspired Leader, the builder of Iraq's towering glory, the patriotic Comrade . . . for restoring right, because he is the father of all revolutionaries and because he knows the value of a reward and the humanitarian meaning of it."[61]

In his first rebuttal, Ali al-Bāzirgān picks a passage in which Āl Farʿōn argued that the real revolutionaries were the combatants and the ones who sacrificed everything, lives and property, not the "thinking intellects" who gave speeches but did not lift a finger after the revolution started—although Āl Farʿōn does give credit to the Baghdad intellectuals who joined the revolution in the Middle Euphrates, including a lot of praise to Ali al-Bāzirgān. In response, al-Bāzirgān states the following:

> There is a sad truth that must be mentioned first . . . that the tribal leaders and *ʿiqāl*-wearing deputies feel inferior to the *effendiyya*, because of their lack of general knowledge and their ignorance of the direction of political currents. They became the flock of cattle for every government . . . and their positions in the parliament became the subject of mockery and humor everywhere. That is why they waste no chance to attack the men from Baghdad.[62]

In his anger toward Āl Farʿōn and his book, Ali al-Bāzirgān makes many mistakes and attacks people whose role in resisting the British was unquestionable. One stark example is his treatment of the expulsion of the mujtahid of Baghdad, Shaykh Mahdi al-Khāliṣi, to Iran. Here, al-Bāzirgān approvingly claims that al-Khāliṣi was sent into exile because he was meddling in governmental affairs. While this was true, the example given falsely portrays the mujtahid's dispute with the government. Al-Khāliṣi, says Ali al-Bāzirgān, once recommended to King Fayṣal I the hiring of a certain Mirza Muḥammad al-Hindi as a mayor in Sāmarrāʾ. Al-Bāzirgān reports that Fayṣal showed him al-Khāliṣi's letter and told him, "What would people say about me if I hire an Indian in this position? Why then have you revolted against the British? Was it so that I would hire Indians in government positions? Isn't there anyone in Iraq who is fit for these jobs?" Ali al-Bāzirgān then went to al-Khāliṣi and convinced him to drop his request and support another man, Jalāl Bābān, who ultimately got the job.

While this anecdote has no relation whatsoever to the exile of al-Khāliṣi, whose expulsion was due to his opposition to the Anglo-Iraqi Treaty and his fatwa considering Fayṣal an illegitimate ruler after violating his covenant with the Iraqis regarding the independence, which al-Bāzirgān mentions in passing and in a distorted way, the anecdote itself opens an interesting window on the political games played at the time. Fayṣal pretends to worry about people's opinion regarding the hiring of a foreigner for an insignificant job in a small and faraway town at a time when a visitor to any ministry or governmental agency in Baghdad would have encountered a long line of high-ranking British employees. Also, al-Bāzirgān, who quickly found a replacement for this "non-Iraqi," did not seem to have any problem with hiring Sāṭiʿ al-Hīṣri to be in charge of Iraq's education, whose ethnic and sectarian inquisition caused irreversible damage in the Iraqi educational system for many decades.[63] What seems to be the real problem was that Fayṣal did not want to set a precedent for hiring a man from the Shīʿa for a mayor's job, at least not in a city that was not "purely" Shīʿa.

THE REVOLUTION MUSEUM AND MONUMENT

According to ʿAbd al-Sattār al-Naffākh, a Najafi historian, the Baʿth government allocated funds to build a monument commemorating the 1920 Revolution around 1975, and an art contest was announced to select the best idea. The government decided to have the monument built at the four-way intersection that connects Najaf with the provinces of Dīwāniyya, Ḥilla, and Karbalāʾ, where a statue of General ʿAbd al-Karim Qasim, the founder of the republic, used to be—the statue had been demolished after the 1963 coup against Qasim. A young artist from Kūfa, Muḥammad Ali al-Janābi, won the competition, and his model was adopted. But until 2010, the monument stood unfinished. The part that was erected represents the foundation of the envisioned monument only, while the rest was never assembled. It is supposed to portray an Iraqi fighter seizing a British cannon by using his rural weapon, the *miguār*, which is a yard-long stick with a baseball-sized asphalt mass affixed at one end.[64] *Miguār* can be deadly when used to strike the head or another vital organ. It is said that during the revolution, one Iraqi used his *miguār* to capture a cannon from the British force and began chanting the famous *hōsa* on the way back: "*Il-ṭob aḥsan lo miguāri*?" (Which is better, the cannon or my *miguār*?). It appears that the artist was inspired by this story of the revolution.

According to al-Naffākh, one theory behind the failure to finish the monument was that the government's art advisers interpreted the foundation as depicting the Hashemite crown in an inverted position. The monument was removed in the beginning of 2010 at the orders of the Najaf city council, which authorized plans to construct traffic overpasses to provide relief for one of the most overcrowded intersections in the country. The monument will be built at an alternative location under the supervision of the original artist, al-Janābi, who was asked to "redesign" the monument, according to the mayor of Najaf.[65]

The adjacent 1920 Revolution Museum was not luckier than the doomed monument. On 29 August 2003, a horrific explosion devastated the area around the Shrine of Imam Ali in Najaf. It took place right after the Friday prayer, which was led by the prominent cleric-politician Muhammad Bāqir al-Ḥakīm, who was killed in the explosion, along with hundreds of worshipers. The al-Ḥakīm family used its sweeping influence in Najaf to seize a parcel of strategic real estate in the city where they established a complex that includes the burial place of the slain cleric, a family-controlled political organization, and a charity. Two ironies stand out in connection with this story: first, the confiscated location included the 1920 Revolution Museum, which was removed to prepare the place for the grave; and second, there was no body to bury in the first place, because the blast left nothing to be recovered or buried. Lamenting this atrocity, a Najafi intellectual wrote the following:

> The 1920 Revolution Square and Museum, along with the adjacent former government buildings became a shrine for the niche martyr (*Shahīd al-Miḥrab*), that is Muhammad Bāqir al-Ḥakīm (1939–2003), and headquarters for the Shahīd al-Miḥrab Organization for Islamic Advocacy. . . . With an artful trick, every trace of the nationalist 1920 Revolution in Najaf was removed, and the revolution and its martyrs were replaced with one organization and one martyr. . . . The neo-Semiologists did not see in the revolution, which the Shīʿa consider a testament of their history, anything but a prop for a sort of family, or individual, presence. The revolution, which is a symbol extending beyond Najaf, was not helpful in the land-grabbing battle.[66]

THE REVOLUTION IN THE POST-SADDAM ERA

The U.S. invasion of 2003 recalled the British invasion of 1914–1918. From the route the invading forces used to penetrate Iraq's borders, occupying Baṣra first and then moving north, to the initial Shīʿa resistance in Um Qaṣr and Nāṣiriyya, against all preinvasion assumptions, and finally the Turkish hindrance of the invasion plans, every step of the way carried some historical parallel. In spite of the accusation that the U.S. administration in Iraq had not studied the British experience in Iraq and learned from their mistakes, the repetition of these mistakes gave the impression that the Americans were following the exact policies their British counterparts had crafted eight decades earlier. Recalling an interview with Christopher Segar, head of the British Office in Baghdad in May 2003, Toby Dodge stated the following:

> However, the conversation could well have taken place at the end of May 1920. Instead of Christopher Segar, Head of the British Office in Baghdad, answering the questions, it would,

> in 1920, have been Arnold Wilson, the acting Civil Commissioner, responsible for building a state in Iraq in the aftermath of the First World War. Wilson was a confident and bullish colonial official who was wrestling with a serious dilemma. How, under intense international scrutiny, could he control a well-armed society that had become increasingly resentful about the occupation of their country?[67]

No one was more mindful of the parallels between the two invasions than the Iraqis, whose national memory and current identities were shaped by the eight decades separating them. The first to carefully calculate a course of action were the mujtahids of Najaf. Realizing that they had a unique opportunity to reverse the mistakes of their counterparts in 1920, the Shīʿa mujtahids, particularly Grand Ayatollah Ali Sistani, took no action that might jeopardize a Shīʿa rise to power for the first time in modern Iraqi history. They did not repeat the folly of siding with a Muslim oppressor to repel a non-Muslim invader, who was eventually going to leave.

The post-Saddam era witnessed the continued rise of tribal power, which began in the wake of the 1991 uprising. Shīʿa tribes of the Middle Euphrates began to celebrate the anniversary of their participation in the 1920 Revolution and, for the first time, restore some of the local narratives of the events, which had been suppressed by the previous regimes. Conferences were held on 30 June of every year in the provinces that witnessed the violent events of 1920. While these conferences were held to commemorate the revolution, they also had another agenda: the assertion of legitimacy for a tribal role in the new Iraq, against the calls for reducing tribal influence in favor of democratic institutions and a strong state.

The symbolism of the revolution was present at the state level as well. In 2004, Iraqis agreed with the U.S. officials to terminate the power of the Coalition Provisional Authority on the anniversary of the revolution, but security concerns spoiled the plan, and the transfer of power to the Iraqis was held two days earlier. When another opportunity presented itself, the symbolism was cultivated successfully: the withdrawal of U.S. forces from Iraqi cities was scheduled for 30 June 2009—the anniversary of the start of the 1920 Revolution. Prime Minister Nūri al-Māliki addressed the Iraqi people on the occasion: "It is my pleasure to congratulate you on this day, 30 June, the day of the withdrawal of U.S. forces according to the agreement signed by Iraq and the U.S., which is the day commemorating an anniversary dear to the hearts of all Iraqis, the immortal 1920 Revolution, which established the will of Iraqis for freedom and independence."[68]

The worst misappropriation of the revolution's memory came from the terrorist front in Iraq after the collapse of Saddam Hussein's regime. The formation of the so-called 1920 Revolution Brigades was meant to drape pure terrorism, which killed Iraqis and non-Iraqis indiscriminately, with a patriotic mantle. The revolution's name was used to refer to the "militant wing" of the self-described "Islamic Nationalist Resistance" in Iraq. It consisted of eleven brigades, most named after historic figures revered by Sunni Muslims, with the exception of the al-Ḥusayn Brigade, named after the third Shīʿa imam. Some of the names are the usually invoked companions of the Prophet, while others are drawn from recent history, including a theorist of modern terrorism, ʿAbdullah ʿAzzam. The brigades operate in Baghdad, Diyālā, Anbār, Salāhuddīn, and Mosul.

Once again, the name of Shaykh Ḍāri came to the fore, this time through his progeny, Ḥārith al-Ḍāri and his son, Muthannā Ḥārith al-Ḍāri, who became the spokesmen for terrorism and sectarian intolerance in the new Iraq. In the midst of the appalling atrocities committed by al-Qāʿeda in 2007, Ḥārith al-Ḍāri appeared on al-Jazeera television and stated unequivocally, "We are from al-Qāʿeda and al-Qāʿeda is from us."

From the historical misappropriation and the areas of operation, not to mention the terrorist aims, the 1920 Revolution Brigades have done more damage to the revolution's good name than all previous distortions combined.

Having examined the historical significance of the 1920 Revolution and its place in the history of Iraq and in the Iraqi national memory, let us turn to an examination of the causes of the revolution and the local and regional context of its events.

CHAPTER TWO

The Causes of the Revolution

In the four years, 1914 to 1918, British arms completed what three centuries of British commerce and diplomacy had begun.

PHILIP IRELAND, *IRAQ: A STUDY IN POLITICAL DEVELOPMENT*

THE MAIN QUESTIONS TO BE ASKED CONCERNING the 1920 Revolution must focus on the timing as much as on the causes and goals. Why did the Iraqis wait until 1920 to revolt against an occupation that had been completed in 1917? What were the original causes of the revolution, as opposed to the causes that were stated after the fact or the ones that evolved during the course of the revolution? Was the revolution isolated in its timing, causes, and goals, or was there a connection to a regional or global context? And most importantly, was it, in fact, a revolution?

To answer these questions and any others that might occur during this examination of the revolution's history, we have to consider all the possible sources of influence that led to the revolution. Some sources were, of course, only indirect in their influence and perhaps not as demographically far-reaching as others; but this cannot be the basis for ruling out their contribution to the revolution. This chapter will discuss the socioeconomic and political causes of the revolution and how they contributed to the eruption of violence in the Middle Euphrates during the summer of 1920.

POLITICAL CAUSES

From accounts of participants in the revolution, it is clear that the major reasons behind the 1920 Revolution were local. Prominent among them was the British refusal to grant Iraq full independence as promised numerous times, especially in the declaration of General Maude upon capturing Baghdad in 1917 and in the Anglo-French Declaration.[1] These two documents and the Fourteen Points presented by U.S. president Woodrow Wilson in a speech before Congress on 8 January 1918 were omnipresent in the memoirs of the revolution's leaders and the records of their contacts with British officials.[2]

On 19 March 1917, shortly after the capture of Baghdad, the British distributed a proclamation signed by Lieutenant General Sir Stanley Maude, the commander of the British forces, addressing the people of Baghdad. It read in part:

> To the People of Baghdad Vilayet:
> In the name of my King, and in the name of the peoples over whom he rules, I address you as follows:
>
> Our military operations have as their object the defeat of the enemy, and the driving of him from these territories. In order to complete this task, I am charged with absolute and supreme control of all regions in which British troops operate; but our armies have not come into your cities and lands as conquerors, or enemies, but as liberators.
>
> Since the days of Hulaku your citizens have been subject to the tyranny of strangers, your palaces have fallen into ruins, your gardens have sunken in desolation, and your forefathers and yourselves have groaned in bondage. Your sons have been carried off to wars not of your seeking, your wealth has been stripped from you by unjust men and squandered in distant places.[3]

Although the proclamation was read in his name, General Maude, it seems, was not in favor of making such an elaborate promise to the Arabs, even under the necessity of wartime and the need to win the hearts and minds of the population. He considered it "unnecessary and ill-timed."[4] Maude was not in favor of revealing any British intentions concerning the Arab territories and, certainly, not in favor of any policy that might complicate the task of conducting his military mission, which required unquestionable authority. The proclamation, as he correctly predicted, gave the Iraqis high expectations about their future that were contrary to what the British had planned for them.

Maude's attitude was deemed misguided by British officials, who, disastrously, disagreed with him. In a letter dated 10 October 1920, Gertrude Bell impenitently explained the circumstances of the drafting and distribution of the proclamation, as well as Maude's attitude toward it. She also expressed her dislike for him and the British press that held him in high regard:

> On the whole the papers write egregious nonsense in detail—such as, for instance, that the management of Arab affairs has gone wrong ever since the death of Maude!—Maude! Anyone more totally removed from the remotest idea of self-government in Asia it would be impossible to conceive. Keine Ahnung. He indignantly accepted the proclamation drafted at home which is usually attributed to him and published it only under stringent orders. After which Sir Percy spent 6 laborious months in attempting to uphold even the most moderate civil rights for the local population. No one ever chose a more fortunate moment for dying than he.[5]

The proclamation further promised the people of Baghdad the ability "to participate in the management of [their] civil affairs in collaboration with the political representatives of Great Britain who accompany the British Army," in order to ultimately realize their nationalist dream of creating a larger Arab state by joining their "kinsmen in North, East, South, and West" and ending centuries of foreign rule over Arab land since the invasion of Hulaku.

To appreciate the ramifications of the promises presented in those documents, one may turn to the letters of Captain James S. Mann, the assistant political officer in Shāmiyya, a place that became the heartland of the revolution. In a letter to his father dated 4 June 1920, he wrote: "They [i.e., the Iraqis] have of course one absolutely genuine cry, which is that the Allies, ourselves included, have not kept our promises. If you read the Anglo-French Declaration of November 18,

1918, and the address to the town of Baghdad made on our triumphal entry in March 1917, you will see that this is perfectly true."[6]

As the protracted occupation continued to burden the Iraqi population with numerous difficulties and to make clear that the British had overstayed their welcome and were not serious about keeping their word, these politically expedient promises became the Achilles' heel of the British occupation. Initially, Iraqi notables and their delegates peacefully reminded their British governors of the government's declared plans. But their demands either fell on deaf ears or sometimes resulted in hostile treatment. Iraqis reciprocated with violence of their own. Captain Mann reported on a series of botched meetings with the shaykhs of the Fatla tribe that took place in the first half of July 1920, before they joined the revolution. He quoted Sayyid ʿAlwān al-Yāsiri as saying to him: "You have offered us independence. We never asked for it, we never dreamt of it till you put the idea into our heads: for hundreds of years the country has lived in a state as far removed from independence as it is possible to conceive; then you come with your promise of independence, and every time we ask for it you imprison us."[7]

The comment Captain Mann made in response to the above statement captures the essence of the conflict between the colonial political interests with those of local military administrators, not to mention the interests of the colonized: "I don't see what we can do about these broken promises; no one but fools or politicians would ever had made them, but as they were made they are in a way binding . . . the politician must prevaricate in order to live, and thus make things intolerable for an Administration like ours!"[8]

This sentiment was also shared by Gertrude Bell, who, in spite of supporting the Maude declaration, was annoyed by her government planning the Iraqi future in a way that would not be compatible with the Iraqi way of life:

> I pray that the people at home may be rightly guided and realize that the only chance here is to recognize political ambitions from the first, not to try to squeeze the Arabs into our mould and have our hands forced in a year—who knows? Perhaps less, the world is moving so fast—with the result that the chaos to north and east overwhelms Mesopotamia also. I wish

> I carried more weight. I've written to Edwin and this week I'm writing to Sir A. Hirtzel. But the truth is I'm in a minority of one in the Mesopotamian political service—or nearly—and yet I'm so sure I'm right that I would go to the stake for it—or perhaps just a little less painful form of testimony if they wish for it! But they must see, they must know at home. They can't be so blind as not to read such gigantic writing on the wall as the world at large is sitting before their eyes."[9]

Another event that became the focus of heated dispute was the influence of the Arab Revolt in the Ḥijaz area and the subsequent formation of the government of Fayṣal in Syria. Following a series of letters between Sharīf Ḥusayn of Mecca and Sir Henry McMahon, the British high commissioner in Cairo, the former pledged to revolt against the Ottoman Empire and denounce the Ottomans as enemies of Islam, which he did later in a proclamation issued 27 June 1916, shortly after launching the revolt. Sharīf Ḥusayn criticized the ruling Committee of Union and Progress (CUP) for violating settled Islamic rules on fasting and for looking the other way when a paper in Istanbul (*Al-Ijtihād*) "published an article maligning the life of the Prophet . . . under the eye of the Grand Vizier of the Ottoman Empire and its Shaykh al-Islam." The paper also, he added, "adds to this impiety by denying the word of God that 'the male shall receive two portions' and decides that they [male and female] shall share equally under the law of inheritance."[10] Having secured the support of the British, in the form of supplies, arms, and money, Sharīf Ḥusayn launched his revolt on 10 June 1916, by attacking the Ottoman garrison in Mecca. He controlled the entire Ḥijaz region by September except for the holy city of Medina, which was put under siege for the duration of the revolt. It is important to note here that the proclamation makes no mention of Arab nationalism or Arab independence. Indeed, it opens with a paragraph praising "the Great Ottoman Sultans" and it laments the CUP's assault on the sultan's power.

The Arab Revolt was not a popular revolution against the Ottomans, but essentially a Hashemite revolt aided by levies from the Ḥijaz region, led by Sharīf Ḥusayn's son, Fayṣal, with the assistance of former Ottoman officers, mostly Iraqis, who became known later as the sharīfian officers. There was also a contingent of British military advisers; the most well-known among them was T. E. Lawrence (Lawrence of Arabia). The revolt ended with the successful capture of Damascus on 1 October 1918. Following the capture of Syria, Fayṣal began to establish an Arab administration on the basis of assumptions included in the sharīf's correspondence with McMahon.

The presence of Iraqi officers in leading positions in the revolt, along with the large-scale British propaganda in favor of Sharīf Ḥusayn and his efforts, made Iraq, to a certain extent, a party to the revolt.[11] From the attitude of the leaders of Iraq's 1920 Revolution and their demand that the British establish an independent government led by one of the sons of Sharīf Ḥusayn of Mecca, it is clear that the Iraqis, except the pro-Ottoman elite, at least agreed with, even admired, the Arab Revolt.[12] Indeed, they sent a delegate to Mecca and Syria to explain their position and to establish contact with the leader of the Arab Revolt, Sharīf Ḥusayn of Mecca, and his sons. But the delegate, Muhammad Riḍā al-Shabībi, was "shocked," as he put it, by the regression and stagnation of the territory over which the sharīf ruled, especially Mecca. Even the high-ranking officers serving the sharīf complained to him about the "negligence, gross laziness and the lack of attention to the administrative, cultural, military and social affairs of the country."[13]

From al-Shabībi's recollection, it seems that Fayṣal was not in a position to help the Iraqi participants in the revolution except to wish them well. He was hopelessly engaged in lobbying the British to help him with the threats against his throne by the French, who were determined to oust him from Syria. Fayṣal did claim later, however, that he sent 20,000 Turkish pounds in gold to help the Iraqis, but the money was never delivered. When he became king, he investigated the matter and found out that the money had been divided among some people on the way instead of going to help the revolution. Fayṣal did not disclose the identity of those who stole the money—if there was any money in the first place. This cover-up was ably described as "the first mistake in the [modern] history of Iraq."[14]

The revolution in Iraq broke out while al-Shabībi was still in Damascus.[15] Furthermore, Iraqis initially called for another son of Sharīf Ḥusayn, ʿAbdullah, to be king of Iraq, which shows that they were not particularly inspired by Fayṣal, whose weakness in Syria was the opposite of their gathering strength in 1920.[16] As fate would have it, on the same day Fayṣal suffered his devastating defeat at the hands of the French in the decisive Battle of Maysalūn—on 24 July 1920—the Iraqi fighters scored their most impressive victory, at Rāranjiyya.

A number of Iraqi officers, led by Ramaḍān Shlāsh, attacked Dayr al-Zōr in December 1919. It appears that they acted on behalf of the ʿAhd Association. Fayṣal and the Arab administration in Damascus, which did not support this move, worked out the border differences with the British. Also prominent among the Iraqi officers in Dayr al-Zōr was Mawlūd Mukhliṣ, who replaced Shlāsh as part of the deal between Fayṣal and the British. The Iraqi officers who mobilized in Dayr al-Zōr made too much of their supposedly inspiring the Iraqi population to revolt.[17] Indeed, history reveals that they were the ones who asked for help from the Iraqi tribes of the Middle Euphrates. In a letter dated 17 August 1920, addressed to the top cleric, Mirza M. Taqi al-Shirazi, they asked for money to save their movement from collapse.[18] The money was collected but was not sent, because of the objection by Sayyid Muḥsin Abu Ṭabīkh, who held the officers in low regard. He first pledged 800 pounds in gold, but said to his companions: "Ask me to give any amount of money to any group you want; for I am ready and willing to comply with pride. But for those mercenaries, I am not ready to give a penny."[19] Given this low regard, which seems to have been shared by many others, it is not likely that Iraqis looked toward the officers of Dayr al-Zōr for inspiration, but their actions against the British must have contributed to the general atmosphere of resistance against the occupation, mainly by exposing the vulnerability of British forces.

Another major regional event that was perhaps a motivating factor for Iraqis was the Egyptian Revolution of 1919.[20] A delegation of landowners and lawyers was formed in November 1918 to participate in the Paris Peace Conference on behalf of Egypt. The group of delegates (*wafd*) was headed by Saʿd Zaghlul, a self-made lawyer with a European education. Since they did not hold any official status, their request to represent Egypt was denied, and Zaghlul was sent into exile on Malta. This move caused enormous sympathy for Zaghlul and his party, and many riots and violent events ensued in rural and urban Egypt. Ultimately, the *wafd* was allowed to represent Egypt at the conference, but without much to gain. But the *wafd* was allowed to engage in lengthy direct negotiations with Great Britain, during which they pressed for full independence, while the British offered conditional independence under their auspices. Ultimately, this process ended by the British unilaterally declaring Egypt's independence in 1922.

Iraqis were well aware of the situation in Egypt from the Syrian and Egyptian papers. According to Muḥammad Mahdi al-Baṣīr, Egyptian papers continually brought to Iraq the news of Egyptian resistance, and no gathering went without the praise of Saʿd Zaghlul and his patriotism.[21] Also, as early as 1918, there was a bookstore in Najaf owned by a man named ʿAbd al-Hamid al-Zahidi, dedicated in part to the distribution and sale of Egyptian and Syrian papers. This bookstore later became the headquarters of the revolutionary movement in Najaf, with connections to all parts of the Middle Euphrates.[22] The Egyptian Revolution was also present in the minds of Middle Euphrates intellectuals in 1920. *Al-Furat*, the first newspaper published during the 1920 Revolution, referred, in its second issue, to the similarity between Iraq's revolution and "its sisters, the Irish and the Egyptian revolutions."[23] The influence of the *wafd* experience on the Iraqis residing in Baghdad was clear from their attempt to form their own *wafd* to negotiate with the British administration. But the British thwarted the effort of this *wafd* just as it had that of the Egyptian. After a series of contacts, the British administrator, Colonel Arnold Wilson, agreed to meet with the fifteen elected delegates on 20 July 1920. Nonetheless, he arranged to undermine their position by inviting also twenty Iraqis who were known for their pro-British position. But his attempt did not succeed. The two Iraqi groups met before seeing Wilson and agreed on a unified national agenda. After a disappointing showdown at the meeting, the British administration decided to pursue the delegates, who eventually escaped to the Middle Euphrates to join the revolution. Some unfortunate Baghdadis were captured and were either executed or sent into exile on Henjam, an island off the coast of Iran.[24]

In addition to these events, Iraqis were also influenced by the political struggles in Iran and Turkey. The former had maintained its influence on Iraq through the Shīʿa connection and the prominence of Iranian mujtahids who resided in Iraq and provided spiritual leadership for the Iraqi Shīʿa, without completely severing their relations to their homeland. Similarly, the Sunni connection to Turkey and the centuries of Ottoman control of Iraq made Iraq strongly connected to Turkey and influenced by its internal events.

Indeed, the Iranian battle of constitutionalism (*al-Mashrūṭa*) and anticonstitutionalism (*al-Mustabidda*) was fought, in part, in Iraq's holy cities, where prominent Iranian mujtahids resided, such as Kadhim al-Yazdi, Muḥammad Ḥusayn al-Nāʿīni, and al-Ākhund al-Khurāsāni—the last two being the champions of constitutionalism, while al-Yazdi was not in favor of the idea.[25] The Iranian constitutional revolution of 1906 forced the Iranian monarch, Muzaffar al-Dīn Shah, to sign on 5 August 1906 a proclamation to hold national elections for a constituent assembly whose role was to draft a constitution.[26]

In the course of the bitter dispute among the mujtahids in the Iraqi holy cities and their respective constituents, who adopted opposite views depending on whether the mujtahid they followed was a supporter or a detractor of constitutionalism, a general sense of awareness was formed among the Shīʿa of Iraq, who ultimately supported the constitutionalist cause. In fact, the dispute about constitutionalism led to the formation of something close to a popular culture. The historian Ali al-Wardi notes that a Najafi book dealer, who was a child in 1906, remembered that children playing in the streets of Najaf divided themselves into a *Mashrūṭa* team and a *Mustabidda* team, and the games often ended in a fight fashioned after the disputes among the adults.[27]

It was this awareness of the benefits of constitutionalism among the Iraqis that led them to respond to the British plebiscite of 1918–1919 by voting for "a government with an Arab king whose authority is limited by a constitution."[28]

Similarly, the constitutionalist struggle in Turkey, the center of the Ottoman Empire, created a division among Iraqis, whose daily life was directly influenced by the policies and balance of power in Istanbul. The Ottoman reformers, known as the Young Turks, had managed to impose a constitution in July 1908 against the will of Sultan ʿAbd al-Hamīd after threatening to invade the capital. The constitution of 1876, which had been suspended by ʿAbd al-Hamīd in 1878, was restored, and a newly elected parliament was convened in December 1908. But a counterrevolution took place in the spring of next year, mainly by groups supportive of the Islamic identity of the empire. The Third Army marched on Istanbul and crushed the opposition. Sultan

ʿAbd al-Hamīd, accused of encouraging the counterrevolution, was deposed. He was replaced by his brother Rashād, who ruled until 1918 as Mehmet V.

Meanwhile, there had been many separatist movements throughout the Ottoman Empire, from Eastern Europe to the Levant. The news of these movements and the successful quest for independence in some cases—mostly with help from Western powers—reached Iraq and provided hope for self-determination. But this hope began to fade as the British occupation established a colonialist administration in the country, leaving Iraqis no choice other than a violent revolution.

From this discussion of events and movements in the Middle East, it becomes clear that the 1920 Revolution did not occur in a political or ideological vacuum. Every event contributed in some way to the idea or the course of the revolution. Some events may have inspired the Iraqis to revolt, while others presented them with the lessons and tactics of revolution. But these factors notwithstanding, the 1920 Revolution was first and foremost an Iraqi nationalist revolution motivated and executed by domestic elements. As evidenced by the emphatic statements of the participants, its execution and financing were purely local. Almost all the key participants indicated that they were not acting on behalf of, or in consort with, any foreign group or entity. Additionally, all of them said unequivocally that no assistance was given to them by anyone, that they financed the war effort from their own limited resources.

SOCIOECONOMIC CAUSES

In addition to the internal and external political causes, the revolution was also a result of various economic and social pressures that forced Iraqis to react with unreserved violence. To contextualize the local causes and motivations of the revolution, it is important to examine them in light of the events that preceded the eruption of armed resistance, namely, the policies of British officials during the invasion and occupation.

Great Britain invaded Iraq primarily for the purpose of securing its strategic interests, especially the region's oil. The Persian Gulf was also important for the government of India for military and commercial purposes. In the words of Prime Minister Asquith, "The object of sending a force . . . to Mesopotamia was to secure the neutrality of the Arabs, to safeguard our interests in the Persian Gulf, to protect the oil fields, and generally to maintain the authority of our flag in the East."[29] But the British had begun arranging for the takeover of these territories the previous century, in agreement with the French and other Great Powers. By the time of the invasion, Britain had already secured the allegiance of several Arab rulers in the area, especially those who feared Ottoman encroachment on their territories. They had treaties with the shaykhs in Muscat, Bahrain, Kuwait, and other rulers on the shores of the gulf. The British also had amicable relations with Ibn Saud, the founder of modern Saudi Arabia, and Shaykh Khazʿal, the ruler of Muḥammara, southwest of Iran, who feared both the Ottomans and the Persians. All these local rulers aspired to acquire British patronage and protection, thus becoming essential to the British war effort against the Ottomans. They were informed about the scope, objectives, and nature of the hostilities when war was declared in the last week of October 1914.

The first British force landed at the Fao peninsula, in southern Baṣra, on 6 November 1914—three days after the Ottoman Empire entered an alliance with Germany and on the eve of the Ottoman declaration of war against Great Britain and France. But this force had been deployed from India on 16 October 1914[30] and had arrived in Bahrain on 23 October, two weeks before the Ottoman declaration of war, where they remained "watchfully awaiting developments."[31] On 23 November, Sir Percy Cox read in Arabic a proclamation that included the following statement of policy: "The British Government has now occupied Baṣra, but though a state of war with the Ottoman Government still prevails, yet we have no enmity or ill-will against the population, to whom we hope to prove good friends and protectors. No remnant of Turkish administration now remains in this region. In place thereof the British flag has been established, under which you will enjoy the benefits of liberty and justice, both in regard to your religious and secular affairs."[32]

The relatively easy occupation of Baṣra gave the British a misplaced sense of confidence that caused them to direct a weak campaign against the Ottoman army up the Tigris River without the proper support. On 29 April 1916, the entire British army participating in that campaign, commanded by General Townshend, surrendered to the Ottomans in Kūt after a brutal siege for five months. The force included 13,309 soldiers and officers, including 2,870 British soldiers and officers, while the rest were Indians.[33] A commission charged with investigating the defeat concluded that the British "advance to Baghdad under the conditions existing in October, 1915, was an offensive movement based upon political and military miscalculations and attempted with tired and insufficient forces, and inadequate preparations."[34]

Nevertheless, British forces under General Maude occupied Baghdad in March 1917 and finally accomplished the occupation of Iraq as a whole by 1918, when they occupied Mosul. There has been, however, a lasting dispute over the technicalities of Mosul's destiny. As noted by Phebe Marr and others, the Armistice of Mudros, which was announced on 31 October 1918, covered the territories occupied by the British at the time of the signing of the treaty. British forces occupied the city on 7 November, a week after the armistice was announced.[35] This act was justified by the British according to a broad interpretation of the terms of Mudros, which allowed the Allies "the right to occupy any strategic points in the event of any situation arising which threatens the security of the Allies."[36]

Iraqi groups' reactions to the British occupation varied according to their interests. The most favorable reaction came from the merchants, contractors, and farm owners, who made very handsome revenues from doing business with the British, as opposed to their dealings with the Ottomans. The British paid generously for goods and services, while the Ottomans had confiscated and conscripted. Another group amenable to British occupation consisted of aspiring notables, whose loyalty was going to be given to the victors regardless of who they might be.[37] The British also managed to purchase the loyalty of several tribal chiefs, who promised to deliver the consent of their constituents. But British efforts to secure the consent of religious authorities in Iraq proved fruitless. British officials operated under the false assumption that centuries of Ottoman oppression would be enough to make the Shīʿa clergy ready to accept anyone who might deliver them from their ordeal at the hands of the Sunni Ottomans. To the contrary, Shīʿa scholars in Najaf, Karbalāʾ, and Baghdad sided with the Sunni Ottomans against the non-Muslim invaders—many of them, like Muhammad Saʿīd al-Ḥabbūbi, actively participated in the fighting and mobilization of resistance forces, while more senior scholars, including Mahdi al-Khāliṣi and Mahdi al-Ḥaydari, used their religious credentials to call for a binding jihad against the invaders. Their effort reached its climax in 1920 with the countrywide popular revolution, which cost the British more than four hundred lives and forty million pounds.

Following the completion of the occupation, the British divided Iraq into sixteen provinces, each of them called a *liwāʾ*, and each province was in turn divided into several districts. Indian laws and bureaucratic norms were introduced, and Indian currency (the rupee) replaced Turkish currency. On the matter of replacing existing laws by alien alternatives, the question arose from a dilemma faced by the occupation officials when they claimed to be completely unaware of Ottoman laws. When Iraq was being occupied, the Ottoman judges and other court officials fled the region and absconded with or destroyed their records. According to British officials in charge of administering justice in Iraq, they found no English translation of the laws that had been applied in the territory before the British occupation.[38] While it was against international law to introduce foreign laws and legal patterns to an occupied country, as acknowledged by the British officials themselves, they did so anyway, citing necessity and what they claimed was a lack of adequate local laws—this was, in fact, just their lack of knowledge of such laws. The adviser to the Ministry of Justice explained the rationale for the replacement of Iraqi laws: "The abandonment of the legal system to which the people were accustomed must necessarily cause serious inconvenience to them and could not fail to be unpopular; especially having regard to the fact that much of the law is religious in origin."[39] Indeed, the most serious inconvenience came not from the introduction of new laws, although this was illegal and improper, but from the arbitrary appointment of junior officers as judges, in spite of their lack of any aptitude or training to adjudicate the cases before them.

In general, as one historian observed concerning the "relations between the civil population and the military authorities, the fact was never lost sight of that it was a military occupation and that a war had to be won"; given this imperative, "From the first to last, the needs of the inhabitants were subordinated to those of the occupying Forces."[40] British officers were appointed to govern each province with almost full authority to do what they pleased. They used the help of lower-ranking officers (mostly captains) to govern the districts, also with full authority. In a 1920 letter from Ghammas, Captain James S. Mann wrote of his own astonishment at being appointed, at the age of twenty-six, a *hakim* (governor):

> It is odd that an entire stranger, who at the beginning couldn't speak one word of the language, and whose mental make-up was about as different as could be well imagined, should be put straight away to an almost uncontrolled eminence from which to utter his fiats to a perpetual chorus of "*Kull Shay tamur ju-abal* [sic] *Insha'allah yasir*"—Every order given by your Honor shall, please God, be carried out.[41]

Such absolute power, coupled with the predisposition of the officers to feel disdain for their "subjects," made for a dangerous formula that caused many officers to meet violent death at the hands, or at the behest, of the scorned shaykhs. Sometimes, as acknowledged by their colleagues, the slain officers had invited their own demise. Gertrude Bell, known as the architect of modern Iraq, wrote to her father on 16 August 1920:

> The worst news is that Colonel Leachman has been ambushed and killed . . .
>
> . . . I've heard the Leachman story today from my most trusted ʿAqaili—this is what he had heard and I expect it's true. Col. L. stopped at the tents of the Shaikh of the Zoba on his way to Fallujah and abused him in very violent terms for not preserving the peace of the road. He always used extremely unmeasured language to Arabs and Sh.[aikh] Dhari had many grudges against him. Added to which Dari is a mis-stitched vindictive man. Col. L. left his tent alone, and Dhari's slaves ambushed him. He was a wild soldier of fortune but a very gallant officer and his name was known all over Arabia.[42]

According to the records of Ḍāri's trial, he claimed that Colonel Leachman had abused him both verbally and physically: "He called me names, spat in my face and drew his gun on me, then began kicking me—I was sick that day." After being thrown in the station's jail cell, Ḍāri recalled, "I heard three or four shots, then [my nephew] Ṣlaibi opened the door for me. I came out to find the colonel slain." But some witnesses told the court that Ḍāri did participate in the killing.[43] Leachman's behavior with Ḍāri follows a pattern of abuse he displayed everywhere he governed. Bell recalled an instance when an associate told her that he expected Leachman to be murdered eventually, a prediction that she communicated to the political ruler, Arnold Wilson.[44] When Leachman was in Mosul, he insulted the shaykh of the Shammar tribe, ʿAjīl al-Yāwar, causing him to revolt. He told Bell, "It was Leachman . . . He told me I was like a woman and that he would give me no recognition in my tribe." Bell had no doubt that he was telling her the truth: "It's so exactly like Colonel Leachman," she commented.[45]

Such abuses were sometimes due to a lack of cultural awareness on the part of most of the officers who were "put straight away to an almost uncontrolled eminence." They were not made aware of the intricacies of Iraqi culture and thus offended the wrong people inadvertently. One such incident illustrates the danger of a lack of knowledge of Arab customs and decorum. One day an important shaykh from the Āl Bdair tribe named Ṣagban Abu Jāsim was sitting in the office of Captain Webb, the assistant political officer in the ʿAfak district, when the captain's dog came in and began sniffing the shaykh's cloak. The shaykh rudely yelled at and removed the dog. Captain Webb asked him for the reason for his behavior, and the Shaykh told him, "He is *nejis*" (impure). Captain Webb replied, "He is cleaner than you because I bathe him with soap twice a day." The Shaykh stormed out of the office, saying, "God curse your father and the fathers of all the Englishmen!"[46] It is needless to say that the hearts and minds of the whole tribe were lost forever because of that one imprudent statement by Captain Webb.

To further examine the experience of British officers as local governors of Iraqi territories, a thorough consideration of the letters of Captain James S. Mann is appropriate at this point. He governed the Eastern Shāmiyya district, which included Shāmiyya (then called Umm al Baʿrūr), Shāfiʿiyya, Ghammas, Mishkhāb, Shināfiyya, and

Mahannāwiyya.[47] He occupied the post from 26 August 1919 to 22 June 1920—he was killed in July by a sniper's bullet during the siege of Kūfa as he was walking with his superior, Major Norbury. All the existing references attribute his death to an unidentified shooter. But Shaykh Wahaiyd Āl ʿAbbūd al-ʿĪsāwi told me that his late father, ʿAbbūd Āl ʿAnayyid, then the shaykh of the Āl ʿĪsā tribe, was the shooter. Shaykh ʿAbbūd Āl ʿAnayyid

> was jailed in Ḥilla along with more than thirty tribal and community leaders and was not included in the pardon given by the High Commissioner to the others after the revolution, because he killed a British officer. He was then brought to Kūfa for trial before a special tribunal. The prosecutor asked for the death penalty for his killing Captain James Mann, but the judge extended the pardon to him because he killed the officer in battle.[48]

Captain Mann's letters to family and friends were edited and published by his father shortly after his death. There is a thorough description of the district, the people, and the daily activities he had to perform as governor and chief judge of the district. Ghammas, where Sayyid Muḥsin Abu Ṭabīkh lived and owned a vast amount of land, was under Captain Mann's jurisdiction. The two men had a working relationship, but not without occasional troubles dictated by changing circumstances. Also, many other Middle Euphrates notables were residing in this particular district, and their joining the revolution was the turning point in the course of its events.

There are three significant stories related by the letters of Captain Mann: the lack of experience of junior officers who were placed in positions of absolute power over a very recalcitrant tribal population; the general prejudice and condescension felt by almost all British civilian and military personnel toward the local Arab population; and the manifestation of the "white man's burden" ideology among the British officials who wrote off their revenue-increasing measures as a service for the local people, who were often drafted to render free labor.

Undeterred by a lack of knowledge, Captain Mann taught himself some Arabic in a few weeks and began to handle his day-to-day tasks with the limited communication skills he had acquired, including adjudicating land disputes and presiding over criminal trials.[49] His logic as a jurist was very simple, and disturbingly arbitrary, as he revealed in a letter to his father on 15 February 1920: "I hate judicial work, and have an almost irresistible desire to release anyone the moment he pleads not guilty; but we are having a lot of trouble with thieves just now, and as these people [i.e., the accused] all belong to the profession of thieving, they are probably guilty."[50]

Such was his judgment, which could not be subject to appeal. It was backed by the appearance of power and the threat of more punishment for those who objected or failed to cooperate. He wrote to his father on 10 March of the same year, "Why they do what I tell them is something of a mystery to me, but I suppose they think I can do far more to punish them than I really could, even if I wanted to."[51] The extent of his abuse of power is clearly obvious in what he had told his father in a letter dated 1 October 1919:

> To-day I used my maximum power and sentenced three lovely thieves to six months each. I tried to behave legally, but European ideas of giving the accused a fair show are simply ridiculous when applied to these people. Each side can bring fifty witnesses—their whole tribe—to swear exact opposites [...] So I told them that as they were all liars obviously, and one was evidently a thief, I should give them all the same punishment.[52]

It is hard to follow his reasoning in the above opinion, however, for it is not necessarily "obvious," as he claimed, that when two parties swear exact opposites, both parties are liars. What is obvious, however, is that sending all three men to jail was an arbitrary act made possible by the giving of unchecked power to a man with no sense of judicial responsibility and no experience in the administration of justice. The British introduced not only an alien law, the one used by their India administration, but also a novel philosophy of applying the law. When the truth became quite blurred, Captain Mann adopted local customs that relied on human vulnerabilities. The following story, from a letter to his mother on 15 April 1920, demonstrates the arbitrary methods of his administrative and judicial work when challenged by complicated cases. It deserves to be quoted at some length:

> As an example of a silly piece of trouble of a kind aroused daily by our double position as supporters of the tribal system and at the same time lovers of justice, here is a case which has given me some annoyance. I have one tract of land occupied by pieces of several tribes, who before my time were invited and compelled to elect a sheikh to themselves. This they did, and the choice fell on a respectable harmless little man called Ali al Hasan Agha, a loyal subject but not a strong character, and of no special family or warlike claims. However, there he is, and as sheikh has to be supported; and on the whole he does his work better than many a bigger man. He came and complained that two of his sirkals (sub-headmen of sections) owed him trifling sums of money on account of an old affair with Government; they always delayed payment and insulted him, and this was not good for his honour and his authority. I called them both, and they indignantly denied, saying they had paid up their shares in full at the time. I should have let the matter drop at that, as there were no proofs or witnesses on either side; but Ali came again, and practically claimed damages for the insult involved in supposing him a liar. I said to both parties eventually that it was obvious someone was lying and there was no evidence; that my experience of oaths was not very encouraging; but in view of the position of Ali I would send the whole party to Karbala to swear by ʿAbbas the famous oath which few like to perjure against wittingly . . . They have gone off very much displeased with life, to return, I hope, in a suitably chastened frame of mind, when I propose to fine the liar 500 rupees.[53]

The dilemma in Mann's work was to reconcile two imperatives: the idealism of dispensing justice among the population, and the reality of having to work with tribes by securing the loyalty of the shaykhs, who, in turn, would deliver the collective loyalty of their tribes if their own interests were served. It seems, as the above passage demonstrates, that when the two imperatives clashed, the British priority was to support the shaykhs at the expense of justice. British officials rewarded friendly shaykhs with land and tax relief and stood by their side in case of disputes with other shaykhs or even with their own tribesmen. They also upheld the tribal system by the issuing of the Tribal Disputes Regulations in 1918. These British "efforts to restore tribal organization meant the re-imposition of feudalism, contrary to the principle of the evolution of political institutions."[54] It also caused an environment of continued conflict among the tribes and the shaykhs, especially when land awards to friendly shaykhs meant encroaching on land already owned, or claimed, by a rival.

But Mann deserves much credit for using his power to combat some of the most appalling tribal practices, such as the compensation for murder and injuries (*faṣl*) that involved delivering women to the family of the victim. Faced with a dispute on this issue, he told a quite dissatisfied shaykh who wanted to maintain the tribal custom, including the women-for-blood arrangements: "I replied that I knew all about tribal custom, that some of it was good and some very bad, and that they would jolly well have to stop the payment of women as part of blood-money, and that the British Government would never recognize it."[55] The case involved a woman who was engaged to marry one of Captain Mann's low-level officials, but the tribe objected, claiming "that previously this girl had been allotted to someone else in part payment of blood-money, following murder." Mann sent interested parties to Najaf, and the Shīʿa mujtahid ruled against the tribal custom, saying that she could marry the official—a verdict Captain Mann was very happy to affirm. While the religious position was in clear opposition to the tribal custom of using women as a commodity in the settlement of tribal disputes, Captain Mann still falsely claimed later on that this practice was "a private arrangement sanctioned by tribal and religious custom."[56]

This misrepresentation of local religiosity fits into a larger context of a preconceived contempt toward the local customs. The reason for the contempt was a shared belief among almost all British personnel that Iraqis, especially the Arabs, were bad apples. For Captain Mann, Iraq was "a country where everyone lies all the time," as opposed to an Englishman like himself, who was "civilised too much."[57] Mann combined two of his prejudices in one sentence describing the people in his district: "They tell lies like the Irish—art for art's sake; they are temperamentally, I think, pro-British because they always respect military strength."[58] On another occasion, thirty notables sent him "a congratulatory address from Ghammas" to welcome him and to tell him that his order to build a dam to strengthen the bank of the river, a branch of the Euphrates, had been heeded and that the project had been accomplished by the tribes, among many other gracious words and good wishes. He reciprocated by describing "many of them [as] famous scoundrels."[59]

After living among the people of the Middle Euphrates, Captain Mann hardly changed his views. This is not to say that the behavior of local people always confirmed his prejudices—far from it. But it seems that these prejudices were so entrenched that even good behavior had to be explained as conforming to them. In describing a meeting with ʿAzrā, an Iraqi Jewish notable in his district, he did not fail to take a shot at the Arabs:

> Before dinner three tiny little girls, sisters of his new daughter-in-law, came in and very shyly said "How do you do" and when they went out "Good night" in English; and afterwards we heard them in the next room singing "God save the King!" They were dressed just as English children, and were complete with hats: they come from Hillah, where there is a proper school, and are learning English. Being with Jews one realises very sharply how incredibly backward the Arab is; and it is really pleasant to talk to people who, quite indubitably, are solidly delighted to see the British Government, and want nothing but its continuance.
>
> After dinner he and his sons told us endless stories of Turkish times and the way in which Jews and Christians suffered as compared with Muslims. The marvel is how they ever managed to become rich, but somehow they did, and at the moment I suppose that Azra's capital may be £20,000 or more.[60]

The tone of Mann's second paragraph shows clear skepticism about the veracity of the stories ʿAzrā and his sons told him about their suffering under the Turks, but he let it slide by, since the narrators were pro-British. Of course, Mann should have known that it is erroneous to compare three rich Iraqi girls from a big city with their counterparts in his rural district, which had no school or a decent road, even after his government had controlled the country for six years. In his one year as governor, his efforts were focused on revenue- (tax-) generating projects but no school was built; the project was kept as a dream for the future. Also, one must not infer from the above quotation that Mann was appreciative of Jews for any reason other than their exhibited pro-British positions, an attitude that was especially held by the Jewish notables, not unlike their non-Jewish counterparts. In the words of one historian: "It is wrong to assume, however, that Iraqi Jews as a community asked for direct British rule. Such views were most probably expressed by the upper layer of the Jewish trading class, which was the main beneficiary of the British presence. Similar views were also expressed by Muslim and Christian notables in a letter to the high commissioner in June 1921."[61]

In a letter to his mother on 27 March 1920, Mann equated the mind of the Jew and that of the Arab, whom he described as "such an inconsequent mixture of the knight of chivalry, the high-spirited child, and the fawning, false-tongued Oriental." His description of the Arab and Jewish minds as "European, compared with the real Eastern races" seems to be out of place in the same paragraph.[62]

The population of the district that Mann governed was almost entirely Shīʿa, whose religion he had the most negative view of. It is clear that his negativity about the Shīʿa and their religion was not based on any investigation—he did not have the time to do so—but stemmed from the general anti-Shīʿa attitude held by almost all British officials. Gertrude Bell clearly articulated this general viewpoint in a letter to her father dated 3 October 1920:

> The Shiʿah problem is probably the most formidable in this country [. . .] If you're going to have anything like really representative institutions you would have a majority of Shīʿa. For that reason you can never have 3 completely autonomous provinces. Sunni Mosul must be retained as a part of the Mesopotamian state in order to adjust the balance.[63]

But Bell was not after "anything like really representative institutions" so much as a friendly government readily susceptible to manipulation by British interests. The first government Bell helped shape, in November 1920, consisted of twenty-three ministers, of whom only two were Shīʿa. Bell wrote on 3 November 1920, "The Shīʿa complain that they are not sufficiently represented on the Council." She dismissed this complaint on the grounds "that nearly all their leading men are Persian subjects." Then she counters their complaint with one of her own: "They are the most difficult element of the country, frondeur almost to a man, and entirely indifferent to public interests."[64] It was in that cynical atmosphere that Captain Mann and his fellow officers came to form their attitudes toward the Shīʿa. Hence, he wrote to Lady Mary Murray on 4 February 1920:

> The Shīʿa religion is deadening, obscurantist, and definitely anti-human from beginning to end, and it is a curse on the face of the earth. Not one scrap of the ethics of the Prophet is remembered, God is a meaningless term, and all the expressions that I've quoted are survivals of the free desert speech of the Arab before he was spoiled by the fruits of his conquests and particularly the worse side of Persian religiosity. The Qurʾan is in parts magnificent, and there is hope for the Sunni: but the Shīʿah seems to me to be blighted from birth, and that's why the peasant is such a much better and honester man than the Shaykh and the "gentleman"; his religious knowledge being somewhat on the scanty side.[65]

Earlier, he had written that "Islam, cleared of the post-Koranic accretions and all these hateful Shīʿa traditions, is on the whole a clean and decent religion adapted to a nomad people in an early stage of civilization."[66] In spite of Mann's lack of scholarly authority to make such grand statements, having admittedly discovered Islam only a few months before writing his letters, these statements are important because they indicate his attitude as governor and because his daily decisions, arbitrary in nature, were prejudiced by this cynicism. The description of Shīʿa practices seems to have come from a Wahhabi polemic rather than the observations of an outsider. His knowledge of the Shīʿa tradition is no better. In the previous paragraph, Imam Ali's shrine was situated in Karbalāʾ (not in Najaf), and Imam ʿAbbas became Imam Ali's grandson (not his son), and so on.[67] Mann wanted to convince an unsuspecting reader that he knew more about his subject than he in fact did. Therefore, his statement lacks any historical value. Compare it with another comment he made on the basis of personal observation, which comes across as candid, in spite of its pessimism:

> I had a funny experience the other night. When on tour, I made it a rule always to dine in the madhīf with members of the Board and all the crowd that is always to be found in a madhīf. One night, when all had just been cleared away, coffee served, and pipes were going, suddenly I became aware of someone climbing into a high chair in the middle of the madhīf (there isn't much light) and the man next to me muttered "Mustn't smoke now," and before I knew where I was we were off with what you might call evening prayers. This was the private chaplain, so to speak, of my sheikh, and he began intoning in a biting nasal drawl the story of Husain, which is to the Shiʿah very much what the Crucifixion is to us. In two minutes practically everyone except the Shaykh and myself was sobbing as if his heart would break, real tears pouring down their cheeks. The story went on for nearly twenty minutes, and they sobbed nearly all the time. . . . Then suddenly reference was made to our host, Hajji Juwad, and the Mullah vanished as quickly as he had come; and in two or three minutes all were talking, smoking, and drinking coffee as though nothing had ever worried them![68]

In fairness to Captain Mann, he continued to conduct certain parts of his business without giving in to his prejudices toward the locals. He arrived in a land where no previous government had done any work to provide an environment fit for human habitation. His description of Ghammas may present an image of the living conditions of the locals before he began his work to improve the place, what he called, "my great scheme to improve the site of Ghammas" and "my pet scheme at Ghammas."[69] He wrote to Lady Mary Murray on 23 December 1919: "The land of Ghammas is almost level with the river, and in flood time below it; consequently when people built a town there each man built himself a little platform of earth on which to put his hut. The holes from which they took the earth at once filled with water, and the result is an indescribable jumble of smells, flies, malaria and utter filth."[70]

His "great scheme" was to eliminate those holes in the ground in order to deny the flies and mosquitoes a breeding place and reduce the spread of malaria and other diseases. This was not done as a governmental service in the strict sense, but it was accomplished by imposing on the local people to do what they should have done for themselves, or to undo what they should not have done in the first place. Mann was right to be frustrated with a people whose apathy had deprived them of the will to take the initiative to improve their living conditions or, worse, had caused them to act against their own interests. They needed someone to force them to act. Hence, the place was, as he put it, "very much as it was when Abraham moved up from Ur of the Chaldees."[71]

Mann's assertion that the British administration in Iraq was not "very Imperialistic" and that, in the absence of some details unknown to him, he "could honestly state that [they were] running the country solely in the interest of its people," could be most closely seen in this part of his work—namely, the improvement of the area under his jurisdiction, which had been completely neglected by the Ottomans and devastated by the detrimental habits of its populace.[72] But the underlying motivation behind his work and methods was indeed imperialistic from beginning to end. Two immediate causes for British interest in the improvement of the place are apparent in Captain Mann's letters: the increase in revenue (taxes) coming from the projects, and the usefulness of prosperity in dissuading the people from revolting against the British. This was perhaps the reason that constructing a school was not as urgent as completing the revenue-generating items on the agenda of improvement—the first school was built around 1924–1925 by Sayyid Muḥsin Abu Ṭabīkh, who spent his own money to build it, a mosque, a post office, and a police station.[73]

Regarding the revenue incentive, Captain Mann wrote to his sister on 30 April 1920:

> I estimated that we shouldn't get more than 120,000, a 50 per cent increase on last year, which would have been creditable; 150,000 is nearly 100 per cent on last year, and incidentally it

> means that our vegetables for this season will be worth about a million rupees, £100,000; as our population is probably well under 200,000, I think this augurs a good deal of prosperity. The Turks thought themselves lucky if they could raise 1000 in vegetable tax.[74]

In the span of a year, the British raised a hundred times more than the Turks in taxes, attributing this exorbitant increase to the expansion of cultivated areas and the improvement made to the rivers and irrigation systems. However the calculation is made, the bottom line was always how much tax money would enter the coffers of the government: "I am assured that there is a good hope of our realising 50,000 mesharas this year—about 30,000 acres. Last year we realised just over 20,000 mesharas. A meshara of rice may be worth anything from £5 to £15; if we take £8 as a safe figure, this gives a gross value of £400,000 and a Government share of £120,000."[75]

There is no interest in how the increase in wealth might be reflected, if at all, in the lives of the peasants. The main use of this prosperity was to give the people what they might lose in the event of their joining a revolution. In a letter to his father dated 4 June 1920, Mann wrote: "However, in this part at all events, I don't think anything is likely to happen; certainly my people seem to be on the best of terms with me, and the fact that their crops look like being a great success this year makes them strongly in favour of the Government."[76] This calculation proved too optimistic twenty-six days later, when the tribes of the Middle Euphrates began an all-out war against the British, starting the countdown to the end of British colonization of Iraq.

The method of accomplishing these projects was more proof of the imperialistic nature of the British "scheme" for improvement and modernization. Both the financial and labor burdens were almost entirely imposed on the local population, especially those wretched peasants who were coerced into carrying out corvée labor. Mann wrote with manifest frustration about the British media's "gross use of the word 'exploitation' to cover what anyone except an incurable romantic would call 'development.'" What the media called "exploitation" was the drafting of peasants to spend weeks—sometimes months—toiling in "development" projects without any compensation. To that, Mann asked, "Am I 'exploiting' my tribes when I make them build roads and canals and flood-banks without pay in order to increase revenue?"[77]

The banality of Mann's question becomes apparent when we contemplate the repugnance of increasing the tax revenue solely through the labor of poor peasants whose lives had hardly been changed by the nearly 100 percent increase in the cultivated areas. More cultivated land resulted in the employment of more peasants, who would collectively do all the work for a portion of the crop; the other half went to the landowners after, of course, the payment of taxes, which amounted to 30 percent. Notables, tribal shaykhs, and landowners were forced to contribute money to finance the development projects, giving a free ride to the colonizing government, whose obligation was to finance the projects if it were to demand any taxes at all.

CHAPTER THREE

The Revolution in the Middle Euphrates and Beyond

We didn't show any signs of an intention to fulfill our promises; as far as the local administration was concerned we didn't intend to fulfill them if we could possibly help it. . . . Also, the agitation has succeeded. No one, not even H. M. G. [His Majesty's Government], would have thought of giving the Arabs such a free hand as we shall now give them — as a result of the rebellions!

GERTRUDE BELL, 19 SEPTEMBER 1920

Sunday, the 25th July 1922, was a day I shall not easily forget.

LIEUTENANT GENERAL SIR AYLMER HALDANE, 1922

IT IS CLEAR THAT THE BRITISH OFFICIALS DID not see the 1920 Revolution coming. They underestimated the level of influence of the religious leaders on the tribes, including those tribes whose shaykhs stood to gain from their cooperation with the British administration. The spark that ignited the largest revolution in Iraq's modern history was a minor dispute involving Shaʿlān Abu al-Chōn, an important shaykh in the town of Rumaitha, and an 800-rupee (£80) debt he allegedly owed the government. Coincidently, Shaʿlān's town fell administratively under the jurisdiction of the Dīwāniyya region, which was governed by Major Daly, who was one of the cruelest British officers. As Bell testified, Aylmer's "present obsession is that the tribal rising is due mainly to hatred of individual POs [political officers]. It is unfortunate that in the case of Diwaniyah there's some truth in it."[1] Daly ordered one of his subordinate officers to arrest Shaʿlān and send him on the first train to Dīwāniyya. Having sensed the danger, Shaʿlān sent for his cousin to mobilize the tribe and get him out of the local jail before the arrival of the train, which they did; therefore, Rumaitha was lost to the most recalcitrant tribes in Iraq. In the words of one British officer, "the release of Shaʿlān [Abu al-Chōn] from the Rumaitha lock-up by his tribesmen set the Euphrates on fire."[2]

But one should not be tempted to take this incident as the sole cause of the revolution. The truth was that "the ice broke at the thinnest place," as Bell correctly put it.[3] For, as these events were taking place in Rumaitha, there was another movement in progress in the holy cities, Najaf and Karbalāʾ, where leading Shīʿa scholars, chief sayyids, and shaykhs of the major tribes in the Middle Euphrates were preparing for an all-out revolution against the British. In fact, a meeting took place in Mishkhāb (close to Najaf) on 28 June 1920—two days before the arrest of Shaʿlān Abu al-Chōn—to prepare for the revolution. Letters were sent to shaykhs in the regions of Najaf and Dīwāniyya, including Shaʿlān Abu al-Chōn, but the messenger, Sayyid Muḥsin al-Yāsiri, arrived in Rumaitha one day after the revolution had already begun in the town.[4]

While the first spark, as often happens, was related to a particular incident, the arrest and forced release of Shaʿlān Abu al-Chōn, the shaykh of the Ḍuwālim tribe, in Rumaitha, the greatest cause of the revolution was, perhaps, the British policy of denying Iraq its promised independence and harshly treating those who called for it—not to speak of the overbearing military administration of the country, especially in the countryside. Likewise, the external factors mentioned above provided the revolution's leaders with stimuli and designs to further their demands. But it was the direct grievances that brought the situation to a boil.

The failure of the British to keep their promises, an ill-advised and costly policy as it turned out, made the coming of the revolution only a matter of time, whereas the harsh treatment ensured that it occurred sooner rather than later. As Sayyid Muḥsin Abu Ṭabīkh, one of the revolution's main leaders, reflected on the events in his memoirs, the 1920 Revolution was inevitable because of the Iraqi desire for self-determination and the British refusal to make good on the promise to make Iraq independent. But in his view, it took place prematurely: "The British hastened its timing by their ignorance about the proud personality of the Iraqi and the numerous political mistakes that they committed across the country."[5]

In the course of the continual humiliation of Iraqis by British officials, the first spark of the revolution was precipitated by the acts of Major Daly and his subordinate, Lieutenant Hyatt, the assistant political officer in Rumaitha, who summoned Shaykh Shaʿlān Abu al-Chōn, and following an exchange of words, he insulted and imprisoned him. Hyatt further, Abu Ṭabīkh recalls, wanted to teach the tribes a hard lesson by attacking, without cause, a village belonging to the tribe of Abu Ḥassān.[6] Neighboring villages came to the aid of the battered Abu Ḥassān village and defeated Hyatt and his force. This incident led to a wide-scale war between the local tribes and the British in Rumaitha.

When arrested, Shaʿlān was aware of the humiliation from Daly that awaited him in Dīwāniyya; so he used a local form of misleading speech that Hyatt could not have deciphered. This form of coded language, locally known as the *ḥischa* (double entendre), requires exceptional talent and experience from both the sender and the receiver of the message. Shaʿlān told a companion who came with him to the meeting to go to his cousin Ghathīth al-Ḥarchān and ask him to send ten Ottoman pounds in gold before the departure of the Dīwāniyya train. Unlike the unsuspecting Hyatt, who saw no harm in a prisoner's obtaining some money before an awful journey, Ghathīth understood what his cousin really needed. He selected ten vigorous men and sent them to the prison to release Shaʿlān, which they did. The men were Ḥabshān al-Gāṭiʿ, Chinḥīt al-Gāṭiʿ, Ḥmūd al-Rāḍi, ʿAbed al-ʿAbbār, Khḍayyer al-ʿAbbūd, Najm al-ʿAbdallah, Abu ʿUyūn al-Ḥarchān, ʿĀjil al-Rāḍi, Theʿbān al-Ḥāchim and Dākhil al-ʿAbbūd.[7] These men, unfortunately, became a footnote to the story of Shaʿlān's confrontation with the British, and were added to tens of thousands like them who were the unknown soldiers in Iraq's war of independence. But they deserve recognition for their role as the fighters who started the 1920 Revolution in the Middle Euphrates.

TABLE 3.1. STRENGTH OF BRITISH TROOPS IN IRAQ AND PERSIA, 1920

	British	*Indian*	*Others*
Total strength	12,000	61,000	60,000
Noncombatants	3,000	23,000	60,000
Combatants	**9,000**	**38,000**	
Reductions			
Sick	700	1,000	
In transit	600	1,000	
In Persia	3,500	6,000	
Total reduction	**4,800**	**8,000**	
Combatants in Iraq	**4,200**	**30,000**	

Source: Haldane, *Insurrection in Mesopotamia*, 325.

Following the release of Shaʿlān, which was accompanied by the killing of two prison guards, the tribes knew that it was only a matter of time before the British would come after them. They decided to gain some time while preparing to defend themselves against an imminent attack; initially, they destroyed the railroad lines north and south of Samāwa, and soon after, they declared an all-out revolt.[8]

While the British force at Rumaitha was placed under siege, there were several areas elsewhere under similar tension. The British had no more than 34,200 troops available for combat against the revolting tribes, out of a total force of 133,000.[9] In real military terms, however, on 1 July 1920 only one battalion was capable of reaching the Middle Euphrates within twenty-four hours.[10] With the partial destruction of the railway, their march was "a practical impossibility."[11]

The next task for the British was to move against the tribes and make examples out of some weak ones in order to deter any further hostilities against the British forces in the south. An opportunity for such act presented itself when a complaint was raised against the tribe of Abu Ḥassān, alleging that they had attacked the market and caused looting and other damages. The operation began initially as a reconnaissance mission by the two platoons of the Ninety-Ninth Infantry, but it ended in a major atrocity against the whole village. In the words of General Haldane: Lieutenant Hyatt urged the commander of the mission "not to be bound by the letter of his orders, but rather burn the hostile village before he returned to camp."[12] Far from condemning the atrocity, Haldane considered it merely an act based on "rash advice" that was costly to the attacking force. While the troops busied themselves with the burning and killing, some fifteen hundred to two thousand tribesmen arrived to rescue the battered village, and then engaged the British force in a ferocious fight resulting in the loss of some forty-three soldiers and the wounding of two officers, one British and one Indian. The atrocity that was meant to serve as a deterrent ended up inciting more tribal hostilities. The long-term effect of this incident was the shift of tribal attitudes in Samāwa from tacit to unmistakable hostility.[13]

The British force at Rumaitha continued to suffer hardships, especially from the lack of food and supplies. The soldiers finally resorted to looting, raiding nearby shops and food stores and carrying what they could to the garrison. They also suffered casualties, including the deaths of three soldiers, while trying to bring in water from the river. They solved this problem by digging wells inside the garrison.[14]

On 6 July, a British force led by Lieutenant Colonel McVean arrived in the area of ʿĀriḍiyyāt, north of Rumaitha, and was intercepted by a tribal force of just fewer than 5,000 fighters. After a heated battle, the commander managed to cut his losses and withdraw his force under the cover of a dust storm, leaving behind some 48 dead in addition to 167 wounded.[15] From that point on, the garrison had to be supplied with food and other provisions via airborne shipments. But some of the supplies were occasionally dropped off target, and the local villagers managed to get hold of some boxes. At one incident, British soldiers followed the villagers, who took refuge from the bombing in a large house, and massacred twenty people, a "feat" praised by General Haldane as a success equal to that achieved by the force that recovered the scattered food supply.[16]

This battle was followed by another confrontation at the same place, with the British gaining the upper hand. A large force under General Coningham, aided by a train of supplies, advanced toward Rumaitha and engaged the tribes, whose force was about 5,700 fighters. The tribes' successful tactics caused the British, as General Haldane noted later, to believe that they were being helped by Ottoman officers.[17] On

19 July, the fighting began, and after a significant battle that went in favor of the tribes, the first day ended without a victory on either side. On the second day, three platoons of Gurkhas (Nepalese soldiers in the British forces) managed to cross the river and place the tribes in a difficult position, causing them to retreat and leaving a large number of dead fighters, in addition to those wounded. According to Haldane, the British suffered 35 dead and 152 wounded.

The siege of British forces in Rumaitha lasted for sixteen days and caused 148 casualties.[18] But the British did not stay long in Rumaitha. One day after breaking the siege of the garrison, they evacuated their forces and headed for Dīwāniyya to prepare for the evacuation of the forces there. All forces were ordered to gather in Ḥilla to counter a possible tribal attack on the last line of defense before the revolution could reach British headquarters in Baghdad. The rationale for this voluntary withdrawal was not only to have enough troops in Ḥilla, but also, and most importantly, to save those troops from the tribes, as General Haldane explained:

> I was prepared to sacrifice practically everything at Diwaniyah except those supplies which would be necessary for the force during its march to Hillah, and the ammunition, which could not be left behind. My anxiety to avoid the least delay was natural, and was due not only to the necessity for concentrating in Hillah, but to the danger which the troops might run through the marked predilection which the insurgents were showing everywhere for the destruction of railways.[19]

The trouble at Samāwa remained throughout the revolution until 17 October, when a final attempt to relieve the British force was finally successful.[20]

THE SPREAD OF FIGHTING

At the same time, there was another revolt underway in the Abu Ṣkhair area, near Najaf. Tribes from the Shāmiyya district moved to surround the Abu Ṣkhair garrison on 13 July 1920. They were joined on the following day by the Banu Ḥasan tribe. This move ended a period of two weeks of unaided fighting by the Rumaitha tribes. According to one historian, the tribes of the Middle Euphrates had a long history of mutual hostility that inhibited each tribe from joining the fight first and thereby giving its rivals the opportunity to conspire with the British to seek revenge against it. Also, the British were aware of these rivalries, and they exploited tribal divisions at every turn.[21]

It must also be noted here that the exceptional effort by Captain Mann, who took advantage of his excellent relations with the tribes within his jurisdiction, spared the British an earlier encounter with the ferocious tribes of his district. But the unprincipled tactics of his superiors ultimately undermined his success. He was finally ordered by the tribes to leave his headquarters in Shāmiyya and join the British force in Kūfa; as a final gesture of goodwill, the tribes offered him safe passage and a tribal escort to ensure his safe arrival in Kūfa. He agreed and they kept their promise.

The first act was a tribal attack on Abu Ṣkhair, a small town between Najaf and Shāmiyya. The tribes put the town under siege for a week before the British managed to rescue their force through the intervention of the Najaf clergy. In a strategic mistake on the part of the tribes, the small British force was allowed to join the larger garrison in Kūfa unharmed after agreeing to some conditions involving no aggression from either side until a final agreement was reached regarding the demands to grant Iraq full independence. The tribes kept their end of the bargain and allowed the Abu Ṣkhair force safe passage to Kūfa and ceased all activities, but the British took the opportunity to begin fortifying their positions in Kūfa and supplying the garrison with more provisions and ammunition. This breach of the pact signaled to the revolution's leaders that their demands had been rejected and that it was only a matter of time before the British would attack.

On 20 July, the siege of Kūfa began, and a plan was put together to complete the capture of the other towns in the Middle Euphrates. Sayyid ʿAlwān al-Yāsiri, a prominent leader in the Middle Euphrates, was tasked with managing the siege in Kūfa while the shaykh of Fatla, ʿAbd al-Wāḥid Āl Sikar, was in command of the tribes that headed to the town of Kifl and ultimately to Ḥilla. Sayyid Muḥsin Abu Ṭabīkh was asked to coordinate the participation of various tribes, especially those whose commitment was weak, in the campaign to attack the British forces in Ḥilla, the last line of defense for the British command in Baghdad. But the final arrangement left Abu Ṭabīkh in charge of the siege of the garrison in Kūfa, and the rest of his colleagues left for Ḥilla after capturing Kifl on 22 July without major fighting.[22] With the capture of Kifl, the anti-British tribes were in control of the entire Middle Euphrates region except for Ḥilla. They captured Samāwa, Rumaitha, Dīwāniyya, Shāmiyya, Abu Ṣkhair, Kūfa, Najaf, and Karbalāʾ—the last two were voluntarily evacuated by the British. The next step was to capture Ḥilla and be at the gates of Baghdad.

To intercept the looming attack by the emboldened tribal forces, the political officer in Ḥilla, Major Pulley, sent a force under the command of Lieutenant Colonel Hardcastle with the task of intimidating the tribes between Ḥilla and Kifl, lest they decide to join the revolution. The force was then ordered to ultimately end the siege of the garrison of Kūfa. On the second day, the tribes attacked the exhausted British force and scored a major victory in the Battle of Rāranjiyya, a village midway between Ḥilla and Kifl. The report on British casualties ranged from the high end given by the revolution's leaders to a very low estimate given by the British. Sayyid Muḥsin Abu Ṭabīkh claimed that the British lost 200 soldiers and officers, while General Haldane counted 20 dead, 60 wounded, and 160 taken prisoner. But the figure given by Abu Ṭabīkh may be close to the real one. Colonel Arnold Wilson wrote that the force suffered 180 dead soldiers and officers, 60 wounded, and 160 prisoners.[23]

Iraqi tribal fighters also captured a large piece of artillery, an eighteen-pounder gun, with its ammunition, as well as a large number of machine guns with a lot of ammunition, all of which helped arm them for the battles to come. They sent the large gun to Kūfa to help win the showdown with the British force in the well-fortified garrison, but the gun was missing some parts. The tribal fighters had among them some former Ottoman officers with decent knowledge of the use of artillery, and they also made use of their contacts with men in the British army who, for the right sum of money, delivered to them the missing spare parts. The only part they lacked was the breechblock, which had been taken by British soldiers as a standard procedure before abandoning the gun in the Rāranjiyya River. A local gunsmith made a replacement, and the gun was finally fixed. The tribes immediately used it to sink the battleship *Firefly*, which was petrifying the fighters in Kūfa with its heavy firepower.[24] It was also involved in bombing residential areas close to the Euphrates River. Shaykh Wahaiyd Āl ʿAbbūd al-ʿĪsāwi told me that his tribe lost twenty-five members in a British bombing, including his stepmother (Um Ali). His father, then the shaykh of Āl ʿĪsā, was injured in that bombing.[25]

The effect of Rāranjiyya on the morale of the British forces and officials was articulated by Gertrude Bell in a letter to her father on the following day, 26 July 1920:

> When I got to the office I found that the whole complexion on the Euphrates had changed. All the tribes are out; we've evacuated the Barrage and are evacuating Diwaniyah. Whether we can hold Hillah or not, I don't know. Major Norbury is shut up at Kufah, where however he has troops and plenty of provisions so he's all right. But it's a bad business. The military authorities seem to me all through to have [been] more inept than it's possible to conceive. The crowning scandal was the dispatch two days ago of a battalion of the Manchesters from Hillah to Kifl. They were ordered to leave at 4 am and left at 10, with one day's rations and water bottles. You remember that hot and barren road? Think of marching down it in July at midday! 17 miles out of Hillah they were dropping about with heat stroke. The tribes attacked—not viciously, I gather, but it was more than enough for the Manchesters, for there wasn't a kick left in them. The tribes carried off the artillery and ammunition they were convoying down to Kifl and then made no objection to ambulances from Hillah coming out to pick up the casualties, whether from sun or bullets. I believe there are more troops coming from India but unless they send a new higher Command with them, I think they may easily send 20 divisions in vain.

On the other hand, the victory at Rāranjiyya sent a wave of enthusiasm for revolution across the region. This can be seen in the case of Dīwāniyya, where the most oppressive and controlling officer, Major Daly, was forced to retreat to Ḥilla with his force, taking eleven days to make the trip because of the fierce fighting between his forces and the tribes. He did not lose his sense of cruelty, though: he destroyed and burnt to the ground any weak village he encountered on the way.[26]

The tribes that participated in the Rāranjiyya fight used the momentum to push forward toward Ḥilla. Meanwhile, the British felt that the situation was spinning rapidly out of control. It is apparent from the previous passage by Bell that there was a general lack of confidence—among the political officials at least—in the command of British forces, primarily in General Haldane, who had failed to stop the continued success of the less well-equipped tribes, much less display any ability to score a victory against them. Haldane was also experiencing the worst of his moments, as he later reflected on the days following the battle of Rāranjiyya:

> From the date when the news was received of the disaster of the Manchester column until the message came announcing Brigadier-General Coningham's arrival at Jarbuiyah bridge, a period of twelve days, I can recall in my career no cycle—and I use that word advisedly—of quite such tense anxiety, not that it cost me one hour of sleep. From 1914 to the Armistice, except for an occasional brief spell of leave, I was never absent from the Western Front, and my troops often held ground which in the parlance of the time was called "unhealthy." But these twelve days at Baghdad in 1920, days seemed like years, surpassed all earlier ones in the mental strain which they imposed.[27]

The tribes first took the town of Ṭwairīj, midway between Ḥilla and Karbalā', and then attacked Ḥilla from three fronts, but because of some timing problems and a lack of accurate coordination, only one of the fronts began the fight. This flaw in the tribes' execution of the attack gave the British a good chance to repel the first assault, and by the time the second and third fronts were opened, the plan was a failure.[28] Abu Ṭabīkh recalls a conversation he had with a British officer years later, quoting the officer as saying, "Your men fought better than our soldiers in the street fighting of Ḥilla. They surprised us so much that we thought a regular army had attacked us."[29]

The tribes that remained in Kūfa under the command of Abu Ṭabīkh were asked to join the fight in the Hindiyya front, between Ḥilla and Karbalā'. He left the Banu Ḥasan tribe under their shaykh,

ʿAlwān Āl Ḥāj Saʿdūn, in charge of the siege of Kūfa and moved with the other tribes, arriving in Hindiyya on 28 July. The objective was to secure the Hindiyya Dam. At this point, the greatest enemy was not the threat from British forces but the lack of food and provisions—as well as the rumors. As Abu Ṭabīkh recalled:

> We began to prepare for a ruthless war against the British, especially with the shortage of ammunition and food that we had left. We became dependent on what we received from Najaf and from our own homes. In addition to all these [difficulties], we had to fight the rumors spread by the agents of the British about the looming counterattack by the British and the death sentences awaiting us and that they would annihilate the unarmed residents; all were claims for the purpose of discouraging [our] resolve and valor.[30]

The second major battle was also instigated by a British attempt to compensate for previous losses. This time they wanted to capture Karbalāʾ, the capital of the revolution and the residence of its spiritual leader, Ayatollah Muḥammad Taqi al-Ḥāʾiri. The capture of Karbalāʾ by the British would have ended the revolution almost immediately. But the tribes between Ḥilla and Karbalāʾ fought fiercely and stopped the British campaign. The heavy casualties and large amount of ammunition the British forces left behind gave the tribes the means and enthusiasm to officially claim Karbalāʾ to be a "liberated" city. They entered Karbalāʾ and placed its pro-British governor, Ḥamīd Khan, under arrest. After putting things in order, the tribes left Karbalāʾ to continue the fight.

THE LEACHMAN-ḌĀRI AFFAIR

The revolution expanded to regions adjacent to the Middle Euphrates, but with only a limited scope and for a limited time. Notable among the other regions was the Upper Euphrates, which joined the revolution more than a month and a half after it began and ceased taking part long before the revolution in the Middle Euphrates was suppressed. The incident of Colonel Leachman's killing by Shaykh Ḍāri and his relatives forced the region to participate in an open revolt for a short while. But unlike the Middle Euphrates, which conducted an ideological revolution, the Upper Euphrates became involved by accident. The killing of Leachman was in line with the tribal honor tradition. He abused the shaykh of the Zōbaᶜ tribe and lost his life for it. At his trial, Ḍāri and his lawyers never spoke about the revolution or mentioned any reasons for the killing other than Leachman's abuse.[31] Indeed, his lawyer proved to the court that Ḍāri was on good terms with the British and that he had no interest in joining the revolution until the killing of Leachman.[32] The tribe had no choice but to preempt an eminent British retaliation by joining the revolution. But the leading personalities in the region were wholeheartedly pro-British and ultimately were able to contain the contrary impulses of their constituents. According to one historian who was also a participant in the revolution:

> Shaykh Ali al-Sulayman, the head of the Dulaym tribes managed to prevent the expansion of the revolution in the [Dulaym] province and helped the British a great deal in fighting the revolution . . . He was helped in this effort by Shaykh Fahd al-Hadhdhāl, the chief of the ʿAniza tribe and Shaykh Muḥsin, one of the Dulaym chiefs. The British government appreciated the great services of these three shaykhs and acknowledged their favors.[33]

This account was corroborated by General Haldane's report about that critical moment. He credited the security of the Dulaym region to the mutual understanding between the British administration and the local shaykhs:

> Fortunately at this juncture an arrangement was come to with the Dulaim tribe, whereby their head, Shaikh Ali Sulaiman, in return for a subsidy, undertook to garrison Hit until such time as it could be reoccupied. Both he and Fahad Beg ibn Hadhdhāl, Shaikh of ʿAniza, as well as his son Mahrut, stood loyal to the Government throughout the insurrection, and later on received rewards for their good services at so critical a time.[34]

Supporting this analysis is the fate of the region after the end of the Zōbaʿ revolt. The only party to receive punishment was Shaykh Ḍāri himself. His property was destroyed, and he was never pardoned, having killed a high-ranking British officer. He remained a fugitive until he was captured, tried, and jailed in 1928. But he died on 1 February 1928, a couple days after the start of his sentence.[35] This was a very selective treatment compared with the collective punishment inflicted on the people of the Middle Euphrates as a whole, who were compelled to pay exorbitant fines, not to mention the death and destruction they suffered at the hands of British forces and in the air raids.

THE REVOLUTION IN THE SOUTH

The revolution spread for a short time among the towns of the Muntafiq, in the Lower Euphrates. Notables such as Shaykh ʿAbd al-Ḥusayn Maṭar, ʿAli al-Dabbūs, and Sayyid ʿAbd al-Mahdi al-Muntafiji in Nāṣiriyya, Sūq al-Shuyūkh, and Shaṭra, respectively, spent much time and energy on the call to join the revolution.[36]

The British secured some parts of the Muntafiq, mainly by cultivating strong relations between their political officers and the local shaykhs. The case of Shaṭra is illustrative. Captain Bertram Thomas was dispatched to the town, where he had worked in 1919, to ensure the neutrality of its tribes. He realized that one man could make or break the revolutionary movement in the region; that man was Khayyūn al-ʿUbaid, the shaykh of al-ʿUbūda tribe. Captain Thomas recalled that Khayyūn had come to him asking for a pass to go on the pilgrimage to Mecca. Thomas informed him that the British planned to arrest and exile him as a political prisoner if he left his area. He explained to Khayyūn his reasons for divulging this information: "Because I desire your welfare, and I ask in return for your friendship. We are living in troubled times. The Gharraf must remain loyal to Government." Reciprocating the good gesture, Khayyūn replied: "We have often been at cross-purposes. From tonight, we are friends. Have no fears for the Gharraf."[37] This was a clever way of acquiring the shaykh's loyalty for free. According to Thomas, "Khaiyyun himself was notoriously rich, and never profited a penny-piece either during or after the troubles;

the loyalty of the other shaikhs likewise was spontaneous—they received neither payment nor promise of payment."[38]

The first sign of revolt came from the town of Qalʿat Sikar, where the assistant political officer, Captain Crawford, was ambushed following an after-dark visit of some local tribe. He and his escort escaped harm, and the group inflicted only "two horse casualties."[39] The British sent two airplanes to intimidate the town, but one of them crashed, causing the opposite impression of the one intended. The central command denied a subsequent request for more airplanes, in spite of Thomas's strongly worded warning about what would happen if they were not sent: "If . . . we fail to send aeroplanes to Qalat Sikar I feel we shall have to evacuate it, and if Qalat Sikar falls, Shatra will have to give up." The response was: "We cannot send even one aeroplane daily to Qalat Sikar . . . we have only five available altogether in Baghdad, and they have to be used elsewhere."[40]

In light of this situation, the assistant political officer in Qalʿat Sikar was forced to evacuate the town on 12 August 1920, leaving the government offices to be looted by the locals.[41] Just as Thomas predicted, the fall of Qalʿat Sikar brought the action to his headquarters in Shaṭra. The locals cut the telegraph lines on 15 August, and twelve days later, Captain Thomas evacuated Shaṭra, leaving the town and its local force under the command of his friend Khayyūn al-ʿUbaid.[42] As soon as Thomas departed, the locals looted the British offices and his house. Khayyūn's cooperation with Thomas earned him a place in some of the most scathing vernacular poetry, which accused him of being irreligious and a money accumulator.[43]

The British faced similar difficulties in the rest of the Muntafiq region, especially in Sūq al-Shuyūkh, whose security situation deteriorated in spite of a confident assessment made by the political officer of Nāṣiriyya, Major Ditchburn, after a visit he made to the town on 27 August. By 1 September, the British had one man left on the police force in Sūq al-Shuyūkh after a mass defection; as a result, the assistant political officer, Captain Platts, took a military vessel and fled to Nāṣiriyya.[44] No major fighting took place in Nāṣiriyya, mainly because of the weak commitment of the tribes to attack the small British force stationed there. With three thousand tribal fighters surrounding the city, it should not have taken them only a short time to overwhelm the garrison, which "consisted only of three platoons of Indian Infantry and two hundred local levies and police."[45] Instead, they continued to cluster outside the city and engage the British in small fights until mid-November 1920, when the shaykhs of the Muntafiq began to approach the British for a settlement. Since most of the Muntafiq shaykhs were pro-British, the region did not receive any punishment or become subject to the kinds of harsh conditions imposed on the tribes and cities of the Middle Euphrates. As Haldane put it: "Some twenty-five minor leaders in the area . . . had earlier committed definitely hostile acts . . . They were ordered to pay a fine or rifles, which they accordingly did."[46]

THE REVOLUTION IN DIYĀLĀ

The revolution began to spread to Diyālā in the first week of August. By 9 August, the local tribes had cut the railway lines from Baghdad to the east, which forced Haldane to send his only reserve unit in Baghdad, under the command of Brigadier General Young.[47] The force engaged in a predawn fight with a tribal force that was also heading for Diyālā, causing the British force to remain in a state of "almost complete chaos" until it managed to reform at 4:30 a.m., only to suffer another attack.

The force finally reached Baʿqūba in the afternoon, but was ordered to return to Baghdad the same afternoon, in spite of appeals from the assistant political officer, Major Hiles, to keep the force there in anticipation of an imminent attack on the town. Instead, he was ordered to evacuate the town.[48] Arnold Wilson recalled: "The abandonment of Baʿqūba was described in writing at the time by one of the senior General Officers in Iraq as 'disgraceful,' and I see no reason to dissent from this judgment, which was shared by many others."[49]

The evacuation of Baʿqūba opened the town to tribal looting on 12 August 1920. But the residents managed later to form a local government to keep some order. Meanwhile, the town of Daltāwa (al-Khāliṣ) witnessed a similar revolt. Local tribes attacked the government office and managed to capture the assistant political officer, Captain Lloyd, and a few other employees. The tribes looted the office and scattered its documents. To their disappointment, the office had less than 100 rupees.[50] Following the capture of Daltāwa, a group of Baghdad notables arrived, perhaps having fled the British attempt to arrest the leaders of the agitation in Baghdad, on 12 August. Among those who came to Daltāwa were the mujtahid Shaykh Mahdi al-Khāliṣi and Sayyid Muḥammad al-Ṣadr.

Two days after the fall of Baʿqūba and Daltāwa, the town of Shahrabān was attacked by the Banu Tamīm tribe, aided by the local residents. The British force—consisting of six British (military and civilian personnel), one Egyptian, ten Indians, and fifty local levies—refused to surrender to the tribe.[51] After several hours of fighting, five of the British had been killed and the rest captured, except for the levies, who had fled the scene earlier. With the loss of Shahrabān, the British administration had lost control in the entire northeast of Baghdad. As Haldane put it: "By the 25th August practically all the tribes north of the Diyalah became implicated in the rising, and lawlessness and disorder spread as far north as Kirkuk, and later on to Arbil."[52]

As in all other regions outside the Middle Euphrates, the revolution did not last long in Diyālā. The British managed to reestablish their authority in Baʿqūba on 27 August and in Shahrabān on 9 September. They entered Daltāwa on 25 September. Punishment of the residents varied from one town to another. The lightest was in Baʿqūba, where they ordered two men to pay fines; the first was Sayyid Maḥmūd al-Mutawalli, who had been appointed governor of Baʿqūba after the British evacuation, and the second man was Sayyid Ḥabīb al-ʿAydarūsi, who had played a major role in exhorting the tribes to revolt. The former was fined 28,000 rupees, and the latter 10,000 rupees.[53] Also, a British officer went to the house of Sayyid Ḥusayn, who had been appointed judge, and shot him dead.[54]

It seems that the town of Shahrabān was not treated very harshly, considering it had witnessed the killing of five British personnel, including three officers. The British destroyed some houses and arrested a few notables, including Shaykh Majīd al-Ḥasan of the Banu Tamīm tribe. They also executed a man they accused of killing Captain Buchanan, although Buchanan's wife stated that her husband's killer, a man from the Banu Tamīm, was at large and that man was killed for a crime he had not committed.[55]

THE FINAL DAYS

The revolution lasted for several months, costing the British £40 million and a considerable number of casualties. But the cost to the tribes was not less considerable. Having no means to supply the fighters with weapons or food other than what was taken from the British on the battlefield, the tribes deeply felt the impact of the war. By contrast, the British brought more troops to Iraq and took advantage of their more lethal forces from the air and on the ground against the inadequately armed tribal fighters.

On 12 October, British forces advanced toward Ṭwairīj. In spite of fierce resistance, the British managed to capture Ṭwairīj and remove the last barrier between them and Karbalāʾ. To prevent the destruction of the holy city and possible harm to the religious leaders, the city of Karbalāʾ offered to surrender after some negotiations with the local commander of the British force and then with the high commissioner, Sir Percy Cox, in Baghdad. The offer to surrender was accepted, but with very harsh conditions, including the surrender of seventeen men who were considered personally responsible for the revolution; the first name on the list was Sayyid Muḥsin Abu Ṭabīkh, the head of the government that the revolution's leaders established in Karbalāʾ. Additionally, the city was ordered to deliver 4,000 rifles and 400,000 rounds of ammunition, half of which had to be modern (i.e., British rifles) and the other half in working condition (i.e., Ottoman rifles). Knowing that the number was more than what the city actually had, the British demanded the price of the undelivered rifles.[56]

At the same time, another British force headed for Kifl and ultimately arrived in Kūfa on 18 October to lift the siege that had been imposed by the tribes on its garrison since the early days of July. As with Ṭwairīj and Karbalāʾ, the fall of Kūfa caused the holy city of Najaf to surrender without fighting; the town also delivered to the British force seventy-nine British soldiers and officers and eighty-eight Indians, all of whom had been taken prisoner by the tribes in various battles. They were deemed to be in good health and to have been treated well by their captors, according to the official announcement.[57] Similar conditions were imposed on Najaf, including the surrender of five notables and the delivery of more than 15,500 rifles, 10 large guns, and 200,000 rounds of ammunition. But in spite of meeting these conditions, the city was placed under harsh conditions for a lengthy period, leaving more than 60,000 residents without adequate subsistence.[58]

Unlike the residents of the major cities, the tribes refused to surrender easily. In spite of heavy bombardment and fierce battles, the tribal forces of Shāmiyya and Abu Ṣkhair carried the fight well into November 1920. The last British war announcement concerning the Shāmiyya district was made on 26 November, declaring the end of hostilities in the region and asking the residents to go back to their ordinary lives and to cooperate with the authorities.[59]

The Samāwa tribes were among the last fighters standing in the war against the British, having refused to surrender under any conditions. They carried on the fight until the second half of November 1920. When the British saw no easy victory over the Ḥachchām tribes, they agreed to negotiate a cease-fire, which was concluded on 20 November. The tribes managed to avoid the harsh conditions imposed on the cities. Among the terms of the agreement, the tribes did not have to compensate the British for any losses or damages from the fighting in their region, and they did not have to pay any taxes in 1920. They did agree, however, to deliver 2,400 rifles, but without any specification of the condition of the rifles or the requirement to give the monetary value of undelivered rifles. To further save face for the surrendering tribes, the British agreed to include, as the first term of the agreement, the establishment of "an independent Arab government" in Iraq, which had already been decided by London, albeit not as independent as the Iraqis would have expected.[60]

THE POLITICS OF THE REVOLUTION

One of the main controversies that surrounded the 1920 Revolution was the appointment of Abu Ṭabīkh as the governor of Karbalāʾ and the historical significance of this appointment. The leaders of the revolution asked him to go to Karbalāʾ and start a government with jurisdiction over all the liberated territories. The question that is at the core of this controversy is whether Abu Ṭabīkh was appointed merely as a local governor with limited authority within the confinement of Karbalāʾ's borders, or whether he was head of the sovereign government that the revolution's leaders were attempting to establish over all the liberated territories, beginning with the Middle Euphrates and spreading throughout the rest of Iraq.

To shed light on the pivotal role played by Sayyid Muḥsin Abu Ṭabīkh in the 1920 Revolution, it is essential to consider his own recollection about the events that took place in the Middle Euphrates and the aftermath of the revolution. His memoirs chronicle the important events to which he was an eyewitness and a participant. In addition, a wealth of information about his involvement was recorded in the memoirs of his fellow notables, who were unanimous in acknowledging his financial generosity and active participation in the planning and execution of the revolution. Finally, the reports and memoirs of British officials in Iraq at the time help complete the portrait of Abu Ṭabīkh as a revolutionary. Needless to say, the defamatory tone in the British reports about Abu Ṭabīkh places him in clear distinction to those Iraqis who rendered valuable services to the administration and were showered with praise and incentives.

Abu Ṭabīkh's fight against the British began in the early days of the occupation, when he participated in the fight in al-Shaʿaiba, in April 1915, following a call for jihad against the British by the mujtahids in Najaf. This fighting, he recalled, was against his personal preferences. The call for jihad came very shortly after a Turkish assault on his home and the homes of other notables, many of whom were in Turkish detention.[61] When the British occupied Baṣra and weakened the position of the Ottoman troops, Abu Ṭabīkh and other Iraqis wanted to revolt against the oppressive Ottomans and avenge their honor. But they were preempted by the binding calls for jihad against the British on the account of their being a non-Muslim force engaged in a fight against the Muslim—albeit oppressive—Ottomans. After a brief period of soul-searching, Abu Ṭabīkh and like-minded people decided to heed the call for jihad and join their oppressors. In the decisive battle at al-Shaʿaiba, on 15–18 April 1915, Sayyid Muḥsin Abu Ṭabīkh was wounded and his cousin, Sayyid Rāḍi Abu Ṭabīkh, was more seriously injured and taken captive by the British, who treated his wounds and sent him into exile.[62]

After the British subsequently gained control over Iraq, Abu Ṭabīkh—like many landowners—received much patronage and privileges from the new administration, which attempted to make itself tolerated by taking the opposite approach to that of the Ottomans. In the words of Abu Ṭabīkh: "We received the kind of respect and appreciation from the [British] occupying authorities that cannot be compared with what our status was during the Ottoman rule and our share of the harshness of Turkish governors. British governors used to exaggerate in honoring and respecting us . . . and made sure that our needs were met in the best way possible."[63]

This statement may not be construed as a general evaluation of the Iraqi experience under the occupation. First, the British did not extend this courtesy to the average Iraqis; they reserved it only for the key figures in every community. This was a policy to appease the leaders in tribal communities where trouble began and ended with the notables. And second, even these notables were not immune to the aggressive behavior of governors such as Major Daly and Colonel Leachman. Abu Ṭabīkh had the good fortune to be under a less aggressive assistant political officer, Captain James Mann, whom he described as "a humble man who possesses none of the arrogance characteristic of British officers."[64]

The notables of Shāmiyya concluded a pact with Captain Mann on 5 July 1920, which promised that he would relate their demands for independence to the administration in Baghdad if they promised not to attack governmental posts and military bases. They asked for:

1. Full and unconditional independence for Iraq
2. The cessation of hostilities in Rumaitha and neighboring areas
3. The withdrawal of all British political officers from the Middle Euphrates, who could remain in the Baghdad until a final agreement concerning the fate of Iraq was reached
4. The release of the cleric Mirza Muhammad Riḍā al-Shirazi and other persons who had been detained on 21 June and sent into exile.[65]

The problems were that their conditions were not local in nature and that Captain Mann was not the man to negotiate such terms with, since most of the demands would have to be fulfilled by someone higher in rank. When the news arrived about the burning of Rumaitha, Abu Ṭabīkh and his fellow Shāmiyya notables sent a messenger to

Captain Mann, informing him about the annulment of the pact after what the British forces had done to the tribes of Rumaitha.[66]

On another front, the city of Karbalāʾ formally joined the revolution on 25 July, the same day the tribes won the battle at Rāranjiyya. On the following day, two councils were formed under the authority of the highest religious scholar, Muhammad Taqi al-Shirazi, after a meeting at his house: the Council of Scholars (al-Majlis al-ʿIlmi) and the National Council (al-Majlis al-Milli). The first council was made up of five religious scholars with a mandate to provide religious promotion for the revolution and to adjudicate disputes among the people, since there was no other authority in place. The second council was made up of seventeen notables whose task was to administer the affairs of the territory under its jurisdiction.[67]

The death of the mujtahid, Muhammad Taqi al-Shirazi, on 13 August, caused the dissolution of the two councils—he had presided over both of them. The political vacuum led to disorder in the territory, and a replacement for the dissolved councils had to be established immediately. A group of notables—the leaders of fighting forces—met in the revolution's main camp in the area of al-Ḥusayniyya and a national government was formed. Abu Ṭabīkh was chosen to head the new government. According to one historian, "there was a need for a person whose respectability was admitted by everyone."[68] Abu Ṭabīkh described the events as follows:

> The notables attending the meeting decided to establish a temporary national government, and they chose me from among themselves for this task.
>
> In spite of my desire to stay among my brothers in the battlefield, I honored their decision and accepted this dignified assignment and asked permission to leave for Karbalāʾ and assume my responsibilities . . .
>
> The celebration took place in the city hall in the midst of crowds that exceeded tens of thousands, and I raised the first Iraqi flag on the building that I chose to be headquarters for the government.[69]

From this passage, it may be convincingly argued that Abu Ṭabīkh was more than just a *mutaṣarrif* (governor) of Karbalāʾ, because the tribal leaders actually formed a government for the revolution with its headquarters in Karbalāʾ and appointed him as head of the government. He was appointed in the presence of the most prominent figures of the time from many Iraqi regions. If he were merely a *mutaṣarrif,* he would have reported to a higher government. In the case of Karbalāʾ, the revolution's leaders had rejected any government in existence at the time, acting as a sovereign entity in all matters. Abu Ṭabīkh was accountable before the "tribal council," the consociation of tribal leaders and other notables that appointed him.

In a 1956 letter to ʿAbd al-Shahīd Nūr al-Yāsiri, a son of Nūr al-Yāsiri, his fellow revolutionary and a prominent figure in the events, Abu Ṭabīkh wrote:

> As for appointing me a *mutaṣarrif* in Karbalāʾ, the notables chose yours truly to go to Karbalāʾ and form a government, as we were in al-Ḥusayniyya after the tribes captured Najaf, Karbalāʾ and Ṭwairīj. Honoring their desire, I went back to Karbalāʾ and formed a government in it, amid a grand celebration attended by some Baghdadis such as the late Yūsuf al-Suwaydi and Jaʿfar Abu al-Timman, as well as Ali Beg Bāzirgān, who is alive among us. I raised with my own hands the first Iraqi flag on the building of the city hall.[70]

Abu Ṭabīkh spoke on both occasions of the flag that he raised on the government building in Karbalāʾ as the first Iraqi flag. He identified himself as the one who raised the flag because other accounts identify Ali al-Bāzirgān as the one who did that.[71] In another revelation, Salman Hadi al-Ṭuʿma conveniently credited his own relative, Muhammad Ḥasan al-Ṭuʿma, with raising the flag and dismissed al-Bāzirgān's claim that he himself had done it.[72] Writing in the midst of the unfolding events, the correspondent for *Al-Istiqlāl,* the revolution's paper, described the flag's installation as a joint effort by the "noble Sayyids," who brought the flag

> after having it blessed by a tour among the sacred shrines, and they ascended to the top of the building and raised it in the midst of the applause and chants of the audience. After the

> raising of the flag, His Excellency, the *Mutaṣarrif* turned to the audience and gave a speech expressing his joy about what the mujahideen have achieved and urged the people to maintain the order and respect the Ottoman laws that were to be applied temporarily.[73]

This is different from the story given by al-Bāzirgān, who claimed that he bought the fabric in Najaf and took it to a tailor and showed him how to make the flag, and then took the flag to Karbalāʾ to prepare for the ceremony.[74] If the flag was in his custody until the ceremony, it is unlikely that he took it to the Shīʿa shrines.[75]

It is obvious from these passages and the reporter's account that Abu Ṭabīkh was the one who raised the flag, either alone or joined by others; in addition, he made the claim while Ali al-Bāzirgān was still alive and offered the addressee the chance to verify with him what was stated in the letter of 1956. Also, it would be out of character for Abu Ṭabīkh to take credit for what others had done—something he often criticized others for doing. What might reconcile the claims of Abu Ṭabīkh and Ali al-Bāzirgān is the account attributed to Saʿīd Zmaizim: "Ali al-Bāzirgān and Sayyid Muḥsin Abu Ṭabīkh raised the flag on the roof of the city hall in the presence of many men from the nationalist movement from most Iraqi cities."[76]

This controversy over who raised the flag provides an interesting example of the credibility problems of the original accounts given by the participants in the revolution. There is a great deal of honor involved in being the person to raise the first Iraqi flag in the modern history, and plenty of people, or groups, wanted to claim that honor. We can tell by this controversy and others like it that even the firsthand accounts of the participants in the revolution are not free of bias and occasional distortion; they too had a significant interest in portraying the events according to their own partiality.

Whatever the situation might have been, Abu Ṭabīkh thought he was establishing an Iraqi government and not merely a city council. Indeed, he described the government in Karbalāʾ as a "national government." Since there was no Iraqi government in at the time, it is reasonable to argue that Abu Ṭabīkh was the first chief executive in the modern history of Iraq.[77] His administration was authorized by pure Iraqi will, with no British intervention whatsoever, and it was acknowledged by Iraqis throughout the liberated areas as well as by the notables who joined the revolution from Baghdad and other parts of Iraq (mostly Sunnis). This was several months before the British handpicked the government of ʿAbd al-Raḥmān al-Naqīb, which functioned as an Iraqi cover for Sir Percy Cox's rule of Iraq. In his instructions to al-Naqīb's government, Cox wrote, "[In any case of disagreement] the final word will be mine."[78] Also, Abu Ṭabīkh was appointed in the position a year before Fayṣal I was made king by an admittedly rigged British referendum.[79]

In the speech of Ali al-Bāzirgān at the event, one can detect some themes that clearly indicate the general understanding among the crowd that they were gathered at a "national" occasion:

> Here is the leader [*zaʿīm*], Sayyid Muḥsin Abu Ṭabīkh. He came to you and he will undertake the task of governing the country [*al-balad*]. Therefore, it is your duty to assist him in the governance and obey him so that he may be capable of governing the kingdom [*al-mamlaka*] and the news of its [successful] governance will reach the occupying British so they realize that we are a people capable of managing the affairs of our own homeland and not, as they believe us to be, that we have not matured yet and that our culture is backward.[80]

The occurrence of political terms such as "*zaʿīm*," "*balad*," and "*mamlaka*" in the speech was not arbitrary. Rather, these words reveal the prevailing state of mind among the people present or, at the very least, among the leaders who came from Baghdad, Karbalāʾ, and the rest of the Middle Euphrates to witness that day. Furthermore, the same frame of mind was acknowledged by the press report in the revolution's paper, *Al-Istiqlāl*, which reported on the event as a historic day for the nation (*umma*). The reporter stated the Arab flag was "flying over the territories [*rubūʿ*] of Iraq."[81]

Other evidence of the national nature of the government may be seen in the secret reports dispatched from the British administration in Baghdad to the Foreign Office (through the India Office). In the report dated 15 November 1920, the twenty-second paragraph reads as follows: "The members of the provisional government, which had been set up by the insurgents at Karbalāʾ, were summoned to Baghdad, but none of the ʿulemā was called upon to accompany them."[82]

The report referred to the government of Karbalāʾ as "the provisional government," which is the same term given by the report to the government Cox established in Baghdad. Hence, it becomes clear that the British also viewed the government of Karbalāʾ as a potential national government rather than a city government. The only difference was that the government in Baghdad had been imposed by the British administration and the one in Karbalāʾ was established by the Iraqis.

Furthermore, had the revolution's leaders decided to appoint a governor for Karbalāʾ, they would have chosen a man from the city. Abu Ṭabīkh was not a resident of Karbalāʾ at the time. His hometown, Ghammas, was part of the Shāmiyya district, which belonged administratively to a larger province consisting of Abu Ṣkhair and Najaf. Karbalāʾ did not belong to the same district.

Abu Ṭabīkh was appointed on a special occasion, 18 Dhu al-Ḥijja, which commemorates the Prophet's appointment of Imam Ali as his successor, according to the Shīʿa.[83] There is a thick cloud surrounding the exact date when Abu Ṭabīkh became in charge of Karbalāʾ. The only consensus is that he was chosen for the post on the eighteenth day of Dhu al-Ḥijja. Beyond that, accounts give many different dates for when the events took place. Farīq Mizhir Āl Farʿōn gives the same date, 18 Dhu al-Ḥijja, as the day of the inauguration as well, as do Abu Ṭabīkh's printed memoirs. But in Abu Ṭabīkh's handwritten memoirs, the date he wrote was 14 November 1920.[84] The most reliable source is, perhaps, the sixth issue of *Al-Istiqlāl*, dated 27 Muḥarram 1339/10 October 1920. The same date is given by ʿAbd al-Razzāq al-Ḥasani, in his account of the event, and by the Iraqi historian Ali al-Wardi.[85] Ali al-Bāzirgān gives the date as Friday, 23 Muḥarram/8 October.[86] According to a report from the *Al-Istiqlāl* correspondent in Karbalāʾ: "The *umma* came on Thursday, 23 Muḥarram, to witness its historic day in which the War Council decided to fly the Arab flag in Karbalāʾ and to place on its throne [*minaṣṣat ḥukmiha*] one of its men and heroes, that is Sayyid Muḥsin Abu Ṭabīkh."

He was appointed to manage the capital of the revolution, Karbalāʾ, and the areas attached to it in the appointment order issued by the War Council: Ṭwairīj, Najaf, Abu Ṣkhair, and the entire Shāmiyya district; these were basically all the liberated Iraqi territories. He was assigned a monthly salary of 1,000 rupees (£100), but he donated all of it to the war effort.[87]

In his assessment of the revolution, Abu Ṭabīkh exhibited mixed feelings. On the one hand, he felt duty-bound to participate as a patriotic Iraqi and as an Imami Shīʿa whose following of the *ʿulema* (religious scholars) was nonnegotiable. Also, as a notable and a man of financial means, he had to rise to the expectations of his peers and his followers. It is true that his family was well known for a history of remarkable generosity, but his munificence was pulled, or pushed, further by the circumstances and the rising cost of the fighting. He served as an example of sacrifice and grace, as independent historical sources recount. One example of this discretion in spending was his refusal to support the officers in Dayr al-Zōr. He said in a harsh speech, albeit one prophetic in retrospect:

> I lost a lot of money in this revolution, without regret for such loss, and I am ready to spend the last penny in my savings and properties and even sell my home furniture. I spend all this proudly and with a clear conscience. But I am not sure about the sincerity of the men in Dayr al-Zōr. They are part of the Ottoman servants and leftovers that they left in our land, and most of them, if they really did participate with the revolutionary mujahideen, must have done so for the sake of positions and employment. Hence, I am certain that if the British would ask them to take jobs with them, they will not hesitate, forgetting all about patriotism . . . Therefore, I am not ready to give some of my money to men I do not acknowledge as being authentic in their patriotism or their sincerity . . . I am ready, should you order me, to give any amount you want to any area you decide — I am ready and willing to answer the call with honor and pride — but to these mercenaries, I am not ready to give one penny.[88]

This prophecy was fulfilled later when many of those officers returned to Iraq. They divided among themselves virtually all the positions and sent the revolution's leaders to retirement or, at best, to inconsequential roles in the country's political life. With British help and

Fayṣal's deceitful conduct, those officers violated every political and ethical rule to remain in power over the majority of the population, whose disappointment with the new regime caused them to reject the king and his entourage, who allowed themselves to become puppets of the British.

It was with this sense of bitterness that Abu Ṭabīkh wrote his retrospective evaluation of the 1920 Revolution:

> The Iraqi Revolution resulted from our miscalculations and excessive discontent. We received from the occupying British authorities the kind of respect and appreciation that cannot be compared to what we had under the Turkish occupation and the austerity of the Turkish rulers. British governors used to exaggerate in giving us good treatment and to ensure that all our needs were met, especially myself, Sayyid Nūr al-Yāsiri, and Shaykh ʿAbd al-Wāḥid al-Ḥāj Sikar.
>
> But we did not honor their appreciation and made up excuses for revolution and fighting against them in the name of independence, only to prepare the governing positions for the effendis who had already enjoyed such civilian and military positions during the Turkish rule.[89]

This is perhaps one of the most candid assessments Abu Ṭabīkh wrote on the revolution and the people who inherited the benefits in the aftermath. He usually held himself above the fray whenever he referred to other politicians. In this statement, he refers to the naïveté of those who participated, especially the notables, including him, but had not personally suffered any kind of disadvantage in British-controlled Iraq. What is missing from his assessment, however, is the mention of any rationale for a group of Iraqis to go to Ḥijaz and bring an unrepentant British agent, Fayṣal, and make him king over them, thus affirming that Iraq did not have one person worthy of the job.[90] None of those who participated in this fiasco cared to explain this lapse of judgment to anyone's satisfaction. The closest we can get to their state of mind at the time is what Thomas Lyell attributes to the shaykh of the Fatla tribe about his decision to support Fayṣal: "They say he is Shīʿa at heart!"[91]

The revolution, then, was not faithful to its fathers, according to

Abu Ṭabīkh. Instead, the only beneficiaries were those who provided no sacrifices whatsoever, either in money or blood. But who was to blame for this outcome? A careful look at the events and the acts of Iraq's notables indicates that those who imported a foreigner to be the king of Iraq willingly forfeited their right to complain.

That said, Abu Ṭabīkh's disappointment never changed his overall opinion that the 1920 Revolution was "a sacred revolution; a great revolution that influenced history in a significant way." His evidence is that the revolution gave birth to the Iraqi state, which was the revolution's "highest goal."[92]

CHAPTER FOUR

The Journalism of the Revolution

I had just embarked on a heart to heart talk with Saiyid Ḥusain about some leading articles which he proposed to publish in his paper.

GERTRUDE BELL, 24 OCTOBER 1920

I'm now turning very serious attention to the press, a job I hate, but it's necessary. I've arranged with the editor of the moderate paper, the ʿIraq, to come in and see me two or three times a week so that I may give him news and supply him with ideas. He's a good little man but not very brilliant—it's a pity that the rank and file of angels can never contrive to cut so striking a figure as Lucifer!

GERTRUDE BELL, 7 FEBRUARY 1921

IN A LETTER TO HIS FRIEND LADY MARY MURRAY, dated February 4, 1920, Captain Mann wrote, "If I treated my 'flock' (as they call themselves) as I should be obliged to treat Englishmen, it would be simply impossible to carry on at all." He then added, in passing, a remark on what made this different treatment both possible and expedient: "I remind myself that after all it will be a long time before there is an *Umm al Baʿrur Advertiser* to pillory me in its columns, and that I might as well carry on for a time."[1]

The first paper in Iraq, *Al-Zawrāʾ*, was established in 1869, during the governorship of Midhat Pāsha (1869–1872), who also established the first printing facility in Baghdad upon his arrival. This bilingual paper—Arabic and Turkish—continued to circulate as a weekly official publication until the British occupation of Baghdad in 1917.[2] The Arabic section of the paper was discontinued after the constitution of 1908, and the void was filled by Arabic papers.[3] The second government paper, *Al-Mosul*, was established in the *wilāyat* of Mosul in 1885 and continued to appear as a weekly bilingual or Turkish-only paper until the British occupation of Mosul in 1918, when it became "the voice of British authorities for some time."[4] The same can be said about the other paper, *Al-Baṣra*, which was established in the *wilāyat* of Baṣra in 1889, first as a private paper owned by a man named Chalabi Zādeh Muḥammad ʿAli. It was confiscated by the government in 1895 and discontinued in 1914 when the British occupied Baṣra.[5]

The Ottoman constitution of 1908 allowed some freedom of expression in the empire and facilitated the appearance of more than fifty-five papers and magazines in Iraq between 1908 and 1911.[6] These papers suffered from technical and content deficiencies. Anstānce al-Karmali, one of the era's best journalists, wrote: "The language of our papers cannot be weaker. . . . If you browse through any one of them and wanted [to know] which language it uses, you will not find any success . . . The writer has perhaps used Turkish, Kurdish, Persian, Hindi, or spoken Arabic. The truth of the matter is that he used them all at the same time."[7] Many of these papers were discontinued shortly after they began, because of a lack of financial or material resources—the scarcity of printing paper in particular—or because of the hardship of publishing a paper in a time of rampant illiteracy and limited audience. The British invasion and occupation of Iraq during World War I took care of the rest.

British administrators in Iraq recognized from the beginning the importance of mass communication for their success in ruling the country. They either secured the allegiance of existing papers or, at other times, established their own. Upon their arrival in Baṣra in 1914, they bought the three printing shops in the city and began publishing a daily newsletter, consisting mainly of collected translations of Reuters news releases and some other war-related news. The newsletter was developed into a daily paper, which they called *Al-Awqāt al-Baṣriyya* (Baṣra Times).[8] It was published in four languages (Arabic, Turkish, Persian, and English) and edited by John Philby, as Harry St. John Philby was known. After the occupation of Baghdad, they established another paper, *Al-Awqāt al-Baghdādiyya* (Baghdad Times).[9] Other noteworthy papers in circulation during the British occupation were *Al-ʿArab*, *Al-ʿIraq* and *Al-Sharq*.[10]

Al-ʿArab was established to highlight the "generosity" of the British administration and to provide "good news" to the populace. In the words of Ali al-Wardi,

> When the British entered Baghdad, they wanted to publish a paper that would speak on their behalf. Originally, they wanted to call it *Al-Awqāt al-Baghdādiyya*, like the one they established earlier in Baṣra, *Al-Awqāt al-Baṣriyya*, and they asked the opinion of their friend, Father Anstānce Mari al-Karmali, who in turn consulted with Maḥmūd Shukri al-Ālūsi. Al-Ālūsi advised that it be named *Al-ʿArab*. Cox liked the idea.[11]

Al-ʿArab, whose first issue was released on 4 July 1917, advertised itself as a paper "published by the Arabs for the Arabs."[12] In reality, however, it was published by the British for the British. The paper was managed by Philby, and after his departure, he was succeeded by Gertrude Bell.[13] The paper was given the exclusive right to publish the resolutions of the San Remo Conference, coupled with a proclamation from Arnold Wilson to the Iraqi people. *Al-ʿArab* was also concerned with polishing the image of the occupying administration, as by carrying Ali al-Bāzirgān's announcement that the Education Authority had granted him a license to open a secondary school:

> The highly esteemed British Government has permitted us to open a secondary school, known as al-Madrasa al-Ahliyya, whose purpose is to educate and raise our sons. We thank the Government for its sentiments and hope that all the residents will help in achieving this project; and Allah is the best guide and supporter. Signed/ al-Bāzirgān, Ali.[14]

Among the other tasks of *Al-ʿArab* was to advertise Sharīf Ḥusayn's Arab Revolt and the Hashemite family. It recruited the help of Iraqi intellectuals, who used pseudonyms for their essays, for obvious reasons.[15] The last issue appeared on 31 May 1920, with an announcement: "The first issue of *Al-ʿIraq,* a daily paper concerned with politics, literature and economics, will be released tomorrow, and will be solely owned by Razzūq Dāwūd Ghannām; this is the last issue of *Al-ʿArab.*"[16] Razzūq Ghannām, an Arab nationalist, was an editor at *Al-ʿArab.*

Al-ʿIraq became the main medium for disseminating British announcements and directives to the general public. It was also used as a forum for sending open letters to the leaders of the revolution and the mujtahids, such as Arnold Wilson's letter of condolence—or threat—to Shaykh al-Sharīʿa al-Isfahāni upon the death of Ayatollah Muhammad Taqi al-Ḥāʾiri.[17] *Al-ʿIraq* was established just a month before the start of the revolution.[18] It goes without saying that this paper as well as the other pro-British publications in Iraq helped many social and literary causes and gave voice to Iraqi writers, poets, and other intellectuals. For that they deserve praise and recognition. But as far as the 1920 Revolution is concerned, their contribution was very negative. They served as media for the British and participated as outlets for their propaganda. For this, no praise is due. *Al-ʿIraq* continued in circulation until the last decade of the monarchy.[19]

This was also the function of *Al-Sharq,* which was established to serve the ambitions of Ṭālib al-Naqīb, a Baṣra notable of great political ambitions with a mixed record in his relations with the Ottomans and the British. Its editor was Ḥusayn Afnan, who had been employed by the British in both India and Iraq.[20] In the words of Ali al-Wardi, "It is fitting to say that '*Al-Sharq*' was the only Arabic paper in Iraq that wrote candidly and audaciously to glorify the mandate. Also, it continued to publish the petitions it received from the tribal shaykhs in support of the British mandate."[21] *Al-Sharq* was blatant in denouncing the 1920 Revolution and praising the "restraint" exhibited by the British government toward the tribes:

> It is not a secret that the British Government, with all its power and means, is capable of crushing the Iraqi movement [*ḥaraka*] with its great power as other governments have done

> elsewhere. But it finds it distressing—as the only government deep-rooted in intellectual freedom and independent orientation and foremost in the fields of civility and development and truthful to its promises in liberating peoples—to replace leniency with cruelty and patience with anger.[22]

A word about *Al-Sharq*'s editor, Ḥusayn Afnan, is in order here to illustrate the type of Iraqi he was. In a letter dated on 10 October 1920, Gertrude Bell wrote the following:

> I had my usual group of colleagues, Major Yetts, Captain Clayton, and Major Murray to dine last night, and with them Saiyid Husain Afnan, the editor of one of the vernacular papers . . . He . . . talks English as well as I do, almost, is bi-lingual as far as Persian and Arabic are concerned and has a profound knowledge of the near East *coupled with a complete understanding of the European point of view and a great sympathy with it. . . . He is not very hopeful about the East. What strikes him . . . is the viciousness of private life and the entire lack of morals.* The mode of existence of most of the young and ardent nationalists would surprise you, added to which, says Saiyid Husain "*What can you expect of people who never go to bed sober?*"[23]

With this kind of sycophancy, the likes of Afnan managed to escape being categorized with those Iraqis lacking, in Bell's words, a "reasonable minimum of virtue and honesty," a deficiency that plagued their anti-British fellow citizens. Instead, he managed to be a frequent guest at Bell's parties and, ultimately, to be promoted from being an "editor of one of the vernacular papers" to being, shortly thereafter, the secretary of the Council of Ministers while retaining the role of personal translator and informant for Bell and Sir Percy Cox.[24]

While the revolution was gaining ground, *Al-Sharq* published a letter addressed to al-Naqīb from someone whose name was not disclosed, asking al-Naqīb, who was addressed with more honorary titles than the British king, to reveal his plan for Iraq. Two days later, on 21 September 1920, al-Naqīb replied in the same paper, explaining his "plan of action," which included some generic statement of "patriotic talk" but no actionable plan. Al-Naqīb did not pass up the opportunity to attack the revolution and the tribes. Indeed, his plan was vaguely described in the first five lines, whereas a scathing attack on the revolution took twenty-four lines:

> On one hand, they call for complete independence, and then at the same time they loot and cause children to be orphans. Rightful claims are made, yet the laws are broken. They unjustifiably cause women to be widows and kill the prisoners of war. . . . How can they call for rightful demands and, at the same time, misbehave and bring the biggest harm to the people and the country?[25]

Al-Naqīb's accusation about the killing of prisoners of war by Iraqis who participated in the revolution calls for careful examination. Indeed, the British acknowledged the good treatment given to their prisoners of war. On 2 August 1920, Gertrude Bell wrote: "The Manchester episode, of which I told you last week, created a very unfortunate impression, as you may imagine. Of the 400 men who went out 199 are missing. They are most of them, in all probability, safely in the hands of the tribes who are not at all vindictive." General Haldane's account of the prisoners' treatment is chaotic. He speaks of unspecified mistreatment, reported by Ḥamīd Khan, the assistant political officer in Najaf, who apparently was trying to appear loyal by claiming that "he was sending these unfortunate men such clothes and comforts as he could procure, and that each prisoner would be given a small sum of money." But Haldane admits that a Muslim doctor was summoned from Baghdad to see wounded prisoners, and "in the end that their treatment had been good was evident from their healthy and well-nourished appearance when released." In general, Haldane's statements regarding possible mistreatment were either speculation or reports by informants, but his personal observations revealed good treatment.[26] The British cannot claim to have shown much mercy toward the Iraqis who were unfortunate enough to meet their forces. Haldane admits in his book that British soldiers burned the village of Ālbu Ḥassān, near Rumaitha.[27] The good treatment of British prisoners of war was mandated by a binding decree from the leading mujtahid, Shaykh al-Sharīʿa, to their caretakers, describing the good treatment of prisoners as a "religious, civil and human obligation." This fatwa was used to refute Arnold T. Wilson's 30 August 1920 address to Shaykh al-Sharīʿa, published in the last issue of the revolution's paper, *Al-Furat*.[28] Moreover, Haldane's account of the alleged mistreatment of prisoners is refuted by Arnold Wilson, who was not a strong friend of the revolution: "I can recollect no case in the voluminous records of the Intelligence Branch or the Political Service of deliberate or calculated torture of prisoners by Arabs."[29]

JOURNALS OF THE REVOLUTION

Opponents of the British occupation had no means of counteracting propaganda such as Al-Naqīb's accusations, communicating their own messages, or publishing articles to influence public opinion. Other than some papers smuggled in from other Arab countries, such as *Lisan al-ʿArab* and *Al-ʿUqāb*, which were published in Damascus, and the *Falaḥ*, which was published in Mecca, in addition to others from Egypt, there were no papers in Iraq that could be described as friendly to the tribes at the beginning of the revolution.[30] The only nationalist paper in Baghdad at the time, *Al-Lisān*, did not print any articles "calling for revolution or revolutionary thought," although it did "publish articles about general notions of patriotism."[31]

The nationalists' failure to produce their own papers was mainly due to the administration's rejection of their petitions for a license, in addition to a lack of resources, especially printing presses. For instance, the authorities in Baghdad denied the petition presented by Muhammad ʿAbd al-Ḥusayn and ʿAbd al-Ghafūr al-Badri to publish a paper, which forced the former to go to Najaf, which was controlled by the tribes, and petition the city council on 15 August 1920. His request was approved four days later, but he had a hard time finding a place to print the paper, in spite of his willingness to pay. The governing council in Najaf had to issue a directive to "nationalize" the Najaf Printing Shop, placing it under the management of the revolution.[32] In its first editorial, the new paper, appropriately called *Al-Istiqlāl* (Independence), presented its purpose and raison d'être as follows:

> We were offended by the lack of patriotic papers in the country and the apathy of writers, therefore, our patriotism com-

> pelled us to publish *Al-Istiqlāl* in the holy city of Najaf after we originally intended to publish it in Baghdad in order to refute the misleading statements of the occupiers and their accusations and to publicize their barbaric injustices and expose their true nature. We also intend to articulate the just demands of the nation before the rest of the world and publish the news about the battles [i.e., the revolution] and the local events.[33]

The writer ends by citing the financial and technical difficulties facing the paper, promising to overcome all hardships and calling on everyone in the community to help in any way possible. The paper promised to appear in two pages four times a week, and if the readers showed adequate support, it would appear every day in four pages. To make it accessible to all, the paper was offered for a nominal monthly subscription.

The life span of *Al-Istiqlāl* was a little more than two weeks. It was first published on 1 October 1920 and closed on the fourteenth of the same month. Its publication was regular and impressively professional in spite of the difficulties of wartime and a lack of resources. Its superior language was but one of the memorable attributes of the paper, which came out of Najaf, the center of gravity of Iraq's literary tradition. This is especially important considering the general deficiencies in content and appearance of many papers in circulation during the same era. But the paper did make some informational errors, such as the publication of a false report of the death of Colonel Arnold Wilson, the military administrator in Iraq at the time; this type of problem still hampers papers today, in spite of advancements in the tools for verifying such news. To its credit, the paper published a correction on the first page of a later issue and explained the cause of the error after admitting its mistake:

> Concerning the killing of Wilson
>
> We published the news about the killing of Wilson, the outgoing ruler of Iraq, in an earlier issue relying on a letter from Shaykh Ḍāri. But we have ascertained that it was the governor of Kūt [who was actually killed] and his name is Wilson also. He was killed by ʿAbdullah in the town of Ḥayy, and that was the genesis of the misunderstanding.[34]

Although it was published to serve the revolution and the cause of independence, the paper seems to have followed its own course when it came to expressing concern about certain events. On one occasion, *Al-Istiqlāl* published an editorial about the arrival of winter and questioned the revolution's government—while praising the revolution and its leadership—about its preparations for the coming days of scarcity and cold weather.[35] This article triggered a harsh response from Sayyid Muḥsin Abu Ṭabīkh, who sent a warning to the owner of the paper and an injunction against publishing such materials in the future:

> To the owner of *Al-Istiqlāl* Newspaper
>
> Your article published under the title "Winter Is Approaching" is part of what can discourage the resolve of the mujahideen and lower their morale. It may also reveal to the enemy a sense of weakness in the fighters. Therefore, we warn you against publishing anything that may insinuate, or indicate, [our] weakness.[36]

This incident may be interpreted as a lack of tolerance by the Abu Ṭabīkh administration, but it highlights an interesting competition between two agendas: the paper was trying to be loyal to its journalistic mission to exercise oversight of the work of government and distinguish itself from the subservient papers of Baghdad, while Abu Ṭabīkh, who was establishing himself as an exemplary wartime administrator, was more interested in the higher good of keeping up the morale of an army made of irregular tribal fighters who had no proper inoculation against rumors and negative propaganda. His letter was meant to warn about the effect of publishing such articles on the war effort and the morale of the fighters, while his injunction covered only the publishing of what might indicate weakness. It must be said that in Baghdad, the British, who were better trained and equipped, hardly allowed any voices of dissent to exist alongside their official papers.

To be sure, ʿAbd al-Ghafūr al-Badri was granted a permit to publish a paper in Baghdad, which he called *Al-Istiqlāl*, too. The first issue of this weekly paper appeared on 28 September 1920, two days before al-Badri's would-be partner published his *Al-Istiqlāl* in Najaf. The Baghdad *Al-Istiqlāl* was concerned with propagating the Hashemite cause and praising Fayṣal's work, so much so that the sign of the paper was written in the colors of the Hashemite flag. Additionally, the paper soon became preoccupied by the development of the provisional government the British had installed in Baghdad.[37]

When Sir Percy Cox arrived in Iraq, the editor of Baghdad's *Al-Istiqlāl* was the first to secure an interview with him. In it, Cox granted the Iraqis permission to hold "peaceful gatherings" and publish newspapers, pending the granting of permits. He also sent a message to the revolution's leaders about his desire to reach an understanding with them to end the revolution. Finally, he promised to establish an Iraqi military after the creation of a permanent Iraqi government and other relevant institutions.[38]

Conversely, the Najaf *Al-Istiqlāl* greeted Cox with a cautious analysis titled "The Arrival of Cox and the English Policy in Iraq." After explaining the British dilemma in Iraq, the article describes the conflicting factions in London: those who wanted "to evacuate Baghdad and withdraw to Baṣra," and the camp of "Lloyd George, who recommends the use of force to suppress the Iraqi independence revolution and keep Iraq forever, contrary to all treaties and declarations that call for its independence and leaving it to its people." The paper then urges the people to give Cox the benefit of the doubt, in light of the latest changes in British policy, citing the removal of Arnold Wilson, the replacement of British employees with Iraqis, and the use of Arabic as the official language. It was ultimately up to Cox, wrote the editor. He could meet the Iraqis in battle, or do the right thing and "stay as a welcome guest among the Iraqis."[39]

Before the publication of *Al-Istiqlāl* in Najaf, another paper, *Al-Furat* (the Euphrates), was published there by Muhammad Bāqir al-Shabībi. The first issue came out on 7 August 1920.[40] The opening editorial declared the paper's purpose in a very authoritative tone: "to show the nation how to acquire virtue and keep away from vice, and to explain the benefits of unity and solidarity, and the good traits of sharing and mutual support."[41]

The paper promised to be a weekly publication, and in due course, a larger-sized format was to replace the small-sized initial issues; but *Al-Furat* did not appear regularly, and it was discontinued after the publication of the fifth issue, which was published on 1 Muḥarram 1339 (15 September 1920).

The most important among the five issues of *Al-Furat* was the last. It was released a relatively long time after the fourth issue appeared, and it was apparently published to send a scathing response to an open letter from Arnold Wilson to the top Shīʿa scholar, Shaykh al-Sharīʿa al-Isfahāni.[42] The author of the response was the paper's owner, al-Shabībi himself. A quick examination of the Wilson communiqué and the responses it received may illustrate the vital role played by the journals of the revolution.

Following the death of Ayatollah Muhammad Taqi al-Shirazi, on 13 August 1920, and at the peak of revolution's violent events throughout the Middle Euphrates, Wilson seized the opportunity and wrote an open letter to al-Shirazi's successor, Shaykh al-Sharīʿa al-Isfahāni. The letter was ostensibly an expression of Wilson's congratulations to al-Isfahāni on his ascendance to the religious leadership of the Shīʿa community and, at the same time, his expression of condolences for the loss of al-Shirazi. But the manner in which it was communicated violated proper protocol, to say the least. It is true that the two men were on opposite sides of a bitter conflict, but there was nothing to prevent Wilson from sending the letter with an envoy rather than dropping thousands of copies from the sky like a warning.[43] Furthermore, the contents of the letter included a mix of diplomatic words, unfounded claims, blatant threats, and provocative slander against those who took part in the revolution:

> The people of Iraq accepted the British State and they were happy to have its armies remain in this country after they defeated the Turks. But, when some corrupt and selfish crooks saw the reduction of its armies, they began to perplex the minds and confuse the opinions [of the people] . . .
>
> Currently, ships are coming to Baṣra every day, full of troops, artillery, guns, bombs, machine guns, ammunition and all the other necessary war supplies. If it is your honorable opinion that someone should be sent to Baghdad to personally observe these things, we will welcome him and promise his safe and speedy return.[44]

To refute the letter, Muhammad Bāqir al-Shabībi resumed the publication of *Al-Furat*, releasing in it a scathing point-by-point rebuttal written in a superb linguistic style. He held Wilson personally and exclusively responsible for having "desecrated the good traits of British civilization and caused three million innocent Iraqis to lose trust in every Englishman even if he be a good example of honesty and pure conscience." He goes on to scornfully refute the main points in the letter: "When did [the Iraqis] accept the British Government and when did they express joy about having your army stay? Here are the referenda documents that prove their resentment against you and their refusal of your stay. Their men and children, young and old, all are alike: they reject you and feel no attraction toward you and you know it."[45]

He then replies to Wilson's calling the revolution's leaders "corrupt criminals," pointing out that Wilson's statement was referring to the leaders of national awakening and the scholars of religion who were directing the revolution, asking him on what grounds could he "call the defenders rebels, the scholars of religion corrupt, and the spiritual leaders deceptive?" As to Wilson's proposal that an envoy be sent to Baghdad to see firsthand the British military capability, al-Shabībi replies: "This nation is well aware of your power, your supplies and your readiness to kill and shed the blood. It has no need to send an envoy to see the war supplies you have assembled . . . Is this your idea of winning the hearts of the Iraqis? How far away have you become from wisdom and right! It is as if military equipment can be the means to ending freedom and independence. Do you need an envoy for this purpose, to see the military horrors? Then what has become of humaneness?"

These two newspapers, *Al-Furat* and *Al-Istiqlāl* (Najaf), serve as the best original documents on the declared motives of the Iraqis who participated in the revolution, their goals, and their demands. Time and again, they made the revolution's case to their readers and clearly stated the demand for independence. Indeed, *Al-Istiqlāl* was published under the slogan *"la ḥayāta bila istiqlāl"* (There can be no life without independence), which appeared as a heading on each issue of the paper. This is why Thomas Lyell commented on Cox's promise of peace and goodwill by writing: "Good will meaning in their eyes an immediate *'istiqlāl'* or independence."[46] This message was repeated in an article published in the seventh issue, which presented the Iraqis, and maybe the British, with a stark choice, *"al-mawt aw al-Istiqlāl"* (death or independence), in a tone resembling the words of the American Patrick Henry, who stated on 23 March 1775, "Give me liberty or give me death!" The last paragraph of Henry's speech expresses well the feelings of those who fought in the Iraqi Revolution of 1920:

> Gentlemen may cry, Peace, Peace—but there is no peace. The war is actually begun! The next gale that sweeps from the north will bring to our ears the clash of resounding arms! Our brethren are already in the field! Why stand we here idle? What is it that gentlemen wish? What would they have? Is life so dear, or peace so sweet, as to be purchased at the price of chains and slavery? Forbid it, Almighty God! I know not what course others may take; but as for me, give me liberty or give me death!

Similarly, *Al-Furat* presented an identical rationale for resorting to violence: "The nation's patience ran out as Iraq's shouting in support of full independence [*al-istiqlāl al-tām*] filled the horizons. . . . Iraqis realized that legal demands and peaceful rallies are useless as they recover no rights."[47]

Al-Furat, along with other means of communication, took particular interest in the religious dispute between some British officers and the Iraqis. It referred, for example, to the tone of religious fanaticism in materials published by a British officer in the pro-British paper *Al-ʿIraq,* and presented this, along with restrictions placed on religious rituals, as evidence of Britain's disregard for freedom of religion.[48] While the British invasion and occupation of Iraq was essentially an imperialist quest rather than a crusade, it goes without saying that some officers did not faithfully observe the dividing line between the two motives. Or as one British colonial official put it: "Individual members of the British executive may confess themselves to be atheist or agnostic, but the laws and the justice they administer are the direct outcome of the community-life with which the Early Church was saturated."[49]

This position was most obviously present in the deep convictions of Arnold Wilson, who held the highest military rank in Iraq during the revolution. In an article he published before his departure from Baghdad, Wilson wrote that Iraq needed more than the material benefits of civilization; if Iraq did not absorb the principles of Christianity, it would not be fit for practicing its freedom. He went on to say that this desire to Christianize the Iraqis inspired, and was imbedded in, the acts of almost all British officials.[50] Elsewhere, Wilson described the invasion of Iraq in both religious and strategic terms: "By occupying Mesopotamia during the war we drove a wedge into the Muhammadan world, thereby preventing the possibility of a combination of Muhammadans against us in the Middle East."[51] This strategy manifested itself occasionally in acts of religious intolerance, such as the bombing of the Grand Mosque in Kūfa and some transgressions on religious endowments (*waqf*, i.e., properties used exclusively for religious purposes). These acts were aptly highlighted by *Al-Istiqlāl* and *Al-Furat*, particularly in the latter's lengthy address to Wilson in its last issue.

PAMPHLETEERING

Journalism also took the form of occasional pamphlets addressing specific issues and responding to particular events in the course of the revolution. They were either distributed in the streets and markets or glued to the walls of mosques and other public places. One of these pamphlets, written by al-Shabībi, was cited in the Intelligence Report of 15 November 1920 as a response to British attempts to question the genesis of the revolution and the motives of the people involved in it. The text of the pamphlet was published in *Lisan al-ʿArab*, a Syrian paper, on 9 October 1920. According to the British Intelligence Report:

> [*Lisan al-ʿArab*] publishes an article entitled, "What is going on in Iraq." It states that the English have claimed in their official *communiqués* that the love of anarchy and plunder has been the greatest cause of the present rising in Iraq, while some articles in Europe say that it is engineered by Bolshevik hands or by the Turks. In order to dispel this doubt the paper publishes a proclamation issued by the insurgents in Najaf. This states that the responsibility of the rebellion rests with the British authorities and that the following conditions

should be observed by those who defend themselves and their country: —

1. Independence should be the war-cry in all battle-fields.
2. Roads should be kept secure and communication maintained between the centres of rebellion in Iraq.
3. Each leader must explain to his followers that the object of the present rebellion is to obtain independence.
4. Discipline should be adhered to, movements duly organized, and there should be no murder or plunder.
5. Due attention must be paid to prisoners, whether officers, English or Indians.
6. Telegraphic instruments and telephones must be preserved, but the wires must be cut in order to interrupt British communications.
7. Transport carts, motor-cars and vessels captured must be safeguarded.
8. Guns and maxims captured must be kept intact.
9. Ammunition, such as cartridges, shells and gun-powder, must be preserved.
10. When a town or village is occupied, it should not be abandoned without a provisional government.
11. Government offices and buildings, unless these were strongholds, should not be destroyed.
12. Protect hospitals and medical instruments.
13. Be kind to wounded, especially those who have fallen in battle-fields.[52]

In some of its points, the pamphlet seems to be a counterpropaganda communiqué. The British continued all along to accuse the revolution's leaders of being foreign agents or selfish exploiters of the popular sentiments for their own aims.[53] Therefore, the first and third points urge the leaders to dispel these accusations and refocus attention on the main goal of the revolution, namely, full independence for Iraq. Other items in the pamphlet show the sophistication of the revolution's leaders in balancing the need to preserve the infrastructure of the country with the goal of disrupting the operations of their enemy. This shows their difference from mob movements that burn and loot without any sense of direction or planning, which is how the revolution and its leaders were commonly portrayed.

Another pamphlet, dated 25 July 1920, was titled "To the Civilized World." It described a British air raid the previous day that killed two women and three children and wounded more than twenty people inside the Grand Mosque of Kūfa.[54] This pamphlet was distributed everywhere in the Middle Euphrates, with several copies being sent to foreign diplomatic missions in Baghdad and Tehran. Realizing the magnitude of the atrocity, British officials published an explanation in their usual outlet, *Al-ʿIraq*, essentially blaming the Iraqis for the incident. The announcement claimed that shaykhs were using the mosque as a center of operations, and alleged that shots had been fired at the airplanes, which "returned fire, not knowing it was a mosque." They promised not to bomb mosques in the future.[55] The British claim that their fighters did not know what they bombed was a mosque qualifies as "the mother of all falsehoods," to borrow a well-known modern Iraqi expression. By 1920, the British knew the small town of Kūfa like the backs of their hands. This important holy site is too obvious to miss and too important to ignore. For the Shīʿa, the Grand Mosque of Kūfa is considered the fourth-holiest site in the world, after the mosques of Mecca, Medina, and al-Aqṣā. Yet the statement made it look like an innocuous mosque on some city corner. The fact that this bombing took place on a sacred site the day after the tribes had attacked and occupied Kifl on their way to Ḥilla, the last trench before Baghdad, gave the act a clear stamp of frantic retaliation. The week of the Kūfa atrocity was by far the worst period for the British in the entire period of occupation.[56]

Although short-lived and lacking resources, the journalism of the 1920 Revolution played a remarkable role by providing press services for the tribal fighters at the time of the revolution and by presenting a counterview of the events for future historians. It is unfortunate that many historians have failed to appreciate the effort of the two papers. This is especially true in the case of ʿAbd al-Razzāq al-Ḥasani, whose book on the revolution discusses the journalism vaguely and briefly. Similarly, his other book, on the history of Iraqi journalism, devotes one paragraph only to each of the revolution's papers.[57]

CHAPTER FIVE

The Revolutionary Networks

Meantime the Baghdadis who are the authors and begetters of all this trouble, have created a monster which they now can't control. The tribes are in full enjoyment of rebellion and they're not going to listen to anyone. . . . Once the tribes get out on the warpath it takes all the King's horses and all the King's men to bring them to order. In fact I don't know what's going to happen.

GERTRUDE BELL TO HER FATHER, 26 JULY 1920

THE 1920 REVOLUTION REPRESENTED THE CONfluence of many intellectual and combative efforts. Nationalist awareness, mainly emanating from the cities, was the contribution of the educated Iraqis. Among these were the Iraqi officers in the Ottoman military, whose organizing efforts date back to the establishment of the ʿAhd Association (Jamʿiyyat al-ʿAhd) on 28 October 1913.[1] Iraqi officers in the Ottoman military joined al-ʿAhd from the beginning and dominated its activities. Among these were Nūri al-Saʿīd, Yāsīn al-Hāshimi, Ṭāha al-Hāshimi, Jamīl al-Madfaʿi, Mawlūd Mukhliṣ, Ali Jawdat al-Ayyūbi, Taḥsīn Ali, Taḥsīn al-ʿAskari, and ʿAbd al-Ghafūr al-Badri.[2] Although the members of al-ʿAhd, which was founded as a secret organization, demanded autonomy for the Arab territories, they also called for the continuation of the caliphate in the possession of the Ottomans, while the Arabs were to serve as "a reserve power" for the Ottoman Empire against the encroachment of the West.[3]

The founding members of al-ʿAhd went on to establish branches in cities such as Beirut, Damascus, Baghdad, Mosul, and Baṣra. But the eruption of World War I caused its members to disperse among the war fronts and froze their political activities. Those of them who joined the Arab Revolt regrouped in Damascus and revived the association, but in two branches: al-ʿAhd of Syria and al-ʿAhd of Iraq.[4] The group shifted its allegiance several times, from being pro-Ottoman during the association's founding era to pro-British when it joined the Arab Revolt, then to being anti-British in late 1919 and early 1920; but it returned to the pro-British position after the selection of Fayṣal for the throne of Iraq.[5]

During its anti-British phase, al-ʿAhd was involved in events that are worth noting. The first act was the occupation of Dayr al-Zōr on 10 December 1919. Ramaḍān Shlāsh, a son of the chief of the neighboring Ālbu Sarrāy tribe, attacked the town and arrested the British force there. But both al-ʿAhd and the Arab government in Damascus dissociated themselves from the incident.[6] Indeed, Fayṣal quickly sent a telegram from Paris, denying any knowledge or approval of the attack and promising to punish the perpetrators, describing them as being in the service of the Turks.[7] The Arab government finally dismissed Ramaḍān Shlāsh and replaced him with Mawlūd Mukhliṣ on 17 January 1920. Joined by more than 30 officers and 250 soldiers from the Iraqis in Syria, Mukhliṣ continued the hostility toward the British, but the adventure in Dayr al-Zōr ended in a dispute among the Iraqi factions over a shipment of gold estimated at seventy thousand Ottoman lire that was supposed to be smuggled across the border. The Dayr al-Zōr police intercepted the shipment, and a dispute ensued between Mukhliṣ and those who wanted to distribute the gold among the tribes and the fighters.[8] Soon thereafter, the Arab government made a deal with the British concerning the border and ended the anti-British hostilities in Dayr al-Zōr.

The second incident involving al-ʿAhd was the attack on Talʿafar, a small town near Mosul. Iraqi officers dominated the administrative and military posts in the Arab government in Syria. Unsurprisingly, this provoked the resentment of their Syrian counterparts, and it was made clear that Iraqi officers were not welcome. Counting on help from the Russians and the Ottomans, the officers approached Fayṣal, who had been enthroned in Syria on 8 March 1920, asking for weapons and money and for his brother, Zayd, to accompany them to Dayr al-Zōr. Fayṣal gave them the money and some weapons, but refused to involve his brother, so as not to give the British any evidence of his involvement in the hostilities against them.[9]

After settling in Dayr al-Zōr, a force of 200 officers and soldiers under the command of Jamīl al-Madfaʿi, one of the sharīfian officers, set out for Talʿafar, arriving on 2 June 1920. They were joined by tribal forces from Shammar and al-Jubūr, and by other tribes and local residents. By 5 June, they were in full control of the town, having overwhelmed the small British force. Al-Madfaʿi, who signed his correspondence "Commander of Northern Iraq Forces," sent a letter to the Mosul branch of al-ʿAhd that read in part: "We entered Talʿafar without giving casualties, and seized twelve vehicles and eight machine guns, four of which are armored. We also shot down an airplane and killed more than a hundred British soldiers. . . . God willing, we will enter Mosul tomorrow, so we ask you to make the necessary preparations."[10]

The attack on Mosul took place on 8 June, which was met by the British artillery with the help of two airplanes. The local tribal fighters were the first to flee, and they were followed by the sharīfian force. This was the end of al-Madfaʿi's adventure in the north, and the British were again in control of the region.[11]

Just like al-ʿAhd, whose establishment went through early setbacks and had to be revived years later, the other association, Jamʿiyyat Ḥaras al-Istiqlāl, was first established in Baghdad in February 1919. It was founded by ten Iraqi intellectuals, including Jalāl Bābān, Ali al-Bāzirgān Ḥusayn Shlāsh, and Muḥyi al-Dīn al-Suhrawardi.[12] Soon after Ḥaras al-Istiqlāl was founded, a bitter rivalry broke out between it and the Baghdad branch of al-ʿAhd, which was headed by Saʿīd al-Naqshbandi. Each side accused the other of treason or of being the agent of a foreign power: Al-ʿAhd accused Ḥaras of being agents of the Turks, and Ḥaras accused al-ʿAhd of working for the British, among other spiteful attacks.[13] The feud seems to have reached Syria, which caused al-ʿAhd to send a delegation led by Jamīl al-Madfaʿi, who attempted to reconcile the two groups, but failed in spite of trying to buy some goodwill. Ultimately, both groups were dissolved.[14]

These clashes between the two groups were perhaps the reason for their failure to present themselves as serious partners to the Middle Euphrates tribes and the mujtahids of Najaf. For example, Farīq Mizhir al-Farʿōn credits the two groups with having made some demonstrations during their brief period of cooperation, but affirms that they were not known to the Middle Euphrates tribes during the revolution. He further notes that their roles were inflated "after the end of the revolution and the formation of the national government and the passing of the ordeal."[15]

Toward the end of 1919, some former members of Ḥaras al-Istiqlāl decided to reestablish the group, and this time its membership included more Shīʿa figures, such as Muḥammad al-Ṣadr Bāqir al-Shabībi and Jaʿfar Abu al-Timman, in addition its original founders like Jalāl Bābān, Ali al-Bāzirgān, and others.[16] Unlike al-ʿAhd, whose goals and loyalties kept changing, Ḥaras al-Istiqlāl insisted from the beginning to the end on the full independence of Iraq. It demanded a constitutional monarchy, one of Sharīf Ḥusayn's sons as king, and the rejection of any ethnic and sectarian discrimination. To be true to these goals, Ḥaras included Kurds, Sunni Arabs, and Shīʿa as members. It established branches in Baghdad, Ḥilla, Najaf, Shāmiyya, and Diyāla. Unlike al-ʿAhd, it had no branches outside Iraq. Ḥaras al-Istiqlāl began to have a very high ratio of Shīʿa members when another group, Jamʿiyyat al-Shabība al-Jaʿfariyya, decided to merge with it.[17]

In 1920, Baghdad intellectuals and notables were divided into three groups by interest, preference, and political position. First, there were those who disliked the Shīʿa and did not want any association with their leadership. Among those were Maḥmūd Shukrī al-Ālūsi and ʿAbd al-Raḥmān al-Gaylāni, the *naqīb* of Baghdad, for whom three kinds of people were worse than Satan: the Jews, the Shīʿa, and the French.[18] The second group consisted of the politically ambitious, such as many former Ottoman officers and some notables of Baghdad, such as Muzaḥim al-Pāchachi, Ḥusayn Afnan, and Ḥisqail Sasūn; their allegiance continued to shift from one patron to another, always siding with the winner, until it rested finally with the British. The third group was made up of nationalist Iraqis, who detested the British occupation and worked diligently toward the full independence of Iraq. Most of them joined Ḥaras al-Istiqlāl.

The inclusion of Sayyid Hādi Zwain in the Ḥaras membership, along with Bāqir al-Shabībi, created a strong link between them and Najaf and, by extension, with the rest of the Middle Euphrates.[19] But this link did not extend as far as involving Baghdad in the revolution. The only activities there were peaceful demonstrations and participation in religious events. Tawfiq al-Suwaydi and other members of Ḥaras were arrested and sent into exile, while some other Baghdadi notables, like Yūsuf al-Suwaydi, Jaʿfar Abu al-Timman, and Ali al-Bāzirgān, managed to escape arrest and ended up in the Middle Euphrates. The one who faced the harshest punishment was ʿAbd al-Majīd Kanna, who was tried for inciting violence and was executed in Baghdad on 25 June 1920. Baghdad was completely pacified after these measures.[20]

THE TRIBAL SETTING

As in previous revolts and uprisings, activities in Baghdad and other urban centers were pointless without the full involvement of the tribes of the Middle Euphrates, which were, as Gertrude Bell described them, the "monster" that became the body and soul of the revolution. To understand the social dynamics in the Middle Euphrates region and the networks of loyalty that facilitated the 1920 Revolution, we must take a closer look at tribal networks and the life and times of some leaders of the revolution.

A pre-Islamic Arab poet once said, "I am only from the Ghaziyya [tribe]; if they go astray, I go astray; and if they go righteous, so will I." In this commitment to one's community, that is, tribe, the interests and concerns of the individual were always secondary, or even sacrificed altogether when they collided with the interests of the community. In return, the tribe always stood by the individual, guilty or innocent, when threatened by members of other tribes. A tribe also stood by its members in times of need. By contrast, selfish individuals, who preferred to pursue their own interests or betrayed the tribe, were cast out and disowned, thereby losing the protection and support of their tribes. The tribe would announce that such a person was no longer a member and that therefore his blood might be shed with impunity.

To make matters worse, he would not be allowed to reside within the territory of the tribe. If the dispute with the tribe were over a matter not in conflict with the values of society, the banished member would generally find another tribe to give him refuge and allow him to live as a second-class member on the condition of good behavior. Otherwise, he was left to fend for himself against all kinds of adversity.

Oftentimes, a band of banished persons from various tribes would form an alliance and live together, displaying loyalty to the group the same way a true tribe would, such as raiding other tribes for subsistence and defending the group against all adversaries, although they could not be considered a tribe in the proper sense and could never gain the legitimacy of a true tribe. This custom gave rise to a new social class known as the *ṣaʿālīk* (singular, *ṣuʿlūk*)—outlaws pursued by all tribes. To avoid this dreadful punishment, a tribal person had to be immersed in the tight network of tribal loyalties and had to adhere to the tribe's collective values and customs, often against his personal convictions, because there was no moral or political authority above the authority of the tribe.

The coming of Islam presented perhaps the first significant opportunity to change the complex structure of tribal loyalties and introduce a space for individual conduct. The concept of the *umma* (the Muslim community) meant loyalty to a group that transcended tribal affiliation. Also, the Islamic privatization of ethics, crimes, and rewards called for a different dynamic in social relations. The *umma* does not stand by a guilty member in the same way the tribes did. Loyal to the *umma* or not, those who offend others will have to answer for their offenses. But many tribal customs survived the onslaught of Islam, coexisted with it, or even took precedence ahead of Islamic teachings—the treatment of women in certain Muslim countries is only one example. Also, the Muslim state after the death of the Prophet, with one or two exceptional episodes, did not pursue the original philosophy of Islam, which considered tribal loyalty to be contrary to the interests of the larger Muslim community. Muslim armies in the first century AH still organized themselves into fighting units by tribe as a way both to take advantage of the impulse to aid blood relatives and to compete with other tribes for having a reputation for valor and heroism. Non-Arab joiners of Islam were forced by some Muslim rulers to affiliate themselves with particular tribes and were called *mawāli* (singular, *mawlā*; client), in clear violation of Islamic law and affirmation of the retribalization of Islam.

When the Muslims came to Iraq, many Arab tribes were already living in the area, which was ruled by the Persians. New cities, such as Baṣra and Kūfa, were established to serve as garrisons for the armies and places of residence for the families of soldiers. Those cities were divided into quarters where members of each tribe resided in spaces of their own. While urban life and centuries of social changes caused space to be shared, and complicated the network of personal loyalties, the primordial loyalty to the tribe hardly faded. One's tribe remained the main source of support, of a sense of belonging, and even of one's last name — a status the tribes maintained well into the twentieth century to varying degrees, depending on the strength of the state and the nature of tribe: urban, rural, or mixed.

To appreciate the role played by the tribes in the 1920 Revolution and during the era of British occupation, it is important to map out the tribes' territorial influence in the Euphrates area, from the Syrian border to Baṣra in the south. While many tribes had moved from Arabia to Iraq as early as the beginning of the Islamic conquest, some of the largest tribes in the country were very recent settlers, such as the Shammar tribe, which moved from Najd around 1790 after losing their territories to the Saudis, who were taking advantage of the weakness of the defeated Ottomans and, later, the tacit consent of the British to consolidate their power in the Arabian Peninsula.[21] The Shammar, mainly a tribe of shepherds, settled in the Jazīra region between the Euphrates and the Tigris, with a territorial influence extending from northern Ramadi in the west to Mosul in the north. But the main influence in the Ramadi area was the nomadic confederation of the Dulaym tribes, although some of the Dulaym were farmers dwelling in tents made of goat hair and temporarily placed near the bank of the Euphrates, which gave life to a narrow strip of cultivated land. But these tents were frequently moved to cope with the flood in the spring. Although sometimes the river did not offer them a chance to flee.[22]

The other part of the Dulaym tribe consisted of nomads dwelling closer to the Syrian border. They did not cultivate the land, because of the lack of fertile areas on the riverbanks. Hence, their main occupation was the herding and breeding of sheep and camels. Those who owned large herds of camels often brought them to the agricultural areas in the Upper and Middle Euphrates to transport the field crops and dates during harvest. The domain of this confederation extended from Fallūja, west of Baghdad, to ʿĀna at the western border.

There was also the nomadic tribe of the ʿAniza, which had its roots and main extensions outside Iraqi territory—toward the Arabian Peninsula. One of the confederation's main branches, the ʿAmārāt, lived in Iraq in the area southwest of the Euphrates. They frequented the cities of Najaf and Karbalāʾ for trade and shopping. Their shaykh, Fahd al-Hadhdhāl, was the most frequent guest at the British administration's offices in Baghdad, along with the shaykh of the Dulaym tribe, Ali al-Sulayman.[23] These two shaykhs went out of their way to prove their loyalty to the British. According to one historian, when they gave their allegiance to Fayṣal, they stated: "We give you our allegiance only because the British agree to your appointment."[24]

The Dulaym region was, and remains to date, predominantly Sunni. In 1919, the population of the region consisted of 247,000 Sunnis and only 200 Shīʿa (as well as 2,600 Jews and 200 Christians).[25]

In the Middle Euphrates, the area south and southwest of Baghdad to the Samāwa region, many tribes resided in and shared the best-cultivated land in the country.[26] The large confederations, predominantly Shīʿa, were divided into smaller subtribes called *ʿashāʾir* (singular, *ʿashīra*). The most well known are the Khazāʿil, who held undisputed influence in the Dīwāniyya region; their subtribe, the Fatla, whose two branches dominated the areas of Hindiyya and Abu Ṣkhair. The Khazāʿil shared the Middle Euphrates with other tribes, including the Ḥmaidat, the Āl Shibl, the Banu Ḥasan, and many others.

In the Samāwa region, the tribes of Ḍuwālim, Banu Salāma, Ḥachchām, Āl Zayyād, Izairij, and Aʿājīb occupied most of the territory. To the south of these tribes lies the territorial continuation of the Muntafiq confederation, which dominated the area from Samāwa to the south of Dhi Qar province, with the town of Sūq al-Shuyūkh, as their marketplace. Unlike the tribes of the Upper Euphrates, whose rank and file are Sunni Muslims, the Middle and South Euphrates tribes were predominantly Shīʿa. In the one exception, the Muntafiq federation, the ruling shaykhs, the Saʿdūn family, were Sunnis, while their constituent tribesmen were predominantly Shīʿa.

According to the same estimate of 1919, the population of the Middle Euphrates had 537,197 Shīʿa and 17,428 Sunnis—the vast majority of the Sunnis resided in the Ḥilla region. There were 7,595 Jews, residing mainly in Ḥilla and Dīwāniyya, and 5,047 Christians, residing mainly in the Dīwāniyya region.[27]

Tribal shaykhs enjoyed undisputed status within their respective tribes. They derived their authority from the loyalty expected from every member. Also, the shaykh acquired a level of eminence according to his personal characteristics, such as generosity, wisdom, prudence, and the like. Fairness was not always a requirement, whereas the ability to maintain order and keep all members of the tribe marching in lockstep was vital. Punishments for small violations often exceeded any sense of proportion, including humiliation or even corporal punishment for the guilty. Muhammad Āl ʿAzzūz, one of the shaykhs of the Hindiyya branch of the Fatla tribe, used to tie men whom he wanted to punish near a colony of large ants and pour water into the colony's entrance. Such inhumane punishment might be inflicted for failure to comply with the shaykh's summons in a timely fashion.[28] The Ottoman rulers, unable to control the tribal areas, often empowered certain shaykhs to dominate rural regions in return for their allegiance and the promise to keep order and collect taxes from the areas under their control.

A shaykh's authority also came from the economic structure of society. A shaykh owned the land, and the peasants—members of his tribe—worked on it for a portion of the crops. Before the 1958 coup, this system gave the owner full ownership of the date palm orchards and 75 percent of the fruit. The farmer's share was 25 percent of the fruit and wood coming from the trees. After 1958, the farmer's share in the fruit doubled.[29] For farmers who grew field crops and vegetables, their share was 50 percent of the harvested crop.[30] But the farmer received some benefits from the land, such as permission to grow vegetables on it for his consumption and to keep some animals—chickens, sheep, and maybe a few cows—to eat or to sell. Except in very rare circumstances, the farmer always received free housing. Nevertheless, the life of farmers was extremely difficult, and they often ended up owing the landlord and others. Most farmers began the year without any savings. Since they had to wait until harvest to receive their first payment, all their needs, other than what the land yielded, could be obtained only through primitive forms of credit. The lack of a banking system gave rise to small lenders whose operations relied on personal trust, since there were no guarantees enabling creditors to collect their money from debtors. The farmer owed money to the owner of the local store, the butcher, the landlord, and maybe to friends and neighbors. This debt consumed the revenue he received from the year's work, and a new year would begin with fresh debt.

THE NOBLE BLOODLINE

The tribes of the Middle Euphrates shared the space with some of the very influential sayyid (plural, *sādah*) families, who belonged to the noble lineage of the Prophet's family. There were two groups of families that held this title: Sunnis, represented by prominent Iraqi personalities such as Sayyid Ṭālib al-Naqīb of Baṣra and Sayyid ʿAbd al-Raḥmān al-Naqīb of Baghdad, who later became the first Iraqi prime minister under the British mandate; and the Shīʿa sayyids, who were supremely revered among the Shīʿa. Public niceties aside, a sayyid, in the Shīʿa definition, is one who traces his ancestry to the Prophet through the descendants of his daughter Fāṭima and, in practice, must be a Shīʿa to be well regarded and to receive the status of a true sayyid in the Shīʿa community.

The sayyids fell into three categories: the sayyids who joined the religious scholarly community and actively participated in the intellectual activities of the Shīʿa seminary, known as the Ḥawza;[31] the poor sayyids, who made up the majority of the Sayyid population; and the wealthy landowning sayyids of the Middle Euphrates—such as the Abu Ṭabīkhs, the Yāsiris, and Āl Mgōṭir.

The first group of sayyids was integrated into the scholarly guild in the holy cities that provided society with its spiritual leaders, the mujtahids. Their authority and status was due to scholars having the final word in matters of religion. They collectively ruled as spokesmen of the Divine. This was perhaps the only domain in which a non-sayyid could be better regarded than a sayyid, because knowledge is the only criteria used to distinguish the most excellent among the mujtahids.

The second group—the poor sayyids—may be viewed in the same way as the ordinary poor members of society. They worked at hard jobs and shared the hard life of their class. But their sayyid status gave them access to some extra money that came from the religious financial payment known as *khums* (literally, "one-fifth"), a 20 percent tax that is incumbent on every income-earning Shīʿa person to pay at the end of the year to help the poor descendants of the Prophet, among other purposes. While the regard paid by society to the first group of sayyids is one of reverence, the sentiment felt toward the poor sayyids is mainly a feeling of sympathy.

The last group, the landowning sayyids, became, in essence, part of the same social class as the tribal shaykhs. They held land, lived and operated within business and commercial networks, and depended for their power on their economic well-being; their noble lineage was an added windfall that distinguished them from their wealthy counterparts who lacked the advantage of the noble bloodline.

SAYYID MUḤSIN ABU ṬABĪKH

Unlike urban absentee landlords, these were landlords whose lives revolved around the maintenance and care of their land. They were the social leaders of their communities in Iraq's rural regions of the Middle Euphrates, a status reserved for tribal shaykhs and some sayyid families. To understand the dynamics of social relations in the region and the role of such landowning notables, it is useful to sketch a portrait of Sayyid Muḥsin Abu Ṭabīkh (1878–1961), a hands-on landlord whose vast lands were his main preoccupation. He belonged to the aforementioned landowning category of sayyids. He was a descendent of Imam Ali, the cousin of the Prophet Muhammad and his son-in-law, hence the title "sayyid" before his name. His lineage belongs to the seventh Shīʿa imam, Mūsa al-Kadhim, through a highly dignified chain of ancestry.[32] His other title, Abu Ṭabīkh, was first given to his great-grandfather, Sayyid Idrīs, who spent much of his money in a year of famine to feed the people of his area until the famine ended. The meals he made consisted of rice and meat, known locally as *ṭabīkh*. Sayyid Idrīs earned this title as a sign of gratitude from the people who enjoyed his generosity.[33] Idrīs was not the first to acquire such a title after a deed of remarkable generosity. He was evidently inspired by the conduct of the Prophet's great-grandfather, who fed the Meccans in a year of famine, insisting on breaking the bread himself to prepare the food; people in turn began to call him

"Hāshim" (the one who breaks [the bread]). The two stories are finely linked by the fact that Idrīs Abu Ṭabīkh was a descendant of Hāshim.

The Abu Ṭabīkh family resided in Ghammas, a small town in the region between Dīwāniyya and Najaf. They arrived in Iraq from their native land of al-Ḥasā (in the Arabian Peninsula) around 1700. In 1958, the family owned 201,450 acres of land, cultivating rice, dates, and other crops in the Middle Euphrates.[34] Ghammas was founded by Sayyid Ḥasan, the father of Muḥsin Abu Ṭabīkh. Originally, the area was *mīri* land—agricultural land belonging to the Ottoman government—that was offered for rent. Sayyid Ḥasan Abu Ṭabīkh rented the entire area and used it to grow rice. When the Ottoman government auctioned the land, Sayyid Ḥasan purchased it and began investing in its establishment as a town.[35]

There were no schools in Ghammas, so Sayyid Muḥsin Abu Ṭabīkh was first educated in his father's guesthouse (muḍīf) by a private tutor who taught him and his brother, Jaʿfar, reading, writing, some Arabic literature, and Qurʾanic studies. He then went to the neighboring holy city of Najaf to continue his religious studies, but he halted upon his father's death in 1902 and returned to Ghammas to take his father's position as the head of the family. He continued his studies independently, benefiting from the large library his family owned.[36]

Ghammas remained without schools until the sons of Sayyid Muḥsin reached school age. In 1925, he funded the building of the first primary school in the town, near the police station, which he had also built, along with a post office and a mosque. He then petitioned the Iraqi Ministry of Education to assign the teachers and staff. The school continued to expand until there was a full set of classes from the first to the sixth grade. The school mainly served the children of merchants and landowners in the region. Some farmers sent their children as well.[37]

Being a sayyid, Abu Ṭabīkh and others like him were given great privileges, such as unconditional respect and reverence by their community, in comparison with the majority, who are not sayyids—usually called *ʿawām* (commoners; singular, *ʿāmmi*). It was considered an honor for an *ʿāmmi* person when, for instance, a sayyid proposed to marry his daughter; some sayyid families refused to marry a daughter to an *ʿāmmi*, although no Islamic law sanctions such tradition. Also, it was customary for someone who wanted to ask another for a favor

FIGURE 5.1. *Sayyid Muḥsin Abu Ṭabīkh. Photo courtesy of Jamil Abu Ṭabīkh.*

or to solve a dispute to solicit the intercession of a sayyid. Such intercession almost always resulted in considerable concessions and ultimately facilitated the process. Sayyids also received privileges from successive governments as a symbolic way of showing reverence for the Prophet by honoring his descendents. On the other hand, such privileges came with the responsibility of self-discipline on the part of the sayyids, who were expected to live by higher moral and behavioral standards than common people. Unlike *ʿāmmi* Arabs, who divided themselves according to tribal affiliations, the sayyids maintained extended family affiliations. They meticulously recorded their lineages, which trace each sayyid to one of the twelve Shīʿa imams and ultimately to the first imam, Ali b. Abi Ṭālib (died AD 661) and his wife Fāṭima, the daughter of the Prophet Muhammad.

The sound business dealings of Sayyid Ḥasan Abu Ṭabīkh bequeathed his sons a handsome financial status. According to British intelligence reports, "the fortune of the Abu Ṭabīkhs was estimated in 1926 at 50,000 Turkish pounds in gold." This figure did not include the "vast estates" on Shaṭṭ al-Ḥilla and Shaṭṭ al-Shāmiyya.[38] These "vast estates" were acquired through a combination of three ways of ownership: *mulk*, *ṭāpu*, and *lezma*. The *mulk* type of ownership pertained to estates in towns and involved properties owned for centuries. The second form, *ṭāpu*, was acquired through the Ottoman land-tenure-reform law of 1858, which allowed the right of use of state-owned lands to be purchased by individuals and entities. While the state maintained actual ownership of the land, the de facto owners had the right to use the land and transfer that privilege to their progeny or to others. The state maintained the right to confiscate the land if the "owner" did not use it for five years or longer. The *lezma* form of ownership was the most recent kind of land tenure, legislated under the monarchy in 1932; it involved public lands that had been held and used productively by individuals for fifteen years. *Lezma* land could be lost to the state if abandoned for four years or longer. The Abu Ṭabīkh family had land under both *ṭāpu* and *lezma* ownership.[39]

Some of the vast land was given to the Abu Ṭabīkh family by other people merely for being sayyids. These kinds of generous gifts testify to their status in a society with unmatched devotion to the family and progeny of the Prophet. According to a deed dated in 1801, the original owner presented half of his land, hundreds of acres, as a gift to a mem-

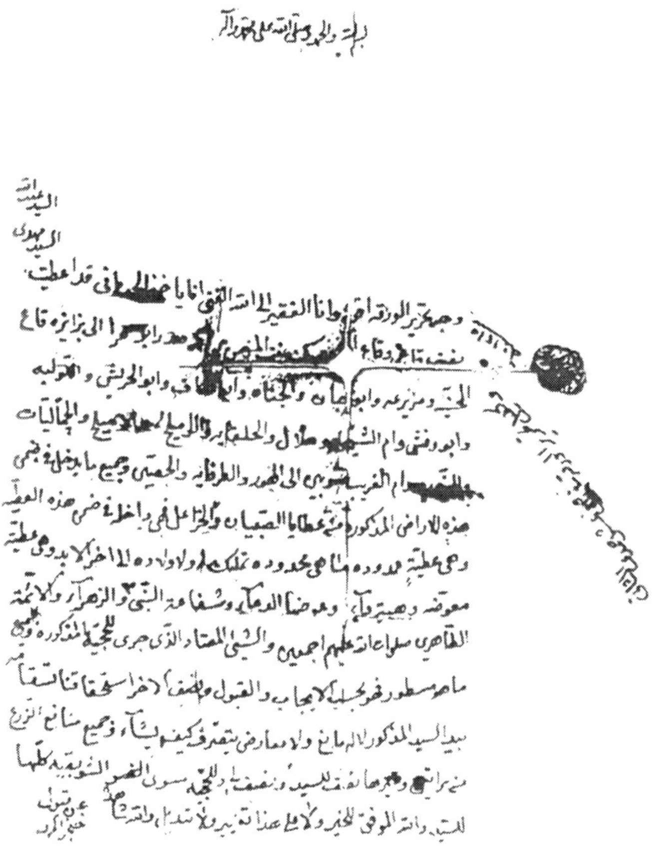

FIGURE 5.2. *Khanjar al-Ḥamad's grant of land to Sayyid Mahdi Abu Ṭabīkh. Courtesy of Jamil Abu Ṭabīkh.*

ber of the Abu Ṭabīkh family. In examining the language of the deed, this apparently wealthy landowner wanted to exchange a piece of land in this world for a better property in paradise. In the grant document, he wrote: "I gave Sayyid Mahdi [son of] Sayyid ʿAbdullah half of my land . . . as a pure gift to be owned by him and his progeny until the end of time. It is a gift in exchange for his supplication [on our behalf] and the intercession of the Prophet and [his daughter, Fāṭima] al-Zahra, and the pure Imams, peace be upon them."[40]

This acquisition of land continued until the passing of the land-reform law after the collapse of the monarchy in 1958. In that year, the Abu Ṭabīkh family stood as the fourteenth-largest landowner in Iraq, with a total property of 124,496 *dunums* (76,939 acres). But this land was not always secure. Before the confiscation and redistribution of land according to the land-reform laws, the Abu Ṭabīkh family faced several confiscations and vandalism during the Ottoman era, the British mandate, and the monarchy. One such incident was the order given by Abu Ṣkhair's governor to distribute Abu Ṭabīkh's land among the local tribes because he and other landowners refused to pay taxes to the Ottoman authorities. The tribes refused to take the land, perhaps out of reverence and fear that such act would subject them to the wrath of God and the Prophet. Other tax evaders were not equally revered. Their lands were taken away, and in one case, it took major tribal fighting to retrieve them from looters. In the case of Abu Ṭabīkh, the Ottoman army occupied the land for more than two months. He ultimately got his land back, but not the two thousand tons of rice that were confiscated and sold in Abu Ṣkhair.[41]

The wealth of Abu Ṭabīkh, as in the case of other sayyids, came with high expectations to help the needy and provide for the common good; when the 1920 Revolution was planned, he was one of the main contributors. When the revolution in Mishkhāb was announced, he contributed 600 Turkish pounds in gold, which was a fortune according to the calculations of the time.[42] He also gave many stockpiled provisions during the course of the revolution. He wrote about the time of the revolution in Karbalā᾽:

> We consumed everything in our food storage, and in any case it was less than we would normally have because of the scarce winter season and the bad summer's rice season before, which exacerbated the bad situation. Making food available took from us all of our financial assets, which would be better used in buying weapons and ammunition. I remember with profound admiration what was generously provided by Sayyid Nūr al-Yāsiri, Sayyid Hadi Mgōṭir, Sayyid ʿAlwan al-Yāsiri, Sayyid Hadi Zwain, and Ḥaj Muḥsin Shlash, as well as the generosity of Ḥaj ʿAbd al-Wāḥid Āl Sikar. If not for their assistance

and generosity, we would not be able to continue the jihad and sustain the fighting effort.[43]

Abu Ṭabīkh, as custom required, omitted his financial contribution to the war effort and praised others for what they contributed. His generosity was acknowledged by Ali al-Bāzirgān, a Sunni notable from Baghdad whose role in the revolution was considerable: "I lived in Karbalā᾽ for a long time [during the revolution] . . . and I must note that Sayyid Muḥsin Abu Ṭabīkh was spending all the money he had to sustain these tribes and providing them with meat and rice, locally called *ṭabīkh*."[44]

In the aftermath of the revolution, the main participants received extraordinary punishments, including a relentless effort to place them in custody for a symbolic trial with a predetermined outcome. Those who owned land and other property suffered grave damage to their property. Abu Ṭabīkh recalls the destruction of his property following the end of the revolution: "They bombed my houses, stores and farms as well as my guesthouse. They also destroyed my village in the Ṭābu and destroyed my guesthouse there and even stole the animals and the hay that was kept for feeding the horses."[45]

When Karbalā᾽ offered to surrender to the British, Sir Percy Cox handed the delegation a list of conditions, the first of which was the surrender—within twenty-four hours—of seventeen men "to face trial because there are reasons to believe that they were criminals." The first name on the list was Muḥsin Abu Ṭabīkh.[46] According to the intelligence report sent by the Office of High Commissioner in Baghdad, Abu Ṭabīkh was named—along with ʿAbd al-Wāḥid Āl Sikar, the shaykh of Fatla tribe; ʿAlwan and ʿUmran, the shaykhs of Banu Ḥasan; and Sayyid Nūr al-Yāsiri—as "the principal leaders of the tribal forces."[47] In a plot to capture the leading participants in the revolution, the British sent to them letters of assurance that they would be treated well if they surrendered. Some leaders, such as ʿAbd al-Wāḥid Āl Sikar, did surrender, perhaps relying on some connections with high British officials.[48] Abu Ṭabīkh and other principal leaders refused to surrender.[49] They chose to leave Iraq and seek refuge in Ḥijaz as guests of Sharīf Ḥusayn of Mecca. This was the first of three forced exiles Abu Ṭabīkh had to suffer in the course of his life.

Abu Ṭabīkh's journey to his first exile began after managing to secure temporary refuge for himself and a few members of his family and associates in the territory of the Banu Salāma tribe. Meanwhile, the British imposed a heavy penalty for his participation in the revolution. He was ordered to pay—or have paid on his behalf—12,000 Turkish pounds in gold and 1,000 rifles;[50] the price of a rifle was £10–£20.[51]

LAND TENURE

Land tenure under Ottoman rule in Iraq was originally vague and contradictory. While the state claimed ownership of the land, the tribes operated under a counterclaim that each tribe, or confederation of tribes, collectively owned its own territory (*dīra*) and defended it against the encroachment of other tribes. Individuals' relation to the tribal land was restricted to right of use.

The Ottoman Land Code of 1858 established several kinds of landholding. As discussed above, *mulk* land was land that had been owned for generations by certain families; it was considered to be owned outright, and its disposition was at the discretion of the owners. This was a very small portion of all land. The vast majority of cultivated land was designated as public (*mīri*) land owned by the Ottoman state. There was also *waqf* land, which was either a private endowment administered by trustees for the purposes specified by the people who established the endowment, or a public endowment normally administered by a religious establishment and used for religious and social purposes. To link the tribes to the land, and to increase revenue and stability, the Ottomans issued deeds of quasi ownership of *mīri* land to those interested in them. This was *ṭāpu* land, as described above.

Suspicious of governmental motivation and lacking legal knowledge about such matters, most tribe members did not register their land or seek deeds for new lands. The people who reaped the fruits of the law were wealthy elites in Istanbul and in the major cities in Iraq. In the Muntafiq area, for instance, the government gave more than 100,000 acres to the Sarkīs family, which resided in Baghdad and had no history of farming.[52] In rural areas, the tribal shaykhs and large landlords used the law to increase their already vast estates. When the twentieth century arrived, about 30 percent of the land in Iraq, "including the most cultivatable and fertile land," belonged to the Ottoman monarch, Sultan ʿAbd al-Hamīd.[53] This practice gave rise to a new category of ownership, absentee landlordism, which later posed a challenge to the British administration. The assistant political officer in Ḥilla wrote in 1918 that absentee landlords were a serious problem that needed to be solved: most were residents of Baghdad, and half of them never laid eyes on the vast fertile lands they had obtained through shady means.[54]

The tribal history of the Middle Euphrates is essentially a history of conflict over land control. This conflict often took place by design: the Ottoman authorities, unable to control the tribes, manufactured feuds and rivalries among them. The Ottomans would occasionally confiscate a territory from one tribe and give it to a rival, causing the two tribes to fight each other for years. As they weakened each other, the winner was the Ottoman administration. Among the notorious land transfers was the granting of the Khazāʿil land in Rumaitha to the shaykh of Izairij, Farhūd Āl ʿAssāf, in 1873. The Ottoman governor of Dīwāniyya, Shibli Pasha, authorized this confiscation to punish the Khazāʿil tribe after arresting its leaders and attacking the tribe with heavy artillery. He also granted their land in Mishkhāb, between Najaf and Dīwāniyya, to the shaykh of the Fatla branch there, Firʿōn Āl Yāqūt. The Khazāʿil recovered the Rumaitha land after six years, but that in Mishkhāb was lost forever.[55]

Similarly, the governor of Baghdad, Jawid Pasha, visited Najaf in the beginning of 1914 to solve a dispute between his local representative, Ḥāmid al-Sāmarrāʾi and the Middle Euphrates tribes — the tribes refused to pay the taxes that year because they were higher than what they owed. He ordered the confiscation of the land belonging to ʿAbd al-Wāḥid Āl Sikar, and then distributed it among his tribesmen. Āl Sikar finally recovered the land with the help of his well-armed followers. The land of Sayyid Nūr al-Yāsiri was given to his cousins, who pretended to be against him. The Ottoman troops attacked and occupied the land of Sayyid Muḥsin Abu Ṭabīkh and confiscated more than 2,000 tons of grain. They remained on his land until the beginning of World War I later that year.[56]

The British adopted similar policies, but mostly as retaliatory measures. Following another dispute between ʿAbd al-Wāḥid Āl Sikar and men from his tribe, a British official, Captain Jeffries, allocated the entire disputed land to the tribesmen, including ʿAbd al-Wāḥid's share. It seems that this partiality of Captain Jeffries was not mere retaliation—he was known to the tribes for taking bribes. In one instance, Ḥāj Mukhīf, a wealthy landlord from Dīwāniyya, placed a belt made of pure gold around the waist of Jeffries's wife on one occasion, which earned him the captain's support until a strictly honest mayor named Ibrāhīm Kamāl came to the city and put an end to Ḥāj Mukhīf's privileges, telling him, "I have no wife who needs a belt of gold."[57] It is believed that this unfair adjudication was the reason behind ʿAbd al-Wāḥid's bitter hatred for the British. Although his tribesmen were willing to give him his share of the land to end the costly conflict, ʿAbd al-Wāḥid insisted on having all of the land in question, according to Sayyid Nūr al-Yāsiri, who was asked to mediate between the two parties. ʿAbd al-Wāḥid got nothing in the end.[58]

Some of the disputes took a long time and involved protracted court proceedings and high-profile figures, especially when some disputants had roles in the national government. A series of confiscations that began in 1922 and was resumed in 1928 between Sayyid Muḥsin Abu Ṭabīkh and the British and lasted until after the independence of Iraq in 1932. Abu Ṭabīkh describes them as retaliatory measures against him and other participants in the revolution. In both cases, the land taken from Abu Ṭabīkh was given to Ilyāhu ʿAzrā, "a Jewish man from Dīwāniyya with connections to the British," as Abu Ṭabīkh described him.[59] It is most likely that the British could not find a local Shīʿa who would accept the land that once belonged to a Sayyid, as the Ottoman governor experienced a decade earlier. As Abu Ṭabīkh recalls, the land of ʿAbd al-Wāḥid Āl Sikar, who was not Sayyid, was distributed among "those who carried their weapons against" the revolting tribes.

It must be noted that the dispute over Abu Ṭabīkh's land was not between him and Ilyāhu ʿAzrā. That is why Abu Ṭabīkh sued the government, which had confiscated his land. As far as ʿAzrā was concerned, it was land that belonged to the government and was going to end up in the possession of someone other than Abu Ṭabīkh anyway. Also, Ilyāhu was not the only notable with connections to the British.[60] Those tribal notables who were awarded the land of ʿAbd al-Wāḥid Āl Sikar, for instance, were equally well connected. Ilyāhu's being non-Shīʿa freed him from the social expectation specifically imposed on the Shīʿa to reject land that once belonged to a Sayyid, even though the acquisition was legal. As a Jew, this rule did not apply to him.

The high-profile dispute that ensued ultimately involved the interference of King Fayṣal himself. An out-of-court settlement was reached that restored Abu Ṭabīkh's ownership of 900 *dunums* (556 acres) after he agreed to give up his claim for the rest of the land—1,100 *dunums* (680 acres).[61]

Hanna Batatu, perhaps because of his expressed lack of regard for Muḥsin Abu Ṭabīkh and his brother, Jafar,[62] mistakenly reported that in 1935, "Sayyid Muḥsin Abu Ṭabīkh was rewarded with a grant of land in Dīwāniyya province for his political services to the government of Yāsīn al-Hāshimi, but lost the grant after the military coup of 1936, only to regain it subsequently."[63]

The account given by Batatu seems to misrepresent the facts about the land in question. What Batatu incorrectly described as a "reward" and a "grant" was in fact the settlement that gave Abu Ṭabīkh less than half the total land that was confiscated from him in 1922 and 1928. Batatu's skepticism about Abu Ṭabīkh perhaps led him to believe that this return of the land during the reign of Yāsīn al-Hāshimi, a political ally of Abu Ṭabīkh, was a grant. It is true that previous governments had not liked Abu Ṭabīkh and had ignored his claim for the land until al-Hāshimi came to power and addressed his grievances, but this was not by any means a reward. Here is how Abu Ṭabīkh himself described the events:

> When the Hāshimi government was formed [in 1935], I became certain that the case was going to be settled according to whatever I desired. But to protect my own dignity and the dignity of my friends, the ministers, I proved to be free of selfish personal interests. When Yāsīn al-Hāshimi asked me how I wanted to solve the dispute, I gave up [some of] my rights and accepted 900 dunums instead of 2,000 dunums, which was mine. He issued an order accordingly and I received it . . .
>
> When the government of Ḥikmat Sulayman came to power

> [in 1936], and only ten days after he grabbed the position of Prime Minister, he issued an order to the mutaṣarrif to take the land from me and give it to the same Jewish man.[64]

There is no indication in Abu Ṭabīkh's memoir that the land was later returned to him. According to Jamil Abu Ṭabīkh, the land was never returned to the family after being confiscated for the second time in 1936.[65]

CHAPTER SIX

The Revolution's Aftermath

If we had begun establishing native institutions two years ago! by now we should have got Arab govt and an Arab army going; we should have had no tribal revolt; all the money and lives wasted this year would have been saved. Damn AT Wilson.

GERTRUDE BELL TO HER FATHER, 10 JANUARY 1921

I have endeavoured to show that the Muslim, and particularly the Shia, is — and for many years must remain — totally unfit for self-government, which he only "desires" as an opportunity to escape from all law and order.

THOMAS LYELL, *THE INS AND OUTS OF MESOPOTAMIA*, 1923

ALTHOUGH THE MANDATE FOR IRAQ WAS GRANTED to Great Britain in April 1920, its implementation did not begin until the end of the year, mainly because of the pressing military situation caused by the 1920 Revolution. The revolution was instrumental in changing Britain's plans for Iraq from annexation, in the way India was dealt with, to the creation of an independent state with the preservation of British interests in the region as the first priority. The immediate result of the revolution was the replacement of the heavy-handed acting commissioner Arnold Wilson by Sir Percy

Cox. It was, and still is, considered by Iraqis to be the war that brought about the country's eventual independence from British colonization. Given the vast difference in power and resources between the British Empire and the Iraqi tribes, it was a matter of time before the revolution was crushed. But the £40 million and the many British lives it cost brought the Iraqi question to the fore. Captain Mann's statement "that after all it will be a long time before there is an *Umm al Baʿrur Advertiser* to pillory me in its columns"[1] could not hold true any longer, because the revolution featured in many columns in the largest newspapers of London.

On 6 June 1920, Sir Percy Cox, then the British ambassador in Tehran, was summoned to London to consult on the future of Iraq. While he was en route, the 1920 Revolution erupted, and by the time he arrived, the British press and public opinion had been mobilized against involvement in Iraq because of the loss of blood and treasure. Among the British, two opinions collided: leave Iraq immediately and cut their losses, or stay the course until Iraq was pacified and ready for annexation. The latter approach was obviously the choice of Wilson and a number of his assistants in Iraq.[2] Cox was more interested in preserving British investment in the country and the potential interests that might still be salvaged. He had a third option in mind. The first order of business, Cox suggested, was to suppress the revolution and then, instead of withdrawing from Iraq and giving up the mandate, establishing a local, Iraqi government.[3]

On 1 October 1920, Cox arrived in Baṣra with a mandate to create an Iraqi national government. He was received by many Iraqi notables, and a party was organized the next day to honor him and bid Wilson farewell. Several political hopefuls gave speeches praising the "noble efforts" of Great Britain and accusing the revolution's leaders of shortsightedness. Of these, it is worth quoting the revealing speech of Muzaḥim al-Pāchachi:

> I very much regret that the follies of some individual Arabs have served to disappoint the British nation in its honorable undertaking [i.e., the occupation of Iraq]. These acts were committed partly owing to unattainable dreams and partly owing to selfish material interests. The present movement is

> not purely an Arab movement, but it is mixed with an alien element, which has been, to my deepest regret, successful in using Arab fame, wealth and blood for its own benefit, in the hope of weakening the position of Great Britain elsewhere. Do not believe in appearances, which are mostly deceptive, especially in the East. Do not consider the present revolt of some nomad tribes to be really a national revolt seeking independence. Such a movement cannot be taken as representing the feeling of the whole community. The influential families of Baghdad have no sympathy with a movement that has ruined their country.
>
> Such are the feelings of the people whose views carry weight. They are anxious to convey what they think and feel to those in England who are advocating the withdrawal of Britain from this country. They cannot realize that withdrawal means no less than the breaking up of law and the ruin of a people, followed by anarchy throughout the country, which might involve an Asiatic war, in which Britain could not stand aside.[4]

Muzaḥim al-Pāchachi, who, as Wilson notes, conveniently "described himself as 'an extreme Nationalist,'" continued to serve the interests of his British patrons in every subsequent capacity he held. For example, he signed the agreement that virtually gave away Iraq's oil for seventy-five years to a foreign company whose main owners were British. The ministers of education and justice, Muhammad Riḍā al-Shabībi and Rashīd ʿĀli al-Gaylani, resigned over this decision, which, in the words of al-Shabībi, "squandered Iraq's rights." After signing the contract on 14 March 1925, al-Pāchachi added the Ministry of Justice to his portfolio.[5]

Muzaḥim al-Pāchachi was not alone in adopting this position in late 1920. Indeed, he was in a sizable company of ambitious notables who hoped to receive favors from the British and rise politically. There were other types of patronage seekers who stood firm in their support of the British administration.[6] One kind represented the rivalry between Baghdad (and other urban centers) and the powerful tribal and rural regions, especially the Middle Euphrates. It is noteworthy that Muzaḥim al-Pāchachi, like many other Sunni notables, did not pass up the opportunity to present the undying accusation that the Shīʿa, the backbone of the revolution, were not "pure Arabs," a charge that persists until the present time.

When Cox arrived, the tribes still held the Middle Euphrates, including Karbalāʾ and Najaf. Kūfa was still under siege, and they were trying to capture Ḥilla. In the Lower Euphrates areas, most of the region was in revolt. Samāwa and Rumaitha—the first home of the revolution—were safely in the hands of the tribes. But the major cities of Baghdad, Ḥilla, and Baṣra were not part of the revolution. Baghdadis who supported the resistance fled to the Middle Euphrates and joined the revolution there. Baṣra, whose population and notables prospered from the presence of the British at the port, was never interested in joining the fight.

Cox started his mission by assembling a team of British and Iraqi officials to help him create the first Iraqi government that would be acceptable to the Iraqis and friendly to the British. But the brunt of the work was performed by Gertrude Bell, who became his secretary. Bell was a well-educated civil servant who worked in Baṣra after serving in many other Arab countries. She had a good command of Arabic and a remarkable knowledge of the Iraqi tribes, along with the skill to identify which locals possessed any inclination to establish alliances with her government. She arrived in Baghdad for the first time in April 1917—the first British woman to be there in an official capacity—and began a tireless mission to maintain an orderly occupational bureaucracy. As personal secretary to Cox, she played an essential role in the molding of modern Iraq.

PUTTING AN IRAQI FACE ON THE OCCUPATION

On 25 October 1920, Cox, with the help of Bell, formed an Iraqi government with ʿAbd al-Raḥmān al-Naqīb as prime minister. Al-Naqīb was an old religious leader of Baghdad's Sunni establishment with no political experience whatsoever, which was perhaps the main reason for his selection. He accepted the assignment reluctantly, and only after considerable persuasion and pressure from Cox and Bell, who thought his appointment would not interfere with plans to place the country in the hands of Cox and his assistants. Helping al-

Naqīb was a cabinet of twenty-one ministers, twelve of whom were without portfolio. Of course, none of these positions went to those who took part in the revolution. The following conversation, recorded by Bell in one of her voluminous letters, reveals how the ministers felt about their countrymen. They were either patronizing, hostile, or condescending:

> And I ended the day by giving a dinner party to Sasun Eff, Jaʿfar Pasha and ʿAbdul Majid Shawi, with Mr Philby, Capt Clayton and Major Murray to help. For I wanted to bring the first named 3 into touch with one another. It was immensely interesting. ʿAbdul Majid told Jaʿfar the whole story of the origins of the tribal rebellion. Jaʿfar, with great eloquence, pleaded the need of an immediate settlement with the insurgents. "The peasant must return to his plough and the shepherd to his flock. The blood of our people must cease to flow and the land must once more be rich with crops. Shall our tribes be wasted in battle and our towns die of starvation?" "Effendim, true," said ʿAbdul Majid, "but do you know why it is that we can now hope to bring the tribes to submission? It is because they have seen the might of the British army." And Sasun Eff. agreed.[7]

Once the government was established, every minister was coupled with a British adviser, who was the actual authority in the ministry's day-to-day affairs. The nominee for prime minister insisted on a cabinet in which no Shīʿa minister would receive a portfolio. Aided by a general Shīʿa aversion to assuming any employment in the government, the *naqīb* eventually got his wish. In the words of the historian Ali al-Wardi: "Cox desired from the beginning to give a ministry with a portfolio to a man from the Shīʿa, but his desire was met by two obstacles; first, the Naqīb and some influential ministers objected, and, second, the Shīʿa themselves despised any member of their community who would agree to participate in the cabinet."[8]

This account echoes the one given by Bell in a letter to her father on 7 February 1921: "The Shiʿahs are sore because they are not sufficiently represented in the Cabinet, which is mainly Sunni and very determined to remain Sunni. There are a number of duds in the Council and the Cabinet—the worst being those who were selected by the Naqib himself—and there are also one or two really efficient men out of office, but they are all Sunnis and it's difficult to see how a reasonable number of Shiʿahs is compatible with a reasonable efficiency. You see the problem isn't easy!"[9]

The appointment of an Iraqi government was a departure from the heartfelt attitude most British officials held, namely, that Arabs were not even close to being capable of self-rule. A year before this policy was put into action, Arnold Wilson, then acting commissioner in Iraq, had stated: "It is impossible to install a real Arab Government in Mesopotamia and for us to make an attempt will be to abandon the Middle East to anarchy."[10] Perhaps that was the reason Cox wanted to choose a government that would ensure his supremacy, not to mention be dominated by the British advisers within the ministries. In the provisional government's first session, it requested that Cox clarify, in writing, the relation between the advisers and the ministers. He responded to their request with a document that remained in effect until the end of the mandate in 1932. According to the instructions, Cox retained the exclusive right to manage the country's affairs. If a disagreement were to occur between him and the government, Cox wrote, "the final word will be mine."[11] In Bell's words, the members of the government were "merely an apparition created by Sir Percy."[12] As for the British advisers, they had the right to block any decision a minister took, until the next meeting of the government. They also were given the option of taking the issue to Cox himself for final arbitration. If an adviser suggested a course of action and a minister disagreed, the minister had to go to the government in order to overrule the advice.[13]

The most important revelation in the document was that the government was not given any jurisdiction outside Baghdad. In article 13, Cox wrote, "As you know, the provinces and districts in Iraq remain as they were. They are administered by British Political Officers with the help of national [i.e., Iraqi] subordinates as Assistant Political Officers and mayors."[14] In the districts where security was still lacking, British governors would remain in charge. But where it was possible to appoint Iraqis, the role of the government, as stated in article 14, was limited to nominating such persons. The decision to appoint any of them was the prerogative of Cox himself.

The new government began its work under great disadvantages besides the meddling of British officials, not the least of which was a lack of funds. According to ʿAbd al-Razzāq al-Ḥasani, "The occupation government withdrew all the money in Iraq and considered it income for the administration of India . . . including thirty thousand rupees of religious endowment money that was deposited as a trust in the treasury."[15] Nonetheless, the government accomplished a few goals, such as securing the return of some exiles from India and Henjam, with the help of the press and popular demands for their return. They also managed to establish the national army, at the encouragement of Sir Percy Cox. On 26 May 1921, they passed the law regulating enlistment in the Iraqi army.

The largest accomplishment of the first government was perhaps due to chance more than to design. The governor of Sulaymaniyya, Shaykh Maḥmūd, had double-crossed the Turks and delivered their military contingent to the British in October 1918 in exchange for British recognition of his rule over the region. But he became more acquisitive, and declared independence. The British retaliated by arresting and sending him into exile in India. Sensing the interest of Cox to add the region to his domain of influence, the Naqīb government urged him to annex the Sulaymaniyya province to Iraq, citing its geographic importance and its economic and political relations with Iraq. Adding the Sulaymaniyya province to Iraq, they argued, would safeguard the country's northern frontiers against foreign threats.[16]

A SECOND CHANCE FOR FAYṢAL

The next task for Cox was to recruit a head of state for the country. The new king had to meet two conditions: be acceptable to the Iraqis and be willing to serve the interests of Great Britain in the region. It became clear from the first days of the search that no Iraqi would gain the confidence of Bell and her superiors. She wrote on 3 October 1920: "If only we could manage to install a native head of the state. I agree with A. M. that Talib is out of the question and there's no possible alternative but a son of the Sharif. I hear that the Young Arabs of Baghdad are now running down ʿAbdullah on the ground that he's a savage and Fayṣal seems to be barred by French susceptibilities, so that the prospect in that direction doesn't seem very hopeful. Damn the French."[17]

But some Iraqi officers who had returned from abroad began a propaganda campaign for Fayṣal, the son of Sharīf Ḥusayn of Mecca, with whom they had served in the Arab Revolt against the Ottomans. The idea of installing Fayṣal on the Iraqi throne was also supported by British officials, especially Bell. The British at last set their mind on Fayṣal to be king. To ensure, through their own Iraqi agents, that Fayṣal was chosen by the Iraqis themselves, the British pretended to be against the choice. The assumption was that Iraqis would always act contrary to the wishes of the British, as Bell knew.[18]

During World War I, Fayṣal led an army from Ḥijaz to fight the Ottomans on behalf of Britain and France with the understanding that his father, Sharīf Ḥusayn of Mecca, would be rewarded with a kingdom in Arabia, Iraq, and Greater Syria. Feeling betrayed by his former allies, especially the British, who declined to honor their prewar agreement without telling Fayṣal that they had promised Syria to France, Fayṣal appointed himself king of Syria in March 1920. But at the San Remo Conference, held on 19–26 April, the mandate for Syria was assigned to France. It took the French little effort to defeat Fayṣal's army at the Battle of Maysalūn and then to dismantle the new kingdom in Damascus on 25 July 1920, five months after its establishment.[19] Fayṣal lived in exile until he was contacted by the British to rule Iraq, after a decision to that effect had been made at the Cairo Conference in March 1921, which was presided over by Winston Churchill.

The main task was to "sell" Fayṣal to the Iraqis, who were predisposed to reject anything pleasing the British. The process began in Mecca, when a number of the leaders of the 1920 Revolution, led by Sayyid Muḥsin Abu Ṭabīkh and Sayyid Nūr al-Yāsiri, took refuge there after the suppression of the revolution.

It seems that Sharīf Ḥusayn was trying to use his Iraqi guests as part of a grand scheme that he had planned with the British. As he sanctimoniously told them at one of their meetings: "We have divided these peoples into kingdoms and distributed their crowns among our sons; King Ali will be my heir to the throne of Ḥijaz and Najd, King Fayṣal for Syria and Lebanon including Palestine and East Jordan, and you are calling for ʿAbdullah for the throne of Iraq. And we will send Prince Zayd to Yemen."[20]

But Sharīf Ḥusayn could not market Fayṣal to the French, who rejected him because of "a personal dispute."[21] Hence, it was up to the Iraqis to help him out of his quandary. If the Iraqis were to give up their demand for ʿAbdullah and request Fayṣal instead, the French would not object to having ʿAbdullah on the throne of Syria and Lebanon.

It is clear that either Sharīf Ḥusayn was deceived by the Allies, or, more likely, he was not candid with his guests. For the French were not interested in giving Syria to any of his sons. Also, the decision to promote the candidacy of Fayṣal for the throne of Iraq was made at the Cairo Conference. On 12 March 1921—fifty days before Ḥusayn's conversation with Abu Ṭabīkh and his group—Gertrude Bell had written: "Among the decisions taken at the Cairo Conference on our policy in the Middle East, Britain agreed to support the candidature of the Amir Fayṣal for the throne of Iraq."[22] For the plot to reach a perfect conclusion, the Iraqis had to believe that they had made the choice of who was to rule them, because any indication that Fayṣal had been chosen by the British would cause an immediate reaction by the Iraqis. As Bell wrote later, describing the success of this particular manipulation, "Last year when they were all crying for Abdullah it wasn't for his *beaux yeux* nor because they were inspired by nationalist enthusiasm, but because they thought the cry was anti-British."[23]

All the Iraqi refugees learned, from someone identified as "a trustworthy clandestine source," was that Fayṣal and the British had agreed to form a government under the mandate. Abu Ṭabīkh and Jaʿfar Abu al-Timman confronted Fayṣal with this knowledge without informing other members of the refugee group.[24] They met with Fayṣal in his private residence, where he confirmed to them what they had learned but added that the mandate was to last only until Iraq's petition for a full membership in the League of Nations was approved; 1930 was the date for ending the mandate.[25] They left Fayṣal without revealing to him their true feelings. In a meeting attended by all the refugees, as Abu Ṭabīkh recalls, there were two opinions about how to react to this news. Sayyid Nūr al-Yāsiri and his faction decided to take a realist stance: they would accompany Fayṣal to Iraq, taking the advantage of an amnesty offered on the condition that they accept the scheme of appointing Fayṣal to the throne of Iraq. Abu Ṭabīkh and Abu al-Timman headed a faction that wanted no part of the scheme, but they did not openly oppose it. Instead, they made an excuse, stating that they wanted to perform the hajj.

After quoting Abu Ṭabīkh's version of the events, the historian Ali al-Wardi interprets this difference of opinion between the Abu Ṭabīkh–Abu al-Timman faction and the faction of Sayyid Nūr as a sign of deeper division caused by their "competition for political gains."[26] He supports this conclusion by quoting an off-the-record conversation with Sayyid Nūr's son, ʿAbd al-Ḥamid al-Yāsiri, who allegedly heard from his father that "the Mandate issue was the outward manifestation of the dispute, while the real reason was much deeper; it stemmed from their competition for higher positions, which was natural, and it existed during the time of the revolution, but it intensified in Mecca because King Ḥusayn gave Sayyid Nūr special treatment which caused the resentment of Sayyid Muḥsin Abu Ṭabīkh."[27]

This account does not match Abu Ṭabīkh's report of the course of events. Indeed, he presented Sharīf Ḥusayn's special treatment of Sayyid Nūr as an attempt to manipulate the group in order to secure its support for Fayṣal. Abu Ṭabīkh went out of his way to play down the decision of Sayyid Nūr to accompany Fayṣal, implying that it had been done more from necessity than ideology:

> I must note that Sayyid Nūr al-Yāsiri explained to me the night when I visited him to say farewell that his rheumatism has become worse because of the trip across the desert and that was the reason he had to accompany Fayṣal to arrive quickly in Iraq and receive medical treatment. Indeed, had [Fayṣal] delayed his trip, Sayyid Nūr would have traveled with his family without waiting for the royal parade. While the rest of his faction had clearly indicated that the whole matter was in the hands of the British, no matter who was going to sit on the Iraqi throne. They were tired of staying away from their homes and being treated like outsiders. They felt a duty toward their tribes and families calling on them to return to their homeland.[28]

Abu Ṭabīkh maintained remarkable respect and appreciation to the other leaders of the revolution, especially Sayyid Nūr al-Yāsiri and ʿAbd al-Wāḥid Āl Sikar. But this appreciation was not likely to cause him to overlook what he would consider traitorous conduct, if it had occurred. Hence, from Abu Ṭabīkh's account of the circumstances that led Sayyid Nūr to accompany Fayṣal, it seems that the competition among these men in the court of Sharīf Ḥusayn was either imagined by Ali al-Wardi or maybe exaggerated. Abu Ṭabīkh did, however, allude to the state of anxiety and homesickness that affected the resolve of other members of the group. Also, it is clear from the joint activities against the Anglo-Iraqi Treaty and the elections that Abu Ṭabīkh and Sayyid Nūr al-Yāsiri were on the same side again after their return from exile.

Fayṣal was brought to Iraq on a British military boat in June 1921 and enthroned on 23 August after a national referendum.[29] The people of each province were asked to sign a document authorizing a delegation to go to Baghdad and give their allegiance (*bayʿa*) to Fayṣal; he carried all Iraqi provinces except Kirkuk, were he was accepted by twenty documents and rejected by twenty-one.[30]

The referendum was by no means a free one. The British administration spared no effort to guarantee the approval of Fayṣal by a handsome 97 percent.[31] One incident may illustrate the charade of claiming that Fayṣal was a "popular choice." The local official of a town in the Kirkuk province received an order to prepare a document affirming the choice of Fayṣal as king, but a rumor reached him later that the British had decided to abandon Fayṣal and appoint someone else. Not knowing what the truth was, he asked his people to sign two documents, one for Fayṣal and another against him, and sent both documents to the headquarters.[32] Further evidence comes from a letter written by Gertrude Bell to her father on 7 July 1921:

> The leading Christian here, ʿAbdul Jabbar Pasha, came in with the Mutasarrif and Naji Suwaidi to urge that once Faisal had come we couldn't afford to wait for elections and must resort to a Referendum to place him on the throne. ʿAbdul Jabbar is a member of the Council. We were all fully aware of this, indeed Faisal had talked of it when I saw him on Saturday, but

he added that the one thing he feared was a coup d'état and we must continue to make the proceedings as constitutional as we could. The only show of Arab Govt is the Naqib in Council, though they are merely an apparition created by Sir Percy. Still the next move must come through them. Accordingly Sir Percy saw the Naqib and it has been arranged that the Council shall ask him how soon the elections can take place, since there is obviously urgent need to come to a settlement. Sir Percy has ascertained that we can't get the registration of electors through under 2 months, which is longer than we can afford. He will therefore reply in that sense to the Council, but add that if the Council approves we can resort to a speedier process [i.e., a referendum]. It will then, to put it quite baldly, be up to us to rig the Council which no doubt we can. I would rather have had elections but 2 months is too long to wait and I hope that in our present extremely favourable position we can get the country to accept anything we approve.[33]

FAYṢAL ON THE THRONE

The choice of the coronation date was made by Fayṣal himself, who chose 18 Dhu al-Ḥijja, the last month in the Islamic calendar, when the Shīʿa celebrate the Eid al-Ghadīr, the day the Prophet Muhammad appointed Imam Ali for the caliphate.[34]

Once again the Shīʿa got a share of the symbolism, whereas the Sunnis carried the substance. Fayṣal began his reign by appointing a legion of former Ottoman officers who had served him in his conquest of Syria during World War I and during his short-lived kingship thereafter, all of whom were Sunnis. These officers, known as the sharīfians, continued to fill both the military and civilian ranks of government throughout the monarchy era (1921–1958). To ensure the triumph of Fayṣal and his officers, the British manipulated the elections, supported the deportation of the Shīʿa ayatollahs who opposed the political process, and, worst of all, established minority rule in Iraq, putting to rest any hopes for establishing a free and democratic society in the country for the next eight decades. In Fayṣal's own words, "Iraq is a kingdom governed by a Sunni Arab government established on the ruins of Ottoman rule."[35]

From the outset, the British planned to use Fayṣal as a puppet and rule Iraq indirectly through him, just as they had done with the provisional government during the previous months. A week before Fayṣal was enthroned, the Colonial Office instructed Sir Percy Cox to make sure that Fayṣal declared in his coronation speech that "the ultimate authority in Iraq lay with the High Commissioner."[36] This would be a continuation of the status quo ante, as declared in the instructions given to the al-Naqīb government when it was formed in the previous year. Fayṣal refused to go along with this plan, citing prior agreements that he would be given full dignity. He also argued that any form of incomplete sovereignty would reduce his legitimacy and anger the Iraqis. The high commissioner settled for a less obvious exercise of control over the government, and the enthronement went as planned.

In his coronation speech, the new king thanked the Iraqi people for their allegiance and for "freely" choosing him.[37] Then he remembered with great affection the dead Arabs who had fought at the side of the Allied forces, and he did not forget to "recite the verses of gratitude for the British Nation that supported the Arabs, in critical war times, and sacrificed its treasure and sons for their liberation and independence."[38] It goes without saying that the speech included no tribute to the treasure and sons sacrificed by the tribes, which had paved the way for Fayṣal to become the king of Iraq.

Upon their return from exile, the revolution's leaders found that their worst fears had become reality in the new Iraq. Although the government included Iraqi ministers and governors, actual power rested in the hands of British "advisers," who were the actual ministers and governors and were ultimately accountable to the British high commissioner, Cox. Their dominance and the concomitant impotence of their Iraqi counterparts became so obvious to Iraqis that, as one historian put it, Iraqis who visited a ministry would bypass the Iraqi official and take a short cut to the British adviser to save time and effort.[39] For their part, Iraqi officials dealt with this situation as a fact of life, accepting the titles and relinquishing the power that should have gone with them. Those who were not happy with the arrangement kept their complaints private, as in the case of ʿIzzat al-Karkukly, who had been a high-ranking Ottoman officer. He commented on being "reduced" to the status of minister: "In all the posts I previously held, I was a full-fledged commander. But when I became a minister, my orders did not extend beyond this desk."[40]

In response to this loss of sovereignty and the brutal conduct of British officials, a grassroots movement was begun to oppose the policies and plans to consolidate British control over the country. In the vanguard of this movement were the mujtahids in Baghdad and Najaf and the shaykhs and sayyids of the Middle Euphrates.

His own opportunism notwithstanding, it must be said that Fayṣal was torn between his loyalty to the British, who had sponsored his bid for the throne of Iraq, and his obligation to the Iraqis, whose notables were anti-British nationalists. In spite of his vigorous effort to strike a balance between these two loyalties, he ultimately failed to reconcile them, or perhaps did not make the requisite effort. The British saw in him a recalcitrant man without loyalty, and the Iraqis were disappointed in what they considered his compromising, even traitorous, politics. Bell described her views of him—she was also speaking for the British—as follows: "Faisal is one of the most loveable of human beings but he is amazingly lacking in strength of character."[41] Other British contemporaries were even more unflattering. Writing in 1923, Thomas Lyell, the former British civil administration official, assistant director of the Tapu, and district magistrate in Baghdad, described the arrival of Fayṣal in Iraq and his appointment as follows: "Finally, Feisal himself (aptly termed the 'jack-in-the-box' king) came up the river, accompanied by an arch-rebel or two. He was duly enthroned as Amir of Iraq, *without* the issue of a single voting-paper, as it was now entirely certain that, except by the tribes of the Middle Euphrates, he was nowhere wanted. But the debt had to be paid!"[42]

Nor were Fayṣal's Iraqi constituents pleased with him. As Bell reports, "On Monday morning all the anti-Mandate lot went out to Kadhimain to consult their oracle Shaikh Mahdi al Khalisi who told them that as H. M. had not fulfilled the conditions of his election to the throne, namely that he would preserve the independence of ʿIraq, their oath of allegiance was null and void."[43] This difference of opinion about Fayṣal's true character was sorted out, in a rare moment of frankness, by Fayṣal's biographer, Amin al-Rayḥāni, who described Fayṣal's policies as neither pro-British nor patriotic (*waṭaniyya*), but "pro-Fayṣal (*Fayṣaliyya*)": "His first concern was to preserve the throne, so that he could enhance his position as a king in order to be capable of enhancing the Iraqi side in the Treaty"—that is, the 1925 treaty drawn up to govern Anglo-Iraqi relations until the end of the mandate.[44]

Among the challenges facing Fayṣal was the Kurdish question, which was not settled by the British until later in the mandate era. Meanwhile, they used it to pressure Fayṣal in the ongoing treaty negotiations. Another point of pressure was the Mosul question. The legal status of Mosul, which had been physically occupied by the British since the conclusion of the armistice with the Ottomans, remained unclear, to Fayṣal at least, although the British seem to have already made up their minds about the future of Mosul. Bell bluntly articulated the British intentions and rationale of the Mosul policy in the aftermath of the revolution:

> Sunni Mosul must be retained as a part of the Mesopotamian state in order to adjust the balance. But to my mind it's one of the main arguments for giving Mesopotamia responsible govt. We as outsiders can't differentiate between Sunni and Shiʿah, but leave it to them and they'll get over the difficulty by some kind of hanky panky, just as the Turks did, and for the present it's the only way of getting over it. I don't for a moment doubt that the final authority must be in the hands of the Sunnis, in spite of their numerical inferiority; otherwise you will have a mujtahid-run, theocratic state, which is the very devil.[45]

Indeed, the British kept the fate of the province hanging so that they could use it for more than one round of negotiations with the Iraqis or, sometimes, to blackmail them. By making the status of Mosul part of the package offered to the Iraqis, through Fayṣal, they secured the acquiescence of the staunchest opponents of the 1925 treaty, which was meant to replace the treaty of 1922. Although the former contained better terms than the latter, it was also opposed by most Iraqis because it did not guarantee Iraq's full independence. Muḥsin Abu Ṭabīkh, one of the longest-standing opponents of the treaty, described his conversion to the camp of its supporters in the following words: "His Majesty [i.e., Fayṣal] revealed to me the British tactics to pressure him and his government so that they would submit to their demands regarding the new treaty, which was to stand in lieu of the 1922 treaty. They made it very clear to him that the price Iraqis would pay, in the case of rejecting [the treaty], was an Iraq without the Mosul Province."[46]

Another, more formidable challenge facing Fayṣal was the need to reconcile sectarian differences in Iraq. The British solution, as articulated by Bell in the above statement about Mosul, granted the Sunnis a greater share of political power, but it did not provide an adequate foundation for granting the Sunnis overlord status in Iraq, for even with the inclusion of Mosul, Sunni Arabs did not make up more than 20 percent of Iraq's population.

Question #2

It is not an exaggeration to state that Fayṣal did not think highly of the Iraqis when he arrived in Iraq, and he continued to hold the same negative attitude until his death. In a memorandum he wrote about the conditions of Iraq, dated March 1932 and circulated to a select group of his confidants in the government, he revealed his thoughts: "It is my belief that in Iraq there is no Iraqi people yet. Rather, there are human masses devoid of any patriotic ideal and imbued with traditions and religious heresies. They are not united by anything. They listen to evil and prefer chaos. They are always ready to revolt against any government."[47]

For an Iraqi people to exist, according to Fayṣal's thinking, they had to selflessly accept him and his exclusive minority (Sunni Arab) rule and reject their identity, be it Shīʿa, Kurdish, or any other—it must be noted that the label "Sunni" is connected with their social identity rather than their religious affiliation. In Fayṣal's essay, he clearly described the men who made up his government as a group of secular young men who did not practice their religion.[48] Had Fayṣal been a little more candid, he would have admitted that it was this minority government, which had been imposed by the British, that caused the divisiveness among Iraqis, who had experienced a remarkable unity before his arrival, as the revolution showed.

Fayṣal's views become even more condescending whenever he spoke of the Shīʿa, notwithstanding the fact that, as discussed, they were the ones who had granted him the throne of Iraq after his devastating failure to establish his own rule in Syria. To continue with Fayṣal's statement: "Iraq is a kingdom governed by a Sunni Arab government established on the ruins of the Ottoman rule. This government rules over a Kurdish part, most of which consists of a majority of ignorant people . . . and an ignorant Shīʿa majority that belongs racially to the same [ethnicity of] the government. But the oppression they had under the Turkish rule did not enable them to participate in the governance or give them the training to do so."[49]

It was convenient for Fayṣal to blame the exclusion of the Shīʿa from his government on Ottoman oppression and not on his lack of fairness and gratitude. As this study demonstrates, the Shīʿa were exemplary in managing their affairs during the short period when they established a national government in Karbalāʾ, in spite of wartime difficulties. Indeed, the Karbalāʾ government provided an era of justice achieved by no previous or subsequent regime. In the words of one historian of the revolution, who witnessed firsthand the unfolding events in 1920: "The management of this province moved at an excellent pace—full of justice, security and prosperity for the population—as more than one Karbalāʾ resident told me, as did many of the residents of other cities. The population of the Karbalāʾ province felt the justice and equal treatment of all citizens then more than in some epochs during the [subsequent] rule."[50]

THE SUNNI MONOPOLY ON THE MILITARY

The minority government set up by the British and gleefully accepted by its Sunni beneficiaries was an inherent flaw in the Iraqi polity, one that paved the way for all the injurious episodes thereafter. One such area of exclusive control by the Sunnis was the Iraqi military, which was perhaps the worst form of monopoly in their favor.

The first unit of the Iraqi army, established on 6 January 1921, was emblematically named Fawj Mūsa al-Kadhim, after the seventh Shīʿa imam, whose tomb is situated under the golden shrine in Baghdad.[51] This was perhaps the first paradox surrounding this institution, which was an army by the Sunnis and for the Sunnis. To be sure, the number of Shīʿa recruits increased in later decades, mainly because of the conscription established by law in 1934. But this increase in numbers did not lead to an increase of Shīʿa power, because the officer corps remained predominantly Sunni.

As stated earlier, Fayṣal began his term in office by appointing a legion of former Ottoman officers—all Sunnis—who had served him in his conquest of Syria during World War I and during his short-lived kingship thereafter. These officers, known as the sharīfians, assumed leadership positions in both military and civilian ranks throughout the monarchy.

When Fayṣal was enthroned, Iraqi defense was the responsibility of Great Britain, according to the mandate.[52] The original reason for forming an Iraqi army was only to ensure the security of the central Sunni government against possible uprisings. In the words of King Fayṣal: "I do not ask of the army to keep the external security at this time, as this will be asked after we call for the general draft. What I ask of it now is to be ready to defeat two revolts that may take place (God forbid) at the same time, in two places far from each other."[53]

It is obvious that Fayṣal was interested in an army that would be able, initially, to crush the anticipated revolutions in the predominantly Kurdish north and the Shīʿa south, the only "two places far from each other" that might have resisted his predominantly Sunni government.[54]

In spite of being selected by the top clergy and the Iraqi elite, the new king was not well connected to the population at large. Further, continual British meddling in every detail undermined Fayṣal's prospects of legitimacy. A national army loyal to the monarchy was a way to enhance his legitimacy and ensure cohesion among the diverse constituents of Iraq's population. But this was easier to propose than to achieve. First, the Ottoman officers were not a monolithic group; while some of them were monarchy loyalists (fewer than two hundred officers joined Fayṣal in the Arab Revolt), the majority espoused nationalist views, and were offended by continued British occupation. Additionally, many officers maintained the old loyalty to Turkey.[55] Second, the recruitment effort did not meet the hopes of the government, in spite of propaganda and the appeals made by the king and his close associates to tribal shaykhs and religious scholars for cooperation.

One of the main reasons for the shortage of recruits was the low pay of soldiers as compared with the pay of other professions. The British decided in 1922 to raise the pay for the military, encouraging young men from all groups to join the army. This measure helped the number rise from just more than 3,000 in 1921 to 12,000 by 1932. But other problems, such as sectarian mistrust of the state, could not be solved. Tribal shaykhs in the Shīʿa areas did not want to offer their young men to strengthen the central government at the expense of their own territorial power. The same can be said about the way the Shīʿa establishment felt, especially since Fayṣal and the British had given the best political and military positions to the Sunnis, thus violating his initial agreements with them. The sharīfian officers were not only placed in favored positions, but also handsomely rewarded for their service in the Arab Revolt. According to the British Intelligence Report of 1 February 1922, the Iraqi Council of Ministers instructed the Ministry of Defense to count, for the purposes of pension and seniority, the period of service in the Arab army of the Ḥijaz as double its actual length for the officers who enlisted before the collapse of Fayṣal's kingdom in Syria.[56] Jaʿfar al-ʿAskari and Nūri al-Saʿīd were among the first beneficiaries of this decision. The first, already the Minister of Defense, was promoted to the rank of colonel, and the second became a lieutenant colonel—an important step to prepare him for the same ministerial position two years later.

The founding of the Royal Military College, whose first graduates assumed their duties in 1927, injected new blood into the Iraqi army. The new graduates were trained by British officers, unlike their superiors, who came from the Ottoman Military Academy, which was dependent on German military expertise. But British policy makers placed a limit on the size of the Iraqi army, against the desires of King Fayṣal and his sharīfian officers, especially Jaʿfar al-ʿAskari. In an attempt to break this restriction, the proponents of a larger military began advocating military conscription. This proposal, however, was wrapped in other claims, the most appealing of which was the purported role of conscription in achieving national cohesion by making the army more inclusive of all components of Iraqi society, especially the Shīʿa majority, whose representation was distressingly below their demographic weight.

It was naïve, even disingenuous, to claim that the systemic problem of Shīʿa underrepresentation could be overcome by conscription. The essence of the challenge was the distribution of power within the state at large, and the military was no exception. Sunni control of the top political and administrative positions created an aberrant environment that had adverse consequences for national cohesion. Similarly, the problem of representation within the army was specific to the officer corps. Therefore, conscription would not ameliorate this inequity because officers were not conscripted. As stated previously, the Shīʿa were not underrepresented outside the officer corps. Indeed, the anti-conscription movement created strange bedfellows when both the British and the Shīʿa rallied their forces against the first bill after its introduction in the legislature in 1926, and ultimately managed to defeat it in 1929. The British lacked the desire to strengthen the Iraqi government too early, and the Shīʿa tribes did not want to have a strong central government at all. But the bill was reintroduced and passed in 1933 when, after the Assyrian massacre, national support for the army was at its highest level.

It may be misleading to state that the military influence in Iraqi politics began with the rise of the generals at the end of Fayṣal's reign. Indeed, the Iraqi state was dominated by a military mind-set from its inception. King Fayṣal and his sharīfian loyalists divided among themselves both civil and military positions in what could be described as a British-sponsored military coup against the leading social groups in Iraq. In the first year, the cabinet was formed by a civilian prime minister, ʿAbd al-Raḥmān al-Naqīb, with sharīfian officers holding the Ministries of Defense, Justice, and the Interior. In the following seven years, from November 1922 to April 1929, all prime ministers were sharīfian officers, and these ministries and others were also being led by sharīfian officers. This pattern continued—a few exceptions notwithstanding—until the fall of the monarchy in 1958.

THE MISCALCULATION OF THE MUJTAHIDS

Contributing to Fayṣal's failure to include the Shīʿa, unwittingly of course, were the Shīʿa mujtahids, whose lack of political prudence caused them to fail to appreciate the new political reality associated with the creation of a nation-state in Iraq. The mujtahids were mostly Iranian subjects whose residence in the newly formed Iraqi state was subject to termination whenever the government deemed it necessary. While failing to adjust to this change, they continued to act according to the old rules. The first test of their status accompanied the call for a national election for the Constituent Assembly, which was intended to ratify the Anglo-Iraqi Treaty of 1922. The protagonists in the treaty drama were ʿAbd al-Muḥsin al-Saʿdūn, from the government side, backed by the British of course, and, on the other side, the Iraqi nationalists and the mujtahids, led by Shaykh Mahdi al-Khāliṣi. In October 1922, al-Saʿdūn, in his capacity as minister of the interior, issued instructions to the provinces to prepare for the elections. In response, the mujtahids issued a set of binding edicts declaring the elections to be a violation of religion on the part of the voters and the seekers of office alike. Responding to a written question from his constituents, al-Khāliṣi wrote: "We have decreed that the election is unlawful for the entire Iraqi nation. Whoever enters, participates or helps in them would be antagonizing Allah and His Messenger. Allah, the Exalted, has said in His glorious Book, 'Have not they known that whoever antagonizes Allah and His Messenger will enter the fire of Hell for eternity, which is the great disgrace?' May Allah protect all people from such punishment."[57]

Similar edicts were issued by other prominent mujtahids, particularly Abu al-Ḥasan al-Isfahāni and Muhammad Ḥusayn al-Nāʿīni. Initially, these edicts and other calls to resist the elections and withdraw any allegiance to Fayṣal, who had violated the conditions of his contract with the Iraqi people—namely, to secure and protect Iraq's independence—were successful. The mujtahids found allies in some of the tribal shaykhs and sayyids of the Middle Euphrates, particularly those who had led the 1920 Revolution, such as Muḥsin Abu Ṭabīkh, ʿAbd al-Wāḥid Āl Sikar, and Nūr al-Yāsiri. In a series of meetings that began on 2 August 1922, they began demanding that the Anglo-Iraqi Treaty be rejected because it would end Iraqi hopes for any form of meaningful independence.

At that point, the treaty was submitted to the cabinet, and received the approval of the Naqīb government. It was signed in October 1922 by King Fayṣal and Sir Percy Cox. Therefore, the opponents of the treaty also called, in a letter to King Fayṣal, for the dissolving of the government, which they described as "a tool in the hands of the British."[58] While anxious to have the treaty ratified, the British were not interested in repeating the catastrophic events of 1920 in the

Middle Euphrates by risking another showdown with the religious and tribal establishment. The words of Gertrude Bell illustrate how irritated British officials were by the effort to block the treaty:

> This afternoon the treaty will be laid before the Ministers, I am not sure they want to do something silly—put in a rider about their non-acceptance of the mandate, which will let the king down and make the whole thing exceedingly difficult. Sir Percy has done his best to persuade the Naqib not to wander off into that line of country. Three of the newspapers have been publishing petitions against the mandate . . . one of the papers has been suspended by the Ministry of the Interior—I expect they are all in the pay of that wicked old hobgoblin, Sheikh Mahdi al-Khalisi, one of the turbaned lot I want to seal into a bottle.[59]

King Fayṣal, acting on behalf of Sir Percy Cox, was involved in mediation efforts to persuade the shaykhs of the Middle Euphrates to support the treaty. He promised them, in return for their support, a variety of benefits, ranging from political appointments to assorted financial grants and tax relief. It was also made clear that failure to comply would be met with strict measures. But the sway of the mujtahids over their allies was unshakable. Abu Ṭabīkh explained to the king: "I, as an Imami, cannot act contrary to the scholars of religion [the Mujtahids] for whom I am a follower, no matter what punishment Your Majesty will impose upon me. I do express my regret that I have to disagree with you in this regard."[60]

Of no less significance for the initial triumph of the antitreaty coalition than their cohesion was the reluctance of Fayṣal and the prime minister, al-Naqīb, to confront the mujtahids. Sensing the prime minister's weakness, the British promoted a strong replacement, ʿAbd al-Muḥsin al-Saʿdūn, who had previously resigned to protest the failure to use force in dealing with the opposition. He initially brought the Ministry of Justice under his control as prime minister, but later exchanged it with Nāji al-Suwaydi for the latter's Ministry of Interior. In this way, al-Saʿdūn was in a position to supervise the election process and ensure its progress by using any means of coercion necessary. But the resignation of the British cabinet in November 1922, and its replacement by a conservative one that lacked the same enthusiasm for the passage of the Anglo-Iraqi Treaty, caused al-Saʿdūn to slow down on the election progress until more support for the treaty formed in London. In the meanwhile, he adopted a more tolerant policy.[61]

For their part, the British attempted to give more incentives to the opponents of the treaty by reducing the term of the treaty from twenty years to four years and by reducing the burden on the British taxpayers. This shift, however, was only a temporary tactic, because there was a plan to arrange for an extension of the term of the treaty after its passage. Once again, the British found the Mosul question to be a useful card to play. The Iraqi Council of Ministers approved the additional protocol. To leave the door open for the intended extension, the protocol included, after the term-reduction clause, a clause that stated: "This protocol does not preclude making a new agreement to regulate any future relations between the two honorable signatories."[62]

But the rise of a Turkish threat to the northern region of Iraq revived the old question of the religious obligations of the Iraqis in case the Turks invaded. The Mujtahids issued a fatwa to the effect that Iraqis should not fight the "Muslim" Turks in support of the non-Muslim British.[63] As Bell noted on 12 April 1923:

> This morning a fatwah forbidding the defence of the ʿIraq against the Turks was posted up in the Kadhimain mosque. We had heard rumours and denials about it for about a fortnight past. A copy was brought in to me early this morning and I think the Criminal Investigation Dept had it at the same time. I haven't any doubt that it's genuine. The question is now what should the ʿIraq Govt do? I've just been talking to Mr Cornwallis about it. He thinks they ought to deport the Mujtahids who are signatory to the fatwah to Persia—they are all Persian subjects. On the whole I'm inclined to believe that they will have to take this step or go under, but it's a very serious decision.[64]

This was the last straw for al-Saʿdūn and the British. After securing the approval of Fayṣal, who was on a trip to southern Iraq to distance himself from the affair, the government arrested al-Khāliṣi and some of his associates on 27 June 1923, citing in a declaration that he was responsible for posting the fatwa on the walls of the Kadhimain shrine. This move had been preceded by a declaration on the act of posting fatwas on the wall of the shrine, "which desecrates the sanctity of the holy shrines and makes them an exhibition for misleading goals." The declaration, issued by the Ministry of the Interior, did not pass up the chance to remind everyone that the perpetrators were "eccentric foreigners."[65] To determine the reaction of al-Khāliṣi's constituents, the government began by arresting and deporting his son and other associates. When the arrest failed to cause any significant reaction, the plan to arrest al-Khāliṣi and his close aides went forward, and they were sent to Baṣra, to embark on a journey to Mecca and ultimately to Iran, where he remained until his death of a heart attack on 5 April 1925.[66]

The other mujtahids, after their welcome in Iran had expired, began to contact the Iraqi government to arrange for their return. Having enjoyed considerably lower levels of influence in Iran than they had been used to in Iraq, they realized the magnitude of the loss caused by their departure from the holy cities. Against the advice of al-Khāliṣi, before his death, they began to negotiate the terms of their return, which included, inter alia, the issuing of new fatwas legitimating the elections, which they had previously banned, and an emphatic promise not to interfere in Iraqi politics as long as they resided in the country. Al-Khāliṣi, correctly, predicted that "submitting to the British and their Fayṣal" would bring catastrophic consequences to Iraq, declaring that "doing so is one of the greatest religious violations and something not done by any person with dignity and intellect."[67] Acting against this sound advice, the mujtahids—Sayyid Abu al-Ḥasan al-Isfahāni, Mirza Ḥusayn al-Nāʿīni, Sayyid ʿAbd al-Ḥusayn al-Ṭabāṭabāʿi, and Sayyid Ḥasan al-Ṭabāṭabāʿi—struck a deal with Fayṣal, who, predictably, used the affair to his advantage in bargaining with the British. They issued statements promising not to interfere in Iraqi politics. To quote al-Isfahāni's statement: "We have pledged not to meddle in the political affairs and decided to stay away from all of the Iraqi demands, holding ourselves not responsible for that. The one responsible for the people's affairs and their governance is Your Majesty."[68]

Meanwhile, the elections were held in Iraq with no significant opposition after the departure of al-Khāliṣi and the other mujtahids. The only negative consequences from the drama was that Najaf and other Shīʿa centers adhered to the fatwas of their mujtahids and, with few exceptions, refrained from participating in the process, leaving them without influence on the political process. The lack of Shīʿa participation enforced the established trend of excluding the Shīʿa from any meaningful participation in power for decades to come. With the mujtahids' bizarre conduct, their Shīʿa constituents had no one to blame for their political demise but themselves.

THE ANGLO-IRAQI TREATY

The foremost three items on the agenda of the Constituent Assembly, which met for the first time on 27 April 1924, were ratifying the Anglo-Iraqi Treaty, writing the constitution, and writing the law regulating the upcoming parliamentary elections.

The order of these tasks reveals how anxious the British were concerning ratification of the treaty; it would have been more logical for the Constituent Assembly to write the constitution first and then worry about making treaties. Indeed, in King Fayṣal's decree to establish the assembly, the tasks were listed in a more intuitive order: writing a constitution, writing a law for parliamentary elections, and deciding on the Anglo-Iraqi Treaty.[69]

When the Constituent Assembly met, it became clear that the treaty was not going to have a smooth passage. The objecting assembly members considered the treaty unfair to Iraq. They demanded further amendments to include a reference to Iraq's independence and assurances of more sovereignty for the government by reducing the meddling of the acting commissioner in political, military, and financial affairs. The new acting commissioner, Henry Dobbs, insisted on rejecting any amendments to the treaty and the additional agreements before ratification. But he also provided no assurances that amendments would be made after ratification. Since the date by which the treaty had to be ratified was quickly approaching, Dobbs interfered to coerce the members of the assembly to ratify the treaty. Once again, the Mosul question came in handy. Dobbs informed the members that their tardiness in ratifying the treaty would risk further complications for the task of Sir Percy Cox, who was making very slow, but sure, progress in his negotiations with the Turks regarding Mosul.[70]

The assembly was deadlocked until the final day to ratify the treaty, 10 June 1924. Dobbs denied the Iraqis any extension of time and insisted they either ratify the treaty or face the consequences—basically, a negative change in the shape of British involvement in Iraq. He also advised King Fayṣal to arrange a change in the law to grant him (that is, Fayṣal) the right to dissolve the assembly because it has not acted in favor of Iraq's interests. Finally, the assembly members were summoned to a late-night session for a last-minute effort to ratify the treaty before the expiration of the allowed time. Sixty-eight members were present, thirty-two were absent. The doors were closed, and scores of soldiers surrounded the place.

The assembly president, ʿAbd al-Muḥsin al-Saʿdūn, explained the situation and placed before the members a resolution by Yāsīn al-Hāshimi on behalf of those who wanted either to amend the treaty before ratification or to receive assurances that the amendments would be made after ratification. The resolution was defeated by a vote of 43 to 24, with 1 abstention. Then an alternative resolution was presented, calling for the ratification of the treaty, trusting that "the honor of the British government and the nobility of its honorable people would not want for Iraq to be overburdened or its aspirations to be denied."[71] This resolution was passed by a vote of 37 to 24, with 8 abstentions, and the treaty was ratified just before midnight.

Although a quorum was present, the absence of thirty-two members and the fashion in which the attending members were dragged out in the middle of the night gave much ammunition to the nationalists, who opposed the treaty, and increased the resentment of the Iraqis against the British and their own government. Ultimately, there was no illusion anywhere that a free and fair deal could be made between an occupied people and the occupying power. Not bothered by this "minor" question of legitimacy, the British ran with the treaty to the League of Nations, which approved, on 27 September 1924, the British recommendations for the upcoming years.[72]

CONCLUSION

THE BRITISH INVASION OF IRAQ WAS CONducted not only in the World War I context of fighting the Ottomans, but also as part of Britain's large-scale imperialist effort to secure resources, especially Persian oil, and the routes to India. To win over the sympathy of the Iraqi population, the British explained their invasion as hostility to the Ottomans that would result in the liberation of the oppressed Arabs, who would enjoy the friendship of Great Britain and ultimately gain control over their country for the first time since the Mongol invasion of Baghdad in 1258.

It is clear, however, that the British were not candid regarding their motives. Iraq was deemed too important to be given to its Arab population, which the British considered incapable of self-rule. After six years of heavy-handed military administration, the Iraqi population realized that Britain's promises had not been made in good faith, a fact acknowledged by some British officials, as this study has shown. The question then was how to deal with the foreign presence in the country.

Two attitudes dominated the Iraqi scene. On the one hand, some Iraqi notables stood to benefit from the British through contracts, employment, and bribes. Although they had enjoyed a somewhat similar situation under the Ottomans, they fared much better when the British were in control of the country. This group of Iraqis favored the continued presence of British forces and administration, spending much of their energy trying to convince their fellow Iraqis of the virtues of Great Britain. On the other side were Iraqis who stood at the receiving end of British brutality, excessive taxation, and denial of nationalist aspirations. They simply failed to see any benefit from a foreign presence that grew more hostile and insatiable by the day.

But the economic and nationalist factors were not all that triggered the 1920 Revolution. Any effort to explain the revolution as a direct result of heavy-handed policies or excessive taxation or even nationalist aspirations can be only partially true. Furthermore, these claims are problematic because they are often made for the purpose of dismissing the Iraqi Revolution by insinuating that resistance to the British occupation was merely a matter of self-interest on the part of the tribes. This explanation is often coupled with the playing down of any nationalist awareness in the Middle Euphrates, as if nationalism were the only legitimate cause for revolution, not to mention the elitism involved in asserting that nationalism was a monopoly of the urban professionals.

The facts lead in the opposite direction. Restricting nationalist awareness to the cities of Baghdad, Mosul, and Baṣra is not supported by the evidence. Most of the so-called nationalists in these urban centers had changed their colors and allegiances so many times that a chameleon would appear modest in comparison. They were in the service of the Ottoman administration before losing their employment and prestige to the army of foreign professionals who came from Great Britain, India, and Egypt in 1918. During this period, Iraqis of all sects and ethnic groups occupied 3.5 percent of all important positions, and they were completely absent from certain political, administrative, and financial departments. Also, not one Arab was appointed political officer, and among the ninety assistant political officers, only four were Iraqis.[1] The vast majority of these "nationalists" did not raise their voices in support of nationalism after the arrival of Fayṣal and their ensuing appointment to excellent political and administrative positions. Indeed, they became, almost to a man, either openly pro-British or tolerant of the pro-British direction of the new Iraqi government. On the other hand, the revolutionary crowd, which is often dismissed as a self-interested horde, continued to fight the pro-British policies of Fayṣal and his government by using the little clout they were allowed in the parliament and from the outside, enduring exile, property confiscation, and myriad other punishments and exclusionary policies.

The emphasis on Baghdad's professionals unjustifiably deprives the professionals of the Middle Euphrates of much-deserved credit. Najaf in particular, as well as Karbalā', had constituted a cultural and religious center of knowledge for more than a thousand years. The prevalence of the city's religious aspect often diverts attention from the fact that it was one of the most important cities in literature and other intellectual activities. If it was not intellectually superior to Baghdad in 1920, Najaf was certainly not inferior. More relevant to the intellectual framework of the 1920 Revolution than the Baghdadis were Najaf thinkers such as the Shabībi brothers, the Kamāl al-Dīn family, the Ṣāfi family, the Jawāhiri family, and other educated figures from the Middle Euphrates such as Sayyid Hādi Zwain, ʿAbd al-Ḥamīd Zāhid, and many others. In his memoir of the time immediately before the revolution, Muḥammad Ali Kamāl al-Dīn, a Najafi intellectual and political leader, lists the names of sixty prominent intellectuals from the Middle Euphrates who took part in "disseminating the ideas of the nationalist movement." Their main goal, he wrote, was to explain to their community the idea of "the freedom those peoples who were detached from the Ottoman Empire to choose the type of political regime and the government they desire."[2]

Also, the history of revolutions, especially those involving agrarian societies, reveals that unfair taxation is at the heart of every revolution. The same can be said for heavy-handed policies and blatant oppression. No matter how great or little a role these factors play, alongside the nationalist factor, they cannot be used as bases to minimize the revolutionary credentials of a movement like the one that took place in 1920 Iraq.

This study was meant to demonstrate that the British could not have done anything to avoid the revolution. Their oppression and arbitrary policies only hastened its beginning, which became inevitable the moment it was evident to the Iraqis that the British would not be faithful in their promise to grant Iraq full independence. For the Iraqi Revolution to materialize, the British need not have done anything more than prolong the occupation. The style of the occupation was completely irrelevant to how its fate was going to be shaped. It was, however, very relevant to the timing. British officers and civilian officials underestimated the consequences of their mistreatment of Iraqis, especially those in the tribal areas, whose uncompromising tradition placed honor and dignity well above life and property. British triumph over the cities, whose vulnerabilities to siege and military assault gave them no chance of successful resistance, encouraged them to extend their oppression to the rest of the country, a fatal mistake for which they paid dearly.

The revolution did not achieve its military goals, but it ultimately achieved its political goals, in winning Iraq's independence and the founding of an Iraqi state. What was not intended, however, was the composition of the state that came into being. Under the auspices of British colonial-cum-mandate authority, modern Iraq received a government of minority rule monopolized by former Ottoman officers, and the Iraqi throne was given to a foreigner who held most of his subjects in contempt. In the words of a British observer, "There is an artificial kingdom ruled by an unpopular King, Fayṣal, and a doubtful ministry, without the confidence of the people and dependent on a native population which is either suspicious or apathetic. The King does not really trust us [the British] or his Ministers. The people trust neither King nor Ministers."[3]

This outcome was the result of the British scheme to replace the state the Iraqis hoped to establish after the revolution. The British devised this plot to preserve their interests in Iraq; therefore, it was the only action expected of them. But the leaders of the revolution, who accepted the British-Hashemite plan and granted legitimacy to Fayṣal, share the responsibility for allowing their fellow Iraqis to be defeated twice, once when they lost on the battlefield, and another time when they contributed to the establishment of a state that knew no way to communicate with them except through perpetual terror. To quote the same British observer, describing the politics of Fayṣal's government:

> A British official who is fully conversant with the routine of "government by bomb" said to me: "I think it may surprise people at home to know how generally we have been bombing these people. Mind you, I don't say it is not necessary. There is no other way of making them do as they are told. At the same

> time bombing is becoming almost as common as patrolling a disorderly area with military police. On October 14 there were seven distinct bombing attacks in various districts. Hardly a day has passed without the aeroplanes going to some disaffected district and dropping explosives."[4]

Considering the atrocities that were committed during Fayṣal's reign and his general contempt for his Iraqi subjects, the unwavering loyalty he received from the leaders of the Middle Euphrates, including those who disagreed more often than agreed with him, remains a mystery. It is beyond the scope of this study to psychoanalyze these men, but some exploration is in order here. In spite of his willingness to authorize aggressive policies, Fayṣal maintained an image of a reasonable man who was always willing to negotiate and compromise. He also managed, whenever possible, to blame most of the atrocities on others, Iraqi or British. When this plan did not work, he appealed to the Iraqis' sense of patriotism, citing the necessities of appeasing the British until Iraq got what it wanted from them. Some examples of this conduct were presented in this book. Additionally, Fayṣal made sure that certain leaders remained out of harm's way, or when certain harm was coming in their direction, he personally handled the problem. The shaykhs and sayyids of the Middle Euphrates were particularly included in this circle.[5]

Additionally, it is evident that the Shīʿa leaders of the Middle Euphrates became increasingly convinced that Fayṣal was the lesser of two evils, one whose departure would leave them at the mercy, or lack thereof, of the new elite in government and the anti-Shīʿa British officials. The best evidence we can find about the declared reason for their support of the Hashemite throne is presented in the personal notes of Sayyid Muḥsin Abu Ṭabīkh:

> I must explain my position toward the Hashemite throne in Iraq, for my insistence on its continuity stems from my belief that the safety of Iraq and its stability depend on the throne's safety. What worry me always are the prospects of regime change and the opening of the gate wide for internal conflict. Then we would lose all of what was accomplished, and the Iraqis would fall victim to regimes that may be imposed on us

> from the outside, without any connection between them and our religion and traditions.[6]

The Hashemite throne became, for the Shīʿa leaders, the devil they knew. Practically, it was a middle-of-the-road outcome between the government they desired and the feared ambitions of the former Ottoman officers, who ended up dominating the powerful positions in Iraq and were ready to take the country into the abyss. One might find much validity in Sayyid Muḥsin Abu Ṭabīkh's fears when considering the fate of the country after the collapse of the Hashemite throne and the events of the republican era.

Instead of engaging in conflict and destructive politics, the Middle Euphrates accepted the Hashemite regime, which allowed its population some leeway to press its demands and, occasionally, engage in coercive resistance to the government. Meanwhile, this acquiescence led to the gradual erosion of Shīʿa rights and the continued encroachment on their space, politically, economically, and socially, including the outrageous tampering with their dearest source of pride: the revolutionary legacy. The 1920 Revolution was nationalized to become the common property of everyone in Iraq, not only those who missed the chance to participate in it, but also those who missed no chance to denounce it.

The combat element of the 1920 Revolution began as a local affair in the predominantly Shīʿa-populated Middle Euphrates. Most of its participants were rural and tribal people, and with the exception of the holy cities of Najaf and Karbalāʾ, no significant urban participation was recorded. Indeed, the elite in the major cities, particularly in Baghdad and Baṣra, criticized the revolution's leaders and accused them of being unpatriotic rebels or simply ignorant tools in the hands of foreign powers. Yet after the passage of time, the revolution came to be considered a noteworthy chapter in the history of Iraq. All Iraqis, regardless of their past attitudes, strived to claim it as their own—even if they had to tamper with history to do so.

The competition for credit among the various Iraqi factions led to distortions about what had taken place in 1920. On the one hand, the combatants saw the revolution only as a period of fighting against the British. Hence, they did not consider those who had not taken part in the fighting to be contributors to, or participants in, the revolution.

This view was, and to a certain extent still is, prevalent throughout the Middle Euphrates. The words of Farīq Mizhir Āl Farʿōn are representative of this exclusivist opinion: "We say nothing but the pure truth when we declare that the Iraqi Revolution involved no role whatsoever for the residents of Baghdad. They did not start it or even think about it. Yes, some men in Baghdad denounced it." He does, however, acknowledge Baghdadi support through peaceful demonstrations, one of which saw the death of a man he identifies as Ḥasan al-Najjār.[7]

On the other side, there was an elitist attitude in Baghdad that dismissed the people of the Middle Euphrates completely as far as intellectual gifts are concerned, considering Baghdad the brain and the Middle Euphrates the center of ignorance. Here is how Ali al-Bāzirgān puts it: "If we stipulate that the revolution was a result of the people's awareness of the promises of autonomy and independence given by the Allies, then it is natural that Baghdadis and the urban centers were more important than the countryside, that is, the tribes, because of the spread of education in the former and the ignorance in the latter. For the educated person becomes aware of his confiscated rights before the ignorant (*al-jāhil*)."[8] Like Āl Farʿōn, al-Bāzirgān asserts his entitlement to his own facts. The Middle Euphrates, with Najaf and Karbalāʾ as its central nerve, was not inferior to Baghdad in education or intellectual attainment.

Also, a review of the state of mass education in Baghdad in 1920 would reveal that his statement about "the spread of education" in the city is completely out of place. "To judge by the results, the [Ottoman education] system was a 'whited sepulcher.' The schools were rarely as numerous nor as well attended as government statistics indicated; the teachers possessed little learning and even less moral character. Arabic was little stressed as a language."[9] The British did not do much to improve these conditions until September 1918, when Major H. E. Bowman was appointed the first director of education; twenty primary schools were established by year's end. Syrian and Egyptian teachers had to be brought in because of the lack of trained elementary school teachers.[10] As far as secondary schools, there was only one in Baghdad, which graduated students after the tenth grade.[11] Unless merely living in Baghdad somehow made one automatically educated, al-Bāzirgān's statement remains completely unsubstantiated.

These disputants, notwithstanding their audacity, spoke about the revolution with authority. Oftentimes, their disagreements in presenting events and representing their roles, as opposed to the roles of others, can be attributed to their interpretations of the course of the revolution and the value they placed on each form of participation. For the intellectuals of Baghdad, history is made by the ideas that mobilize the masses, which, otherwise, would remain unmoved and lacking initiative. On the other side, the people of the Middle Euphrates saw their historic confrontation with the British as a series of battles that changed the course of the entire British enterprise in Iraq. They could not help but see the revolution as a process shaped mainly by blood and gunpowder rather than abstract theories.

The most inappropriate rendition of the revolution's history, however, was concocted by a third party that was not part of either the theoretical or the practical aspect of events. Whether it was the sharīfians, who were not in the country while the revolution was in progress, or the later Iraqi governments, their "magnanimity" in attributing manufactured credit to personalities and regions that had taken no part in the revolution was nothing short of a historical atrocity. One can only reiterate the words of Eric Davis: "State-sponsored history writing and cultural production complement the state's use of violence."[12]

This book is an attempt to shed light on the revolution's history by presenting the viewpoint of those who took part in the revolution, most of which has not been sufficiently incorporated by other works, because of either inaccessibility or lack of awareness about the materials. When read in light of the British and official Iraqi accounts, the memoirs of the revolution's leaders provide a closer glimpse of this often-misrepresented episode in Iraqi history. They articulated their motives, goals, and feelings about the revolution at the time of its occurrence and in hindsight. They also provided an account of the events to which they were eyewitnesses; these events have often been presented in the existing literature on the authority of speculating British officials and other secondary sources.

However analyzed, the 1920 Revolution was a genuine attempt by the Iraqis to attain their freedom from an oppressive occupation. According to the records, the farmers and landlords fought more ethically than their opponents—officers and politicians—who held high degrees from world-class universities and military institutions. The

Iraqis' treatment of prisoners, as certified by British authorities, was more ethical than the British treatment of Iraqis, and their good-faith adherence to the terms of agreements was superior as well, often to the detriment of their prospects of victory.

Not only the fruits of the 1920 Revolution were stolen from the Middle Euphrates, whose population was marginalized for the next eighty years, but the revolution itself also was misappropriated. Successive Iraqi governments assigned partial or total credit for the revolution to personalities and groups whose participation was subsequent, accidental, or nonexistent. Like all seminal events in every people's history, this tampering with the narrative of a formative revolution is to be expected from politicians, parties, and groups gasping for political legitimacy. The role of the historian is to verify these narratives and, as much as possible, reverse the damage of such tampering or complete the story by supplying the narrative with significant pieces previously omitted or distorted. This book restores facts and sheds light on many events that, when highlighted, shatter many long-displayed historical fallacies.

Although the main goal of the book is to examine the 1920 Revolution and provide as accurate a narrative as possible about its events and participants, it was necessary to provide a context for the revolution's causes and results. Therefore, the book includes a good deal of discussion of the social and political conditions that existed before the revolution, as well as a detailed narrative about the British occupation in the Middle Euphrates. This narrative helps solve the controversy about the causes and motivations of the revolution and puts to rest, hopefully forever, the claim that Iraqis revolted merely because they could not tolerate the taxes and the inconveniences of law and order introduced by the British administration.

Similarly, extending the discussion into the period that followed the revolution illustrates the nature of the social and political struggle among various Iraqi groups, a struggle that shaped the future of the country and left a legacy that still casts its heavy shadows on Iraq. The spirit of cooperation between the Shīʿa and the Sunnis was soon replaced by animosity at the encouragement of the British and in the quest to accumulate political gains. This book shows that the founding of the Iraqi state was a process full of mistrust and manipulation. The desired result was to found a state that would be friendly to British

Chp. 6 #3

interests and vulnerable to their continued meddling. This goal was attained by the imposition of leaders who took no part in the revolution and others who held solidly pro-British positions. Leaders of the revolution were either banished from the political process or relegated to marginal roles.

The monopoly of the sharīfians on the officer class and on sensitive state positions ensured that every possible obstacle was placed in the way of meaningful participation by the Shīʿa in decision making and in shaping the fate of the state. As a result, Shīʿa notables gave up their quest to advocate for the interests of their constituents and, instead, developed shared class interests with the ruling Sunnis. Their access to coveted positions came with the expectation that they would accept them as individuals and not as representatives of Shīʿa collective interests. Therefore, the Shīʿa presence in parliament and in executive positions did not result in the making, or executing, of laws favoring the Shīʿa majority.

In the postrevolution atmosphere, two conditions came into being and continued to coexist for decades: a state of peace and harmony among ordinary Iraqis of all backgrounds, who intermarried, formed business partnerships, accepted one another as friends and neighbors, and struggled to form a sense of national cohesion; and concurrently, a state of conflict and discord among affluent political and social leaders, whose interests collided as they failed to share power and the country's abundant resources, not to mention the symbolism of Iraq's identity and its geopolitical alliances.

The root problem of the modern Iraqi state was, obviously, British-imposed rule of a Sunni minority on the Shīʿa majority—a political formula sustained over the decades by oppression and periodic violence. The Iraqi military was used against the Iraqi people to guarantee this arbitrary political arrangement and subdue dissidents during the reign of every regime throughout the twentieth century.

Finally, it must be noted that the 1920 Revolution is not the only episode in Iraqi history plagued by false narratives. In fact, Iraq's entire historical narrative needs to be revisited. This book is a step in that direction.

Notes

INTRODUCTION

1. Main, *Iraq: From Mandate to Independence,* 76.

2. Wardi, *Lamaḥāt,* 4:127. Unless otherwise noted, all translations are mine.

3. Wardi, *Lamaḥāt,* 4:128. A *mujtahid* in the Shīʿa scholarly ranking is someone who can independently provide original solutions to religious questions and is authorized to issue binding fatwas (religious decrees). He is also referred to as an ayatollah.

4. Ibid., 4:163 ff. Sayyid Mahdi al-Ḥaydari exhibited exceptional courage by keeping his tent in the crossfire between the tribes and the British force. It seems that he assumed command after the Ottoman general was injured and taken to Baghdad for medical treatment.

5. Ibid., 4:145 ff. Another reason for the loss of the battle was the delay in engaging the British. After his injury during the Rōṭa battle, Sulayman ʿAskari took a long time to recover, and the Ottomans refused to appoint a replacement. By the time he was ready to return to the battle, many tribal fighters had already left their positions and returned home.

6. Yūsuf Karkūsh, *Tarīkh al-Ḥilla,* 1:196; Wardi, *Lamaḥāt,* 4:306–310. This act seems to fit a pattern of punishment used by the Ottomans then, including the infamous transfer of Armenians during which many of them perished on the way to their final destination.

7. Jubūri, *Wathāʾiq al-Thawra al-ʿIrāqiyya al-Kubrā,* 2:15. Shaykh Maṭar was a religious scholar from Nāṣiriyya. He led the tribes of Khafāja and Izairij against the British and remained fighting for a whole year. He was among

fourteen men who were denied pardon after the occupation of Baghdad. After the intercession of the representative of Iran's government, Ḥusayn al-Shahbandar, he was finally granted a pardon by the political officer in Nāṣiriyya on 27 March 1917.

8. Najaf was divided into four major quarters at the time: ʿImara, Ḥwaish, Braq, and Mishraq, which were led by ʿAṭayya Abu Gilal, Mahdi Sayyid Salman, Kadhim Ṣubbi, and Saʿad Ḥāj Rāḍi, respectively. Najaf and Karbalāʾ are holy cities for the Shīʿa because they host the shrines of the first and third imams.

9. Wardi, *Lamaḥāt,* 4:199–207. The only exception was Dīwāniyya, which remained loyal to the Ottomans during that period.

10. Selim I, also known as "the Stern" (Yavuz), was the first Ottoman sultan to assume the title of caliph. He expanded the empire to include the Levant, Egypt, and the two holy cities of Mecca and Medina.

11. Wardi, *Lamaḥāt,* 1:45–46. Selim I was retaliating for a similar atrocity committed after the Safavid conquest of Iraq in AD 1508. They massacred numerous Sunnis and desecrated the tomb of the founder of the Ḥanafi school of Muslim jurisprudence, Abu Ḥanīfa, in Baghdad.

12. See S. Ṭuʿma, *Turāth Karbalāʾ,* 376.

13. ʿUthman b. ʿAbdullah b. Bishr, *ʿUnwān al-Majd fi Tārīkh Najd,* 121–122; see also Algar, *Wahhabism,* 24–25.

14. For full details on the Versailles peace settlement and the Anglo-French tactics, see the following: Tillman, *Anglo-American Relations at the Peace Conference*; Levin, *Wilson at the Peace Conference*; Lederer, *Versailles Settlement*; Kleine-Ahlbrandt, *Burden of Victory*; and Sharp, *Versailles Settlement.*

15. Nazmi, *Al-Judhūr al-Siyāsiyya,* 364–365.

16. Wardi, *Lamaḥāt,* vol. 5, pt. 2, 112–120.

17. Ḥamawi, *Muʿjam al-Buldan,* 4:93–95, 3:272–275. Ḥamawi uses the name "Ḥadithat al-Mosul" for the northern part of Iraq. This he describes in volume two as "a little town east of the Tigris near the Upper Zab [River]," which is the same location as today's Mosul. This city, according to Yaqūt, was established by Hirthimah al-Bariqi during the caliphate of Omar b. al-Khaṭṭāb (d. AD 644), who made it a residence for the Arabs.

18. See the famous speech of Iraq's governor, al-Ḥajjāj b. Yūsuf al-Thaqafi (d. AD 714), addressing the people of Iraq (A. Safwat, *Jamharat Khuṭab al-Arab,* 2:274–277). Even before al-Ḥajjāj, the fourth caliph, Ali b. Abi Ṭālib (d. AD 661), used the term in his argument against al-Zubayr, his opponent in the Battle of the Camel. He said to him: "You knew me in Hijāz and denied this knowledge in Iraq; what has changed?" See Ali b. Abi Ṭālib, *Nahj al-Balāgha,* 99.

19. Foster, *Making of Modern Iraq*, 2.

20. Maḥbūba, *Maḍi al-Najaf wa Haḍiruha*, 1:354.

21. A. Ḥasani, *Al-Thawra al-ʿIraqiyya al-Kubrā*, 48. The nature and activities of *al-ʿAhd* will be discussed in detail in Chapter 5.

22. Lyell, *The Ins and Outs of Mesopotamia*, 189 ff.

23. The word "*intifāḍa*" has acquired a more significant meaning in the context of Palestinian struggle for an independent state, which is beyond the scope of this book. The meaning of *intifāḍa* in Iraqi parlance refers to events much smaller and more limited than the events of 1920. The magnitude of the Palestinian *intifāḍa* is perhaps the reason for calling the Iraqi uprising of 1991 an *intifāḍa*. Otherwise it would have been called a *thawra*, according to the Iraqi classification of such events.

24. In my conversations with elderly Iraqis, including my ninety-year-old father, they speak lucidly and consistently about different Iraqi political events with different terms. They refer to "*thawrat al-ʿIshrīn*" when speaking about the 1920 Revolution; "*inqilāb Bakr Ṣidqi*" for the military coup led by General Ṣidqi in 1936; "*ḥarakat Rashīd ʿĀli*" or "*daggat Rashīd ʿĀli*" for the May 1941 coup led by the civilian politician Rashīd ʿĀli and four colonels ("*dagga*" in spoken Iraqi means an immoral or embarrassing act); but "*thawrat 58*" or "*thawrat ʿAbd al-Karim Qasim*" for the toppling of the monarchy in 1958.

25. Farʿōn, *Al-Ḥaqāʾiq al-Nāṣiʿa*, 597.

26. See Marr, *Modern History of Iraq*, 23; Tripp, *History of Iraq*, 40; Nakash, *Shiʿis of Iraq*, 66; Stansfield, *Iraq*, 40; Sluglett, *Britain in Iraq*, 34–35; Batatu, *Old Social Classes*, 166, 175; Davis, *Memories of State*, 48–49.

27. G. Atiyyah, *Iraq, 1908–1921*, 307.

28. Skocpol, *States and Social Revolutions*, 4.

29. Ibid.

30. Marr, *Modern History of Iraq*, 24.

31. Ireland, *Iraq: Political Development*, 274.

32. War Cabinet dispatch, 29 March 1917; for a full statement of the policy, see Ireland, *Iraq: Political Development*, 96–97.

33. Quoted in Wardi, *Lamaḥāt*, vol. 6, pt. 1, 9–10.

34. Bell, *Civil Administration of Mesopotamia*, 142.

35. King Fayṣal I (b. 1885), the son of Sharīf Ḥusayn of Mecca, started his career as an officer in the Ottoman military. In 1916, he switched sides and fought against the Ottomans in alliance with the British, leading his father's forces in what was known as the Arab Revolt. He established an independent government in Syria in 1918, and after his unfruitful participation in the Paris Peace Conference, he became the king of Syria for a brief period in 1920. Ex-

pelled from Syria by the French, he was briefly exiled in Europe, and then recruited by the British to be Iraq's first king. He was enthroned on 23 August 1921.

36. In addition to the Sunni prime minister, there was one Jewish minister; all other ministries with portfolio went to Sunnis (see Wardi, *Lamaḥāt*, vol. 6, pt. 1, 20–31). On 22 February 1921, four months after the formation of the government, the Shīʿa were given the Ministry of Health and Education.

37. Bell to her father, 7 July 1921, in *Letters*. Unless otherwise indicated, all of Bell's letters are found at the Gertrude Bell Archive hosted online by the Newcastle University Library (www.gerty.ncl.ac.uk/index.php).

38. See Abu Ṭabīkh, *Mudhakkirāt*, 111–112, and Haldane, *Insurrection in Mesopotamia*, 76.

39. Wilson, *Loyalties, 1917–1920*, 282.

40. Haldane, *Insurrection in Mesopotamia*, 24–25.

41. Ibid., 155.

42. The description is by Wilson in his book *Mesopotamia, 1917–1920* (the second volume of *Loyalties*), which was published after Haldane's book. But Wilson refers to the description of Haldane's decision as "disgraceful" as being made, and shared by many, during the time of the revolution, indicating that this dispute predated the publication of their books.

43. Bell to her parents, 10 October 1920.

44. James S. Mann, *An Administrator in the Making*, 292.

CHAPTER 1

1. Longrigg, *Iraq, 1900 to 1950*, 122.

2. On the politically motivated manipulation of memory in twentieth-century Iraq, see Davis, *Memories of State*.

3. While well intended, this legislation was a failure. With no banks to lend money to poor peasants and no government subsidies, a large number of new landowners abandoned their land and moved to the cities to become day laborers. For the social consequences of the law, see Baali, "Agrarian Reform in Iraq."

4. It seems that even some of the "informed" suffer from this problem. In his otherwise excellent study (an MA thesis) of British propaganda in Iraq, Hādi Ṭuʿma writes that Henry Foster was mistaken when he situated the Rāranjiyya battle in the Najaf region. He then claims that it took place in Rumaitha. Indeed, Foster got it right by placing the battle in the "Ḥilla-Kūfa area"; see H. Ṭuʿma, "Al-Iḥtilāl al-Biriṭāni wa al-Ṣaḥāfa al-ʿIrāqiyya," 376, and Foster, *Making of Modern Iraq*, 82.

5. Wardi, *Lamaḥat*, vol. 5, pt. 2, 192–193.

6. Against all advice and requests from his fellow revolution leaders and other prominent personalities, he refrained from writing his own memoirs until the last years of his life, almost forty years after the revolution. Among those who asked him to write his memoirs were Fayṣal and Prime Minister Nūri al-Saʿīd; see Abu Ṭabīkh, *Mudhakkirāt*, 17–19.

7. Abu Ṭabīkh, *Mudhakkirāt*, 175. The statement was made in response to a letter from the Iraqi historian Jaʿfar al-Khalīli to Abu Ṭabīkh, asking his opinion about a new book on the revolution by the aforementioned al-Farʿōn, *The Plain Facts*.

8. Ireland, *Iraq: Political Development*, 266.

9. Ibid., 270.

10. Ibid., 271.

11. Ibid., 273.

12. Ibid., 275.

13. Ibid., 274.

14. Ibid., 273.

15. Glubb, *Arabian Adventures*, 28–29.

16. Ibid., 29.

17. Ibid.

18. Batatu, *Old Social Classes*, 23.

19. Ibid., 119.

20. Ibid.

21. Marr, *Modern History of Iraq*, 32.

22. See, for example, Abu Ṭabīkh, *Mudhakkirāt*, 177–179.

23. Marr, *Modern History of Iraq*, 33.

24. Ibid.

25. Nakash, *Shīʿis of Iraq*, 67.

26. Tripp, *History of Iraq*, 40.

27. Ibid., 43.

28. Ibid., 44.

29. Dodge, *Inventing Iraq*, x.

30. Ibid., 8. Ireland cites several Western scholars who share the Iraqi belief about the revolution; see Ireland, *Iraq: Political Development*, 274n1.

31. Dodge, *Inventing Iraq*, 8.

32. Ibid., 135.

33. Ibid., 9.

34. Davis, *Memories of State*, 48.

35. Ibid.

36. Ibid., 49.

37. The film was released under two titles: *Clash of Loyalties* in English,

and *Al-Mas'ala al-Kubrā* (The Great Question) in Arabic, hence the reference to the "Great Question" in the poem.

38. Al-Tikrīti draws his last name from Saddam's hometown, Tikrīt.

39. Mājid Shākir, "The Great Question: When Reasons Are Revealed, Wondering Disappears," *Al-Ṣabāḥ*, 10 April 2010. I still remember the disappointment of al-Baṣīr's grandson, Ḥaydar, who was my classmate at the University of Mosul, after we watched the film when it was shown one winter night on Iraqi television.

40. ʿAlawchi and Ḥijjiyya, *Al-Shaykh Ḍāri Āl Maḥmūd*, 127 (emphasis added).

41. Yaphe, "Arab Revolt in Iraq of 1920," 310.

42. Farʿōn, *Al-Ḥaqāʾiq al-Nāṣiʿa*, 6.

43. Ibid., 118–119. The speech is quoted in full in chapter 6 of this volume.

44. Ibid., 139.

45. Abu Ṭabīkh, *Mudhakkirāt*, 175–176; see also, Khalīli, *ʿAlā Hāmish al-Thawra al-ʿIraqiyya al-Kubrā*, 7–9.

46. Yāsiri, *Al-Buṭūla fi Thawrat al-ʿIshrīn*, 259 ff. There is also a refutation from ʿAbd al-Karim al-Jazāʾiri, considering this position beneath the status of Sayyid Nūr al-Yāsiri.

47. Khalīli, *ʿAlā Hāmish al-Thawra al-ʿIraqiyya al-Kubrā*, 126. This important work appeared first as a series of articles in al-Khalīli's paper, *Al-Hātif*—hence, the lack of details. Al-Khalīli missed the opportunity of ending the controversy when he republished his account as a book, which could use some details.

48. Ibid., 5.

49. Ibid., 34–35; see also, Farʿōn, *Al-Ḥaqāʾiq al-Nāṣiʿa*, 7. Interestingly, al-Farʿōn states in his introduction that he "antagonized history" by not saying enough about his own people (8).

50. Khalīli, *ʿAlā Hāmish al-Thawra al-ʿIraqiyya al-Kubrā*, 59.

51. Ibid., 63.

52. Ibid., 78–79, 88–89.

53. Ibid., 88–89; see also, Farʿōn, *Al-Ḥaqāʾiq al-Nāṣiʿa*, 234, 240. In the footnote to the letter, al-Farʿōn states unequivocally: "The person entrusted to handle the prisoners' affairs was the late Sertīb Mizhir Āl Farʿōn" (234).

54. Published in *Al-Furat*, issue no. 5, 2 Muḥarram 1339 (15 September 1920); see also, Farʿōn, *Al-Ḥaqāʾiq al-Nāṣiʿa*, 365–366.

55. Yāsiri, *Al-Buṭūla fi Thawrat al-ʿIshrīn*, 212–213. Ali Al-Bāzirgān also disputed the story, stating that Sertīb Āl Farʿōn, who had vision problems, could not have handled the prisoners. Bāzirgān stated that the letter was sent to Raʾūf Shlāsh, Muḥsin's brother (*Al-Waqāʾiʿ al-Ḥaqīqiyya*, 166).

56. Khalīli, *ʿAlā Hāmish al-Thawra al-ʿIraqiyya al-Kubrā*, 150–151.

57. Bāzirgān, *Al-Waqā'i' al-Ḥaqīqiyya*; see, for example, 15–18.

58. Ibid., 15–16.

59. Ibid., 277–278.

60. Ibid., 346.

61. Ibid., 3.

62. Ibid., 36–37. The *'iqāl* is part of the male headgear in Iraqi tribal fashion.

63. In a well-known dispute, Sāṭi' al-Hīṣri caused the firing of Muḥammad Mahdi al-Jawāhiri, the greatest twentieth-century Iraqi poet, from a meager job as an elementary school teacher, accusing al-Jawāhiri of being an Iranian. Al-Hīṣri opened education jobs in Iraq to Syrians and other Arabs while opposing the hiring of Shī'a teachers.

64. Ahmad Kadhim, "The 1920 Revolution Monument: An Historical Landmark in Najaf," *Burāthā News*, 8 September 2009.

65. Al-Sumeria News Service: www.alsumarianews.com/ar/6/6487/news-details-Iraq%20culture%20news.html (in Arabic; accessed 16 May 2010). It is not clear what the word "redesign" means. There is a plan to build a monument smaller in size than the one being removed. There is also the possibility of adding details that were not allowed during the Ba'th era. Also possible is the intention to allow the artist the choice of improving on the work he did three decades ago, when he was young and less experienced.

66. Nadhem, "Sīmya' al-Najaf," 145–146.

67. Dodge, *Inventing Iraq*, ix–x.

68. Press release, 30 June 2009, National Media Center, Republic of Iraq.

CHAPTER 2

1. The Anglo-French Declaration, signed on 7 November 1918, states in part: "France and Great Britain agreed to encourage and assist the establishment of indigenous governments and administrations in Syria and Mesopotamia, which have already been liberated by the Allies, and in countries whose liberation they are endeavouring to effect, and to recognize the latter as soon as they shall be effectively established. Far from wishing to impose any particular institution on these lands, they have no other care but to assure by their support and effective aid the normal working of the governments and administrations which they shall have adopted of their free will"; see Ireland, *Iraq: Political Development*, 460.

2. Kamāl al-Dīn, *Thawrat al-'Ishrīn*, 181–186.

3. Many copies of this document are available, including a copy in the published memoirs of Abu Ṭabīkh. The text cited here was included in Ire-

land, *Iraq: Political Development*, 457. Hulaku was the Mongol leader who attacked and destroyed Baghdad in 1258.

4. Ibid., 99.

5. Bell to her parents, 10 October 1920. Bell's dislike for Maude dates back to her early days in Baghdad. On 15 November 1917, she wrote to her father: "Sir S. M. [Stanley Maude] though most polite, is a dull dog and that's the truth." A week later, after his death, when the general manners required kind words, her remembrance of him in a letter to her mother was mixed: "General Maude . . . was essentially a soldier; he had no knowledge of statecraft and regarded it as wholly unnecessary. He was self confident, and with good reason for he was so careful of details that he left no margin for failure. He depended on himself alone, no one had his confidence, and at this moment not one of his staff knows what were his future plans. If we had been in the midst of an active offensive, or still more if we had been hard pressed by the Turks, it might have gone very hard with us."

6. Mann, *Administrator in the Making*, 278.

7. Ibid., 292.

8. Ibid.

9. Bell to her mother, 1 January 1920.

10. For the full proclamation, see *The King of Hedjaz and Arab Independence*, 7–8; the work is attributed to Ḥusayn, Sharīf of Mecca, though there is no author or editor listed on the title page. The reference he makes to the violation of fasting concerns extending the same permission to soldiers in noncombat areas as in combat areas to break their fasting during wartime.

11. A. Ḥasani, *Al-Thawra al-ʿIraqiyya al-Kubrā*, 78; see also Baṣīr, *Tārīkh al-Qaḍiyya al-ʿIrāqiyya*, 44–48. Baṣīr notes that British planes dropped on Iraqi regions a large number of copies of Sharīf Ḥusayn's proclamation, and that British administrators distributed copies of the anonymous *Thawrat al-ʿArab* among the tribal shaykhs, urban notables, and educated youth (45).

12. There were many instances of correspondence between the Iraqis and the Hashemite family, including the authorization of Fayṣal to carry the demands of Iraqis at international conferences. Also, there were direct letters between Mujtahid M. Taqi al-Shīrāzi and Sharīf Ḥusayn; see Jubūri, *Wathāʾiq al-Thawra al-ʿIrāqiyya al-Kubrā*, 2:242–264, 2:307–316.

13. Al-Shabībi recalled his observations in a letter to Farīq Mizhir al-Farʿōn; see Farʿōn, *Al-Ḥaqāʾiq al-Nāṣiʿa*, 568–576.

14. Abu Ṭabīkh, *Mudhakkirāt*, 178.

15. Ibid.

16. ʿAbdullah is the founder of the Hashemite Kingdom of Jordan.

17. See Naẓmi, *Al-Judhūr al-Siyāsiyya*, 178–179. Ali Jawdat al-Ayyūbi,

Taḥsīn Ali, Bakr Ṣidqi, and Yūsuf al-ʿAzzāwi were also former Ottoman officers of Iraqi origin; see Wardi, *Lamaḥāt*, vol. 5, pt. 2, 157–159.

18. Farʿōn, *Al-Ḥaqāʾiq al-Nāṣiʿa*, 283. They incorrectly called him Sayyid Mirza al-Kāshāni.

19. Ibid., 285.

20. For details concerning the 1919 Revolution in Egypt, see Rāfiʿi, *Thawrat 1919*.

21. Baṣīr, *Tārīkh al-Qaḍiyya al-ʿIrāqiyya*, 46.

22. Kamāl al-Dīn, *Mudhakkirāt*, 25.

23. *Al-Furat*, issue 2, 14 August 1920.

24. Muhammad Ali Kamāl al-Dīn, *Al-Thawra al-ʿIraqiyya al-Kubrā*, 218–231.

25. Wardi, *Lamaḥāt*, 3:116. He notes that al-Yazdi was the only important mujtahid who refused to sign the fatwa issued in Najaf in support of constitutionalism.

26. For details on the Iranian constitutional revolution, see Abrahamian, *History of Modern Iran*, 34 ff.; Wardi, *Lamaḥāt*, 3:103 ff.; and Foran, "Iran's Populist Alliance."

27. Wardi, *Lamaḥāt*, 3:117.

28. Wardi, *Lamaḥāt*, vol. 5, pt. 1, 67 ff.; Ireland, *Iraq: Political Development*, 166–175.

29. Quoted in Foster, *Making of Modern Iraq*, 37–38. See also Wardi, *Lamaḥāt*, 4:113.

30. Wardi, *Lamaḥāt*, 4:113.

31. Foster, *Making of Modern Iraq*, 37. To note the exact time line: Ottoman cruisers attacked Russian ports on the Black Sea on 29 October 1914; Russia responded with a declaration of war on 2 November 1914; and three days later, France and Britain made a similar declaration.

32. Wilson, *Loyalties, 1914–1917*, 10–11.

33. Ibid., 99. According to Wilson, there were 277 British officers, 204 Indian officers, 2,592 British rank and file, 6,988 Indian rank and file, and 3,248 noncombatant Indians. During the siege, 1,025 were killed, 721 died of disease, 2,500 were wounded, and 72 were missing.

34. Ibid., 173.

35. Marr, *Modern History of Iraq*, 31.

36. Foster, *Making of Modern Iraq*, 127.

37. If history occasionally repeats itself, then today's Iraq is one such occasion. The progeny of early twentieth-century Iraqis are well represented in the current government, having attained their status by similar means.

38. Bonham Carter, "Report on the Administration of Justice for the Year

1920," in *Iraq: Administration Reports 1914–1932*, 6:441–448. Carter was the adviser to the Iraqi Ministry of Justice in 1920.

39. Ibid., 6:441.

40. Ireland, *Iraq: Political Development*, 75.

41. Mann to Lady Mary Murray Mann, 24 March 1920; in Mann, *Administrator in the Making*, 236–237. In 1920, more than 96 percent of the political officers who governed the Iraqi provinces and more than 87 percent of the administrative staff were less than forty years old. This includes the acting civil commissioner, Arnold Wilson, who was thirty-five; see Ireland, *Iraq: Political Development*, 252.

42. Bell to her father, 16 August 1920; in Burgoyne, *Gertrude Bell*, 2:157. Bell was the British high commissioner's secretary. She played a primary role in shaping every institution in the Iraqi government and in deciding the fate of every politician in Iraq between 1920 and her death in Baghdad in July 1926.

43. Wardi, *Lamaḥat*, vol. 5, pt. 2, 70; see also ʿAlawchi and Ḥijjiyya, *Al-Shaykh Ḍāri Āl Maḥmūd*, 124, 127.

44. Burgoyne, *Gertrude Bell*, 2:163.

45. Ibid., 2:237.

46. Wardi, *Lamaḥat*, vol. 5, pt. 1, 28.

47. These small Middle Euphrates towns are situated near Najaf Province, in central Iraq.

48. Shaykh Wahaiyd Āl ʿAbbūd al-ʿĪsāwi, telephone interview by the author, 9 February 2010. Currently residing in Kūfa, Iraq, Shaykh Wahaiyd told me that he still owns the rifle his father used to kill Captain Mann and has it on display in his *muḍīf* (guesthouse).

49. In a letter to his mother dated 29 August 1919—a few days after his arrival in the district—he wrote, "I can hardly understand a word at present, but I don't think it will take long to alter that, and of course I shall have an interpreter" (Mann, *Administrator in the Making*, 148).

50. Ibid., 218.

51. Ibid., 233. As a district governor, Mann had the authority to hand down a maximum six-month jail sentence for minor crimes such as small thefts, aggressive behavior, and the like.

52. Mann, *Administrator in the Making*, 157–158.

53. Ibid., 247.

54. Ireland, *Iraq: Political Development*, 95.

55. Mann to his sister, 17 February 1920; in Mann, *Administrator in the Making*, 221.

56. Mann to his father, 13 October 1919; in ibid., 162. Indeed, no religious scholar has ever condoned such practice because it is in clear violation of Islamic tradition.

57. Mann to his father, 1 October 1919; in ibid., 157. Mann to Lady Murray, 12 October 1919; in ibid., 160–161.

58. Mann to Mrs. Cumberbatch, 14 January 1920; in ibid., 202.

59. Mann to his father, 1 October 1919; in ibid., 158. He mistakenly interpreted the building of the dam as a project done in honor of his coming to their district. The letter, however, states that it was done in adherence to his orders.

60. Mann to his father, 17 January 1920; in ibid., 204.

61. Shiblak, *Iraqi Jews*, 56.

62. Mann, *Administrator in the Making*, 238.

63. Burgoyne, *Gertrude Bell*, 2:168–169.

64. Ibid., 2:179.

65. Mann, *Administrator in the Making*, 210–211.

66. Ibid., 169. The statement came in a letter to his mother dated 11 November 1919, two months after his appointment.

67. Elsewhere he misidentifies Imam Ali as "the Prophet of God"; see Mann, *Administrator in the Making*, 202.

68. Mann to his father, 20 November 1919; in ibid., 166–167. The madhīf is a guesthouse where the shaykh meets his tribesmen.

69. Mann to his mother, 22 December 1919; in ibid., 186. Mann to his mother, 9 January 1920; in ibid., 195.

70. Ibid., 181.

71. Mann to his sister, 30 April 1920; in ibid., 253.

72. Ibid., 251.

73. Dr. Ali Abu Ṭabīkh, telephone interview by the author, 20 August 2006.

74. Mann, *Administrator in the Making*, 252.

75. Ibid., 253.

76. Ibid., 277.

77. Ibid., 263.

CHAPTER 3

1. Bell to her father, 12 September 1920; in Burgoyne, *Gertrude Bell*, 2:163. She was referring to Sir Aylmer Haldane, the commander of British forces in Iraq at the time.

2. Glubb, *Arabian Adventures*, 102.

3. Bell to her father, 12 September 1920; in Burgoyne, *Gertrude Bell*, 2:163.

4. Wardi, *Lamaḥat*, vol. 5, pt. 1, 215–217.

5. Abu Ṭabīkh, *Mudhakkirāt*, 111–112.

6. As discussed above, the atrocity at this village was one of the reasons that caused the tribes to participate in a wide-scale revolt in the area. See Haldane, *Insurrection in Mesopotamia*, 76.

7. Yāsiri, *Al-Buṭūla fi Thawrat al-ʿIshrīn*, 174–175.

8. Ireland, *Iraq: Political Development*, 266.

9. Ibid., 267.

10. Haldane, *Insurrection in Mesopotamia*, 72.

11. Ibid.

12. Ibid., 76.

13. Ibid.

14. Ibid.

15. Ibid., 78.

16. Wardi, *Lamaḥat*, vol. 5, pt. 1, 227; Haldane, *Insurrection in Mesopotamia*, 77.

17. Haldane, *Insurrection in Mesopotamia*, 85.

18. Ibid., 88.

19. Ibid., 128.

20. Ireland, *Iraq: Political Development*, 267.

21. Wardi, *Lamaḥat*, vol. 5, pt. 1, 239.

22. Abu Ṭabīkh, *Mudhakkirāt*, 132–135.

23. Ibid., 136; Haldane, *Insurrection in Mesopotamia*, 102; Wilson, *Loyalties, 1917–1920*, 279.

24. Haldane, *Insurrection in Mesopotamia*, 189.

25. Shaykh Wahaiyd Āl ʿAbbūd al-ʿĪsāwi, interview by the author. The Āl ʿĪsā tribe resided in a row of houses along the eastern bank of the Euphrates River opposite the Kūfa city center. This must have made them especially vulnerable to the ship's fire. Shaykh Wahaiyd told me that his father retained the shrapnel fragments in his body: "They remained under his skin. I used to feel them with my fingers."

26. A. Ḥasani, *Al-Thawra al-ʿIraqiyya al-Kubrā*, 151–154. The distance between Ḥilla and Dīwāniyya is about fifty-six miles, but the tribes made it an eleven-day journey for the British by destroying the railroad tracks in many areas. The British spent most of their time fighting and fixing the tracks.

27. Haldane, *Insurrection in Mesopotamia*, 139.

28. A. Ḥasani, *Al-Thawra al-ʿIraqiyya al-Kubrā*, 142–143.

29. Abu Ṭabīkh, *Mudhakkirāt*, 141.

30. Ibid., 152–153.

31. ʿAlawchi and Ḥijjiyya, *Al-Shaykh Ḍāri Āl Maḥmūd*, 123–154.

32. Ibid., 142–143.

33. A. Ḥasani, *Al-Thawra al-ʿIraqiyya al-Kubrā*, 163–164.

34. Haldane, *Insurrection in Mesopotamia*, 105. Another acknowledg-

ment of such services was expressed in a letter by Gertrude Bell to her father (23 August 1920): "We have also had the staunchest adherence from Fahad Beg of the ʿAnizah—the donor of my dogs. He wrote to AT [Wilson] and me last week saying that nothing would make him budge from his firm allegiance. From first to last he has never wavered and has given us all the help he can. He is now near Fallujah. All the Dulaym in that part of the world have stood firm also."

35. A. Ḥasani, *Al-Thawra al-ʿIraqiyya al-Kubrā*, 164.

36. Wardi, *Lamaḥat*, vol. 5, pt. 2, 76. Sayyid ʿAbd al-Mahdi al-Muntafiji is the father of the prominent Iraqi politician ʿĀdil ʿAbd al-Mahdi; Shaykh ʿAbd al-Ḥusayn Maṭar was a respected religious figure and the representative of the mujtahid Shaykh al-Sharīʿa al-Iṣfahāni in Nāṣiriyya; ʿAli al-Dabbūs was a tribal shaykh.

37. Thomas, *Alarms and Excursions in Arabia*, 96.

38. Ibid., 101.

39. Ibid., 102.

40. Ibid., 103–104.

41. A. Ḥasani, *Al-Thawra al-ʿIraqiyya al-Kubrā*, 185; Wardi, *Lamaḥat*, vol. 5, pt. 2, 81.

42. Thomas, *Alarms and Excursions in Arabia*, 110.

43. For examples of these poems, see Wardi, *Lamaḥat*, vol. 5, pt. 2, 85.

44. Haldane, *Insurrection in Mesopotamia*, 296.

45. Thomas, *Alarms and Excursions in Arabia*, 99.

46. Haldane, *Insurrection in Mesopotamia*, 295.

47. Ibid., 152.

48. Ibid., 154.

49. Wilson, *Loyalties, 1917–1920*, 282.

50. Wardi, *Lamaḥat*, vol. 5, pt. 2, 37.

51. Buchanan, *In the Hands of the Arabs*, 49.

52. Haldane, *Insurrection in Mesopotamia*, 157.

53. Baṣīr, *Tārīkh al-Qaḍiyya al-ʿIrāqiyya*, 126.

54. Ibid., 127.

55. Buchanan, *In the Hands of the Arabs*, 229.

56. A. Ḥasani, *Al-Thawra al-ʿIraqiyya al-Kubrā*, 192–193.

57. Ibid., 176. See also Haldane, *Insurrection in Mesopotamia*, 190–191: "That in the end their treatment had been good was evident from their healthy and well-nourished appearance when released." For a similar acknowledgment, see Wilson, *Loyalties, 1917–1920*, 298.

58. Wardi, *Lamaḥat*, vol. 5, pt. 2, 119–120.

59. Haldane, *Insurrection in Mesopotamia*, 178–181.

60. Wardi, *Lamaḥat*, vol. 5, pt. 2, 126–129.

61. Abu Ṭabīkh, *Al-Mabādiʾ wa al-Rijal*, 40–45.

62. Ibid., 46.

63. Abu Ṭabīkh, *Mudhakkirāt*, 181.

64. Ibid., 118.

65. A. Ḥasani, *Al-Thawra al-ʿIraqiyya al-Kubrā*, 109.

66. Abu Ṭabīkh, *Mudhakkirāt*, 128–133.

67. Wardi, *Lamaḥat*, vol. 5, pt. 1, 293–295.

68. Jaʿfar al-Khalīli, quoted in Wardi, *Lamaḥat*, vol. 5, pt. 1, 300.

69. Abu Ṭabīkh, *Mudhakkirāt*, 156–157.

70. Abu Ṭabīkh, *Mudhakkirāt*, 174. A copy of the handwritten note is printed in Yāsiri, *Al-Buṭūla fi Thawrat al-ʿIshrīn*, 261.

71. See, for example, Wardi, *Lamaḥat*, vol. 5, pt. 1, 301. Al-Wardi's account, written in 1977, relied on Taḥsīn al-ʿAskari's *Mudhakkirāti* (My Memoirs), from 1938. It is odd that al-Wardi, who was exceptionally interested in such details, did not comment on these conflicting accounts, although he read and quoted the manuscript of Abu Ṭabīkh's memoirs on many occasions.

72. S. Ṭuʿma, *Karbalāʾ fi Thawrat al-ʿIshrīn*, 68–69.

73. *Al-Istiqlāl*, no. 6, 10 October 1920.

74. Bāzirgān, *Al-Waqāʾiʿ al-Ḥaqīqiyya*, 196.

75. Al-Bāzirgān was a Sunni, and so does not mention taking the flag to the shrines himself or letting anyone do so. Such an act is consistent only with the Shīʿi state of mind, as was the idea of having a group of Sayyids take the flag to the roof of the building.

76. Quoted in Madani, "Muḥsin Abu-Ṭabīkh and the National Movement," 48.

77. After making this argument, I came across a similar contention by Jamil Abu Ṭabīkh, who pointed out that Abu Ṭabīkh's "appointment is considered the first popular decision in the modern political history of Iraq to appoint one of its sons on a land liberated from a continuous foreign occupation since the end of the Abbasid era." See Abu Ṭabīkh, *Mudhakkirāt al-Sayyid Muḥsin Abu Ṭabīkh 1910–1960*, 454.

78. Quoted in A. Ḥasani, *Tārīkh al-Wazārāt*, 1:12.

79. See Gertrude Bell to her father, 7 July 1921.

80. Bāzirgān, *Al-Waqāʾiʿ al-Ḥaqīqiyya*, 197.

81. *Al-Istiqlāl*, no. 6, 10 October 1920.

82. Intelligence Report No. 1, 15 November 1920, in Jarman, *Political Diaries: Iraq*, 1:9. The main title of the report was "Formation of the Provisional Government"—in reference to the formation of al-Naqīb's cabinet.

83. Bāzirgān, *Al-Waqāʾiʿ al-Ḥaqīqiyya*, 196; Abu Ṭabīkh, *Mudhakkirāt*, 157; Farʿōn, *Al-Ḥaqāʾiq al-Nāṣiʿa*, 376. In an opportunistic attempt to gain legiti-

macy, King Fayṣal chose the same date for his coronation, in spite of his policies, which reflected no appreciation of the Shīʿa.

84. Manuscript of Abu Ṭabīkh's memoir, 66; the manuscript is kept in the home of Jamil Abu Ṭabīkh. This is more than a month later than the actual date. The reason must have been an error in the name of the month; he meant to write "October"—both months share the same Arabic name, Tashrīn, but are distinguished by addition of the ordinal "first" (*awwal*) for "October" and "second" (*thāni*) for "November."

85. A. Ḥasani, *Al-Thawra al-ʿIraqiyya al-Kubrā*, 189; and Wardi, *Lamaḥat*, vol. 5, pt. 1, 301.

86. Bāzirgān, *Al-Waqāʾiʿ al-Ḥaqīqiyya*, 196. The date should be 6 October.

87. Farʿōn, *Al-Ḥaqāʾiq al-Nāṣiʾa*, 376–378.

88. Abu Ṭabīkh, *Mudhakkirāt*, 183.

89. Ibid., 181.

90. British officials at the time did not consider the sharīf and his sons more than hired collaborators. In the words of Thomas Lyell, who was a colonial official, "Lawrence was the accredited purse-bearer of the British Treasury to Hussein, Shariff of Mecca . . . We found the cash to help him keep up his kingly estate; and paid him £5,000 a month. For every reason, his kingdom must be at peace, and we therefore paid a further monthly subsidy of, I believe £2,000, by way of a bribe to his neighbor and hereditary enemy, Ibn Saud, Sheikh of the Wahabis. . . . Then, finally, we found kingdoms for his two sons, Fayṣal and Abdullah. The venerable gentleman certainly exacted his pound of flesh" (*The Ins and Outs of Mesopotamia*, 199–200).

91. Ibid., 206.

92. Ibid., 175.

CHAPTER 4

1. Mann, *Administrator in the Making*, 209.

2. R. Buṭṭi, *Al-Ṣaḥāfa fi al-ʿIraq*, 9.

3. Ibid., 15.

4. Ibid., 49.

5. F. Buṭṭi, *Al-Mawsūʿa al-Ṣuḥufiyya al-ʿIraqiyya*, 15.

6. A. Ḥasani, *Tārīkh al-Ṣaḥāfa al-ʿIraqiyya*, 59. Prominent among these publications were *Baghdad* (1908), *Al-Raqīb* (1909), *Bayn al-Nahrayn* (1909), *Al-Riyāḍ* (1910), *Miṣbāḥ al-Sharq* (1910), *Al-Ruṣāfa/al-ṣāʾiqa* (1910/1911), *Lughat al-ʿArab* (1911), *Al-Nahḍa* (1913), *Ṣadā al-Islam* (1915), *Al-Īqāẓ* (Mosul 1909), *Al-Tahdhīb* (Baṣra 1909), and *Al-Dustūr* (Baṣra 1912). For a complete

list and brief descriptions, see F. Buṭṭi, *Al-Mawsūʿa al-Ṣuḥufiyya al-ʿIraqiyya,* 29–40.

7. Quoted by Fāʾiq Buṭṭi, "Taṭawwur al-Maqāl fi al-Ṣaḥāfa al-ʿIraqiyya," in Iraq, Ministry of Information, *Dirāsāt fi al-Ṣaḥāfa al-ʿIraqiyya,* 31.

8. R. Buṭṭi, *Al-Ṣaḥāfa fi al-ʿIraq,* 43.

9. F. Buṭṭi, *Al-Mawsūʿa al-Ṣuḥufiyya al-ʿIraqiyya,* 43–44.

10. British intelligence reports labeled *Al-ʿIraq* and *Al-Sharq* as "moderate nationalist" papers; see Intelligence Report No. 1, 15 November 1920, in Jarman, *Political Diaries: Iraq,* 1:21.

11. Wardi, *Lamaḥat,* 4:370.

12. R. Buṭṭi, *Al-Ṣaḥāfa fi al-ʿIraq,* 46.

13. Wardi, *Lamaḥat,* 4:371.

14. Ibid., vol. 5, pt. 1, 95.

15. F. Buṭṭi, *Al-Mawsūʿa al-Ṣuḥufiyya al-ʿIraqiyya,* 47–48.

16. Ibid., 46.

17. The letter, dated 20 August 1920, was printed in a pamphlet and dropped from the sky over the major cities; it appeared in *Al-ʿIraq* on 31 August.

18. F. Buṭṭi, *Al-Mawsūʿa al-Ṣuḥufiyya al-ʿIraqiyya,* 46.

19. R. Buṭṭi, *Al-Ṣaḥāfa fi al-ʿIraq,* 53.

20. There are some conflicting accounts of Afnan's origin. He is said to be a Palestinian who attended the American University in Beirut and then Cambridge University, acquiring an advanced degree in political economics; see R. Buṭṭi, *Al-Ṣaḥāfa fi al-ʿIraq,* 53. Buṭṭi wrote also that Afnan was "Palestinian by birth, Persian by origin, although he is a Ḥasani Sayyid [a descendant of the second Shīʿa imam] and the nephew of the head of the [Bahāʾi sect]" (63).

21. Wardi, *Lamaḥat,* vol. 5, pt. 2, 23–24.

22. Quoted in ibid., 110. It is worth noting that the paper uses the demeaning word "*ḥarakah*" to refer to the revolution.

23. Bell to her parents, 10 October 1920; in Burgoyne, *Gertrude Bell,* 2:172 (emphasis added).

24. For Afnan's relationship with Bell, see ibid., 189, 199, 201, 239, 276.

25. Wardi, *Lamaḥat,* vol. 5, pt. 2, 23–26.

26. Haldane, *Insurrection in Mesopotamia,* 190–191.

27. Ibid., 75–76.

28. Kamāl al-Dīn, *Thawrat al-ʿIshrīn,* 306.

29. Wilson, *Loyalties, 1917–1920,* 299.

30. The third paper was called the *Fallāh* in British intelligence reports, which is a mistake; see also Kamāl al-Dīn, *Mudhakkirāt,* 25.

31. A. Ḥusayn and A. Ḥusayn, *Ṣaḥāfat Thawrat al-ʿIshrīn,* 33.

32. Farʿōn, *Al-Ḥaqāʾiq al-Nāṣiʿa,* 211–212.

33. *Al-Istiqlāl,* no. 1, 1 October 1920.

34. Ibid., no. 6, 10 October 1920. The paper refers to Wilson as "the outgoing ruler" because he had already been replaced by Sir Percy Cox. Wilson left Baghdad on 24 September 1920. He went to Baṣra first to welcome Cox, who arrived on October 1 to assume the duties of British high commissioner.

35. *Al-Istiqlāl*, no. 3, 5 October 1920.

36. Far'ōn, *Al-Ḥaqā'iq al-Nāṣi'a*, 212–213.

37. R. Buṭṭi, *Al-Ṣaḥāfa fi al-'Iraq*, 58–60.

38. Ibid., 59.

39. *Al-Istiqlāl*, no. 1, 1 October 1920.

40. Unlike *Al-Istiqlāl*, which included both the AD and AH dates, *Al-Furat* used the Islamic calendar only, dating its first issue on Saturday, 21 Dhu al-Qa'dah 1338 (7 August 1920). 'Abd al-Razzāq al-Ḥasani incorrectly dates the first issue on 1 Muḥarram, which was the date of the last issue (*Al-Thawra al-'Iraqiyya al-Kubrā*, 191).

41. *Al-Furat*, no. 1, 7 August 1920 (Saturday).

42. The fourth issue was published on 13 Dhu al-Ḥijjah 1338 (28 August 1920), and the fifth followed on 2 Muḥarram 1339 (15 September 1920).

43. The letter was also published in the pro-British paper *Al-'Iraq* eleven days later.

44. Far'ōn, *Al-Ḥaqā'iq al-Nāṣi'a*, 356.

45. *Al-Furat*, no. 5, 2 Muḥarram 1339 (15 September 1920). See also, Far'ōn, *Al-Ḥaqā'iq al-Nāṣi'a*, 365–366.

46. Lyell, *Ins and Outs of Mesopotamia*, 208.

47. *Al-Furat*, no. 2, 14 August 1920.

48. Ibid., no. 4, 28 August 1920.

49. Lyell, *The Ins and Outs of Mesopotamia*, 189.

50. *Sunday Times* (London), 20 September 1920, quoted in Nazmi, *Al-Judhūr al-Siyāsiyya*, 214.

51. Telegram no. 10973, Political, Baghdad, to the Secretary of State for India, 10 December 1918; quoted in Ireland, *Iraq: Political Development*, 139.

52. Jarman, *Political Diaries: Iraq*, 1:22–23.

53. Indeed, some Iraqis who wanted to enhance their pro-British credentials did exactly the same thing. Examples of this trend include the speech of Muzaḥim al-Pāchachi at the welcome party for Sir Percy Cox, quoted in full in Wilson, *Loyalties, 1917–1920*, 321; see also the open letter by Ṭālib al-Naqīb to an anonymous supporter, published in *Al-Sharq* and quoted in part in this chapter.

54. Jubūri, *Wathā'iq al-Thawra al-'Irāqiyya al-Kubrā*, 4:11.

55. Wardi, *Lamaḥat*, vol. 5, pt. 1, 324.

56. For the day-to-day difficulties, see Haldane, *Insurrection in Mesopotamia*, 91 ff.

57. A. Ḥasani, *Tārīkh al-Ṣaḥāfa al-ʿIrāqiyya,* 80–82; see also his book on the revolution, *Al-Thawra al-ʿIrāqiyya al-Kubrā,* 210–212.

CHAPTER 5

1. Some sources refer to al-ʿAhd and Ḥaras al-Istiqlāl, which will be discussed shortly, as a party (*ḥizb*). I use the word "association" because it is closer to the Arabic word *jamʿiyya,* which both groups used to describe themselves.

2. Wardi, *Lamaḥat,* 4:228. Although the ʿAhd Association was founded by the Egyptian ʿAzīz Ali al-Miṣri, most of its initial members were Iraqi officers in the Ottoman military. However, ʿAbd al-Razzāq al-Ḥasani claims that al-Miṣri belonged to an Iraqi family by origin, which makes al-ʿAhd a purely Iraqi movement (*Al-Thawra al-ʿIrāqiyya al-Kubrā,* 47).

3. Naẓmi, *Al-Juddhūr al-Siyāsiyya,* 142–143.

4. A. Ḥasani, *Al-Thawra al-ʿIrāqiyya al-Kubrā,* 47–48.

5. On these changes in loyalty, see Naẓmi, *Al-Juddhūr al-Siyāsiyya,* 145–155.

6. A. Ḥasani, *Al-Thawra al-ʿIrāqiyya al-Kubrā,* 50–51.

7. Wardi, *Lamaḥat,* vol. 5, pt. 1, 130–140.

8. Ibid., 139.

9. Ibid., 150–151.

10. Ibid., 161. See also Haldane, *Insurrection in Mesopotamia,* 39–44. He reported that the airplane was indeed shot down, having "received a shot through the petrol-tank, and had to make a forced landing about one mile from the town, narrowly escaping capture."

11. Wardi, *Lamaḥat,* vol. 5, pt. 1, 164–165. In his 18 June letter to al-ʿAhd, al-Madfaʿi blamed the defeat in Mosul mainly on the Shammar, al-Jubūr, and other tribes, who "unfortunately were occupied by the sale of spoils or taking them to their homes."

12. A. Ḥasani, *Al-Thawra al-ʿIrāqiyya al-Kubrā,* 57.

13. Baṣīr, *Tārīkh al-Qaḍiyya al-ʿIrāqiyya,* 81.

14. Wardi, *Lamaḥat,* vol. 5, pt. 1, 94. It seems that al-Madfaʿi was heading a fact-finding delegation, which concluded that the accusations by al-ʿAhd were false. He then tried to reconcile the two groups; see A. Ḥasani, *Al-Thawra al-ʿIrāqiyya al-Kubrā,* 59.

15. Farʿōn, *Al-Ḥaqāʾiq al-Nāṣiʿa,* 120. He attributes the augmentation of their roles mainly to ʿAbd al-Razzāq al-Ḥasani.

16. Darrāji, *Jaʿfar Abu al-Timman,* 81–83.

17. ʿAbd al-Razzāq al-Ḥasani, *al-Thawra al-ʿIrāqiyya al-Kubrā,* 58.

18. Nafisi, *Dawr al-Shī῾a fi taṭawwur al-῾Iraq al-Siyāsi al-Ḥadīth*, 167. Al-Ālūsi was a religious scholar and a journalist. He was an admirer of the Wahhābi concept of Islam. His writings include some commentaries on the works of Muḥammad b. Abd al-Wahhab, the founder of Wahhabism, and several anti-Shī῾a polemics. The *naqīb* of Baghdad is an honorary office held by a descendant of the Prophet's family who represents his fellow *ashrāf* (descendants of the Prophet) before the state.

19. Sayyid Hādi Zwain, a resident of Abu Ṣkhair, between Najaf and Dīwāniyya, was the link between Najaf and Baghdad in the months leading up to the revolution. He was punished harshly for his participation in the revolution: his house was demolished, his land was confiscated, and he was imprisoned. He died in 1927; see Far῾ōn, *Al-Ḥaqā᾽iq al-Nāṣi῾a*, 101. According to Sayyid Muḥsin Abu Ṭabīkh, Sayyid Hādi Zwain was one of the major financiers of the revolution (*Mudhakkirāt*, 154).

20. Far῾ōn, *Al-Ḥaqā᾽iq al-Nāṣi῾a*, 136–138.

21. Williamson, *History of Shammar*, 48. The author mentions also some earlier waves of migration by the Shammar to the region, but they were not as significant and did not result in a permanent establishment of Shammar territory in Iraq.

22. Glubb, *Arabian Adventures*, 57.

23. Wardi, *Lamaḥat*, 4:357.

24. Rayḥani, *Fayṣal al-Awwal*, 92.

25. Wilson, *Loyalties, 1914–1917*, 236.

26. The Middle Euphrates region includes the cities of Ḥilla, Karbalā᾽, Najaf, Dīwāniyya, and Samāwa.

27. Wilson, *Loyalties, 1914–1917*, 236.

28. Khudheyer Kadhim, telephone interview by the author, 2 November 2006. My late father—age ninety—experienced Fatla tribal life in the Hindiyya region from the 1920s to the 1970s.

29. Jamil Abu Ṭabīkh, interview by the author, London, 22 September 2006.

30. See Sami al-Qaysi, *Yāsīn al-Hāshimi wa Dawruhu fi al-Siyāsa al-῾Iraqiyya*, 125.

31. "Ḥawza" is a term that refers to the Shī῾a traditional school of religious studies. People of any level of education may enter this school and pursue religious studies at their own pace. Those who fulfill the scholarly requirements and exhibit the right aptitude ultimately attain the level of mujtahid, which means that they are able to practice independent reasoning in answering religious questions and possess the authority to guide Shī῾a laypersons. The most distinguished Ḥawza schools at the present time are in Najaf, Iraq, and Qom, Iran.

32. Ali Abu Ṭabīkh, *Shajarat al-Sādah Al Abu Ṭabīkh* (The Genealogy of the Abu Ṭabīkh Sayyids), 3; Jawad Hibat al-Dīn al-Shahrastāni, *Nasab al-Sayyid Muḥsin al-Sayyid Ḥasan Abu Ṭabīkh* (www.almawsem.net/turath/index2.htm). Unless indicated otherwise, all translations are mine.

33. Ibid.

34. Batatu, *The Old Social Classes*, 156.

35. Abu Ṭabīkh, *Mudhakkirāt*, 37n.

36. Dr. Ali Abu Ṭabīkh, telephone interview by the author, 20 August 2006; Jamil Abu Ṭabīkh interview.

37. Ali Abu Ṭabīkh interview. Lack of education in rural areas remained common for a long time after Abu Ṭabīkh's sons started going to school. Before free and mandatory education was instituted in Iraq in 1974, only a small number of farmers sent their children to school; doing so meant extra expense, which was considerable, as well as losing a worker on the farm.

38. Batatu, *The Old Social Classes*, 194.

39. Jamil Abu Ṭabīkh interview.

40. Abu Ṭabīkh, *Mudhakkirāt*, 283. The donor was Khanjar al-Ḥamad, the shaykh of the famous al-Khazāʿil tribe. His father, Ḥamad al-Ḥmoud, was one of the most renowned shaykhs in the Middle Euphrates. Ḥamad also gave a sizable chunk of land to the Abu Ṭabīkh family in 1783.

41. Ibid., 35–38.

42. Wardi, *Lamaḥat*, vol. 5, pt. 1, 244.

43. Abu Ṭabīkh, *Mudhakkirāt*, 154.

44. Bāzirgān, *al-Waqaʾiʿ al-Ḥaqīqiyya*, 173.

45. Abu Ṭabīkh, *Mudhakkirāt*, 163. "Ṭābu" refers to Ṭābu Abu Ṭabīkh, a town north of Samāwa, which is named after the family because it owned the entire territory.

46. Wardi, *Lamaḥat*, vol. 5, part 2, 115–116.

47. Jarman, *Political Diaries: Iraq*, 1:10.

48. Bell to her father, 12 December 1920: "I've had a letter from Abdul Wahid, our host at the luncheon party in the Shamiyah, now in prison at Hillah, asking me not to forget him and I've sent him a friendly message. I think he'll get off lightly for we are not punishing people for leading the rebellion but only for specific proved incitement to murder Govt officers, British or Arab, or destroy Govt property."

49. The one person who trusted the British, ʿOmran al-Ḥaj Saʿdūn, was arrested and thrown in the Ḥilla jail.

50. Abu Ṭabīkh, *Mudhakkirāt*, 202–203.

51. Wardi, *Lamaḥat*, vol. 5, part 1, 343.

52. Abdullah Fayyad, *The Iraqi Revolution of 1920*, p. 27.

53. Hashimi and Edwards, "Land Reform in Iraq," 71.

54. Fayyad, *Al-Thawra al-ʿIraqiyya al-Kubra Sanat 1920*, 27.

55. W. ʿAṭiyya, *Tārīkh al-Dīwāniyya*, 61–62.

56. Abu Ṭabīkh, *Mudhakkirāt*, 38.

57. W. ʿAṭiyya, *Tārīkh al-Dīwāniyya*, 169.

58. Ibid., 166. This story was narrated by Sayyid Nūr al-Yāsiri, whose relations with ʿAbd al-Wāḥid were not very good; see Yāsiri, *Al-Buṭūla fi Thawrat al-ʿIshrīn*, 58. Also, Ali al-Wardi notes some historical inaccuracies in this story: the British official, Jeffries, did not assume his position in Dīwāniyya until the end of the revolution, while ʿAbd al-Wāḥid's hatred for the British predated that, obviously (*Lamaḥat*, vol. 5, pt. 1, 121–122).

59. Abu Ṭabīkh, *Mudhakkirāt*, 279–284.

60. On the difference between the attitudes of Jewish notables and those of the Jewish community at large toward the British, see Shiblak, *Iraqi Jews*, 55 ff.

61. Abu Ṭabīkh, *Mudhakkirāt*, 282.

62. See, for example, Batatu, *Old Social Classes*, 194: "Muḥsin [Abu Ṭabīkh] was a master of intrigue and a man of many faces." He interpreted the difference of opinions between the two brothers, which led them to take different political positions, as a conspiracy to always have "one foot in the right camp." In my interviews with Sayyid Muḥsin Abu Ṭabīkh's son Jamil, he made many references to several genuine political disagreements between his father and uncle that led me to rule out Batatu's analysis of the Abu Ṭabīkhs from the start. Writing about the dispute between Muḥsin and Jaʿfar Abu Ṭabīkh, al-ʿAṭiyya notes that "their dispute lasted for a long time and the traces of it exist until now [in 1954]" (*Tārīkh al-Dīwāniyya*, 164).

63. Batatu, *Old Social Classes*, 165.

64. Abu Ṭabīkh, *Mudhakkirāt*, 282.

65. Jamil Abu Ṭabīkh interview.

CHAPTER 6

Portions of Chapter 6 were previously published in "Forging a Third Way: Sistani's *marjaʿiyya* between Quietism and *wilāyat al-faqīh*," in *Iraq, Democracy and the Future of the Muslim World*, edited by Ali Paya and John Esposito (New York: Routledge, 2010).

1. Mann, *Administrator in the Making*, 209.

2. Wardi, *Lamaḥat*, vol. 6, pt. 1, 12.

3. Ibid., 9–10.

4. Quoted in Wilson, *Loyalties, 1917–1920*, 321; see also Wardi, *Lamaḥat*, vol. 6, pt. 1, 11–12.

5. See A. Ḥasani, *Tārīkh al-Wazārāt al-Iraqiyya,* 1:204–212. Al-Pāchachi was also criticized in the Baghdad press for sending "an infamous telegram to the India Office asking for the annexing of Iraq to British India"; see Baghdadi, *Baghdad fi al-Ishrīnāt,* 28.

6. Illustrative of this group was the poet Jamīl Ṣidqi al-Zahāwi, who praised the revolution and eulogized those who died in it, but participated in the reception for Cox. He recited a strongly worded poem reproaching the participants in the revolution and praising Cox.

7. Bell to her father, 1 November 1920. The conversation took place at a party given by Bell to bring three new ministers together: ʿAbdul Majīd Shāwi, Sasun Ḥiskail, and Jaʿfar al-ʿAskari. The first was given a ministry without a portfolio, the second was to be the minister of finance, and the last of national defense.

8. Wardi, *Lamaḥat,* vol. 6, pt. 1, 30. Three months after the formation of the cabinet, it was decided to give one ministry—the Ministry of Education and Health—to a Shīʿa. Muhammad Mahdi Baḥr al-ʿUlūm, who had been in the British employ in 1918, accepted the job. See also Wilson, *Loyalties, 1917–1920,* 388.

9. Bell to her father, 7 February 1921.

10. Quoted in Ireland, *Iraq: Political Development,* 140.

11. A. Ḥasani, *Tārīkh al-Wazārāt,* 1:12.

12. Bell to her father, 7 July 1921.

13. A. Ḥasani, *Tārīkh al-Wazārāt,* 1:13.

14. Ibid.

15. Ibid., 16.

16. Ibid., 20.

17. Bell to her father, 3 October 1920.

18. Burgoyne, *Gertrude Bell,* 2:220.

19. The French general Gouraud illustrated the mind-set of his campaign when he immediately went to the tomb of Ṣalāhiddīn (Saladin), kicked it, and said: "We are back Saladin." For details on the Battle of Maysalūn, see Wardi, *Lamaḥat,* vol. 6, pt. 2, 161–163.

20. Quoted in ibid., 210.

21. Ibid., 211.

22. Burgoyne, *Gertrude Bell,* 2:211.

23. Ibid., 220.

24. Abu Ṭabīkh, *Mudhakkirāt,* 211–212.

25. Ibid. In fact, the mandate remained in place until 1932, when the British were theoretically no longer in charge of Iraq, although they ran Iraq by proxy throughout the monarchy era.

26. Wardi, *Lamaḥat,* vol. 5, pt. 2, 153. Al-Wardi misquoted Abu Ṭabīkh's

account, stating that the meeting to verify the mandate rumor was with Sharif Hussein. In Abu Ṭabīkh's *Mudhakkirāt* (211–212), he stated that they met with Fayṣal.

27. Ibid.

28. Abu Ṭabīkh, *Mudhakkirāt*, 215.

29. A. Ḥasani, *Tārīkh al-Wazārāt*, 1:40.

30. Wardi, *Lamaḥat*, vol. 6, pt. 1, 115–116. Al-Wardi reports that the support for Fayṣal came from the Arbil region, which was part of Kirkuk at the time, while rejection came from the city of Kirkuk itself. This might have been due to the influence of Turkomans in Kirkuk, who saw Fayṣal as an enemy of the Ottoman Empire.

31. A. Ḥasani, *Tārīkh al-Wazārāt*, 1:41.

32. Wardi, *Lamaḥat*, vol. 6, pt. 1, 113.

33. Bell to her father, 7 July 1921.

34. This gesture coincided with a strange moment when the British band, knowing no Iraqi national anthem, played the British one, "God Save the King"; see Ireland, *Iraq: Political Development*, 336.

35. King Fayṣal, "A Note Concerning the Political and Social Conditions in Iraq," in A. Hasani, *Tārīkh al-Wazārāt*, 3:288.

36. Ireland, *Iraq: Political Development*, 335.

37. It is doubtful that Iraqis chose Fayṣal freely. In the conversation between Sir Percy Cox and John Philby that led to the latter's dismissal, Philby told his superior that if the British government wanted Fayṣal to be the king of Iraq, then why not appoint him directly instead of insisting on the charade of elections? See Wardi, *Lamaḥat*, vol. 6, pt. 1, 94.

38. King Fayṣal's coronation speech; see A. Ḥasani, *Tārīkh al-Wazārāt*, 3:41–42.

39. Wardi, *Lamaḥat*, vol. 6, pt. 1, 26–27.

40. Ibid.

41. Bell to her father, 4 June 1922.

42. Lyell, *The Ins and Outs of Mesopotamia*, 212 (emphasis in the original).

43. Bell to her father, 6 July 1922.

44. Rayḥāni, *Fayṣal al-Awwal*, 125.

45. Bell to her father, 3 October 1920.

46. Muḥsin Abu Ṭabīkh, *Mudhakkirāt*, 271.

47. Fayṣal, "Political and Social Conditions in Iraq," in A. Ḥasani, *Tārīkh al-Wazārāt*, 3:289. According to ʿAbd al-Razzāq al-Ḥasani, the essay was shared with Fayṣal's inner circle, men such as Jaʿfar al-ʿAskari, Yāsīn al-Hāshimi, Nāji Shawkat, Nuri al-Saʿīd, and Nāji al-Suwaydi—Sunni sharīfian officers with high-ranking governmental posts. In the essay, Fayṣal states that he spoke frankly because only a few were going to read his remarks.

48. Ibid., 288.

49. Ibid.

50. Farʿōn, *Al-Ḥaqāʾiq al-Nāṣiʿa*, 382–383.

51. King Fayṣal suggested that this unit be named after Gertrude Bell, but Jaʿfar al-ʿAskari, the defense minister, suggested the name "Mūsa al-Kadhim."

52. Iraq was entrusted to Britain as a mandate at the San Remo Conference in 1920.

53. Fayṣal, "Political and Social Conditions in Iraq," in A. Ḥasani, *Tārīkh al-Wazārāt*, 3:290.

54. Such a revolution did not materialize until 1991, when the Shīʿa and Kurds revolted against Saddam's regime; the Iraqi military was dispatched to crush both groups.

55. One of those officers was Tawfiq al-Khālidi. Cox nominated him for the Ministry of the Interior, but Fayṣal rejected this nomination, accusing al-Khālidi of loyalty to the Turks, as did Jaʿfar al-ʿAskari, who told Bell that appointing al-Khālidi would be detrimental to everyone's interests; see Wardi, *Lamaḥat*, vol. 6, pt. 1, 123–124.

56. Jarman, *Political Diaries: Iraq*, 2:5.

57. Wardi, *Lamaḥat*, vol. 6, pt. 1, 202.

58. Abu Ṭabīkh, *Mudhakkirāt*, 232.

59. Burgoyne, *Gertrude Bell*, 2:275.

60. Abu Ṭabīkh, *Mudhakkirāt*, 247.

61. Wardi, *Lamaḥat*, vol. 6, pt. 1, 210–211; A. Hasani, *Tārīkh al-Wazārāt*, 1:102–103.

62. A. Ḥasani, *Tārīkh al-Wazārāt*, 1:102–110.

63. It should be noted that in 1923, Turkey was well into the secularization project overseen by Mustafa Kamal (Atatürk).

64. Bell to her father, 12 April 1923.

65. A. Ḥasani, *Tārīkh al-Wazārāt*, 1:116–117. Al-Khāliṣi, an Arab, was born and raised in Iraq; he had no connection with Iran. But like many other mujtahids, he acquired Iranian citizenship in order to avoid persecution in Iraq during the Ottoman era.

66. Wardi, *Lamaḥat*, vol. 6, pt. 1, 251.

67. Ibid., 246–247.

68. Ibid., 261.

69. A. Ḥasani, *Tārīkh al-Wazārāt*, 1:99.

70. Ibid., 160.

71. Ibid., 175.

72. Ibid., 164–175.

CONCLUSION

1. Nazmi, "Roots of the Iraqi Independence Movement," 187.
2. Kamāl al-Dīn, *Thawrat al-ʿIshrīn*, 70–75.
3. Phillips, *Mesopotamia: Inquiry at Baghdad*, 11.
4. Ibid., 59.
5. For instance, the two times Sayyid Muḥsin Abu Ṭabīkh was sent into exile were handled personally by King Fayṣal. This courtesy was not extended to the mujtahids of Iranian nationality, who were humiliated and deported to Iran by the police at the orders of Prime Minister ʿAbd al-Muḥsin al-Saʿdūn, as discussed earlier.
6. Abu Ṭabīkh, *Mudhakkirāt*, 405.
7. Farʿōn, *Al-Ḥaqāʾiq al-Nāṣiʿa*, 118–119. According to Ali al-Bāzirgān, the man is ʿAbd al-Karīm al-Najjār.
8. Bāzirgān, *Al-Waqāʾiʿ al-Ḥaqīqiyya*, 39.
9. Ireland, *Iraq: Political Development*, 125.
10. Ibid., 127–128.
11. Baghdadi, *Baghdad fi al-Ishrīnāt*, 250. One of these was al-Thānawiyya al-Markaziyya, opened officially in 1919–1920. He mentions two schools, the second being al-Thānawiyya al-Sharqiyya, but this one was established in the 1930s.
12. Davis, *Memories of State*, 6.

Bibliography

Abrahamian, Ervand. *A History of Modern Iran*. Cambridge: Cambridge Univ. Press, 2008.

ʿAbṭa, Maḥmūd al-. *Baghdad wa Thawtat al-ʿIshrīn*. Baghdad, 1977.

Abu Ṭabīkh, Ali. *Shajarat al-Sādah Āl Abu Ṭabīkh*. Orange County (California), 2001.

Abu Ṭabīkh, Sayyid Muḥsin. *Al-Mabādiʾ wa al-Rijāl*. Edited by Jamil M. Abu Ṭabīkh. Beirut: al-Muʾassasa al-ʿArabiyya li al-Dirāsāt wa al-Nashr, 2003.

———. *Mudhakkirāt al-Sayyid Muḥsin Abu Ṭabīkh 1910–1960*. Edited by Jamil M. Abu Ṭabīkh. Beirut: al-Muʾassasa al-ʿArabiyya li al-Dirāsāt wa al-Nashr, 2001.

———. *Al-Riḥlah al-Muḥsiniyya*. Edited by Jamil M. Abu Ṭabīkh. Beirut: Dar al-Aḍwaʾ, 1998.

Adhami, Muhammad Muẓaffar al-. *Al-Majlis al-Taʾsīsi al-ʿIraqi*. Vols. 1 and 2. Baghdad, 1989.

Aḥmad, Kamāl Muẓhir. *Ṣafaḥāt min Tārīkh al-ʿIraq al-Muʿāṣir*. Baghdad, 1987.

ʿAkkām, ʿAbd al-Amīr Hādi al-. *Al-Ḥaraka al-Waṭaniyya fi al-ʿIraq, 1921–1933*. Najaf, Iraq, 1975.

ʿAlawchi, ʿAbd al-Ḥamīd al-, and ʿAzīz Jāsim al-Ḥajjiyya. *Al-Shaykh Ḍāri Āl Maḥmūd*. 1968. Reprint, London: Dar al-Ḥikma, 2002.

Algar, Hamid. *Religion and State in Iran, 1785–1906: The Role of the Ulama in the Qajar Period*. Berkeley and Los Angeles: Univ. of California Press, 1980.

———. *Wahhabism: A Critical Essay*. Oneonta, N.Y.: Islamic Publications, 2002.

ʿAli, Taḥsīn. *Mudhakkirāt Taḥsīn ʿAli*. Beirut, al-Muʾassasa al-ʿArabiyya li al-Dirāsāt wa al-Nashr, 2004.

Ali b., Abi Ṭālib. *Nahj al-Balāgha.* Beirūt: Mu'ssasat al-Aʿlami, 1993.

Antonius, George. *The Arab Awakening: The Story of the Arab National Movement.* 1938. Reprint, Beirut, 1955.

Arjomand, Said Amir, ed. *Authority and Political Culture in Shīʿism.* Albany: State Univ. of New York Press, 1988.

ʿAskari, Jaʿfar al-. *Mudhakkirāt Jaʿfar al-ʿAskari.* London: Laam, 1988.

Atiyyah, Ghassan. *Iraq, 1908–1921: A Socio-political Study.* Beirut: Arab Institute for Research and Publishing, 1973.

ʿAṭiyyah, Wadday, al-. *Tārīkh al-Dīwāniyya Qadīman wa Ḥadīthan.* Najaf, Iraq, 1954.

ʿAzzawi, Abbas al-. *ʿAshāʾir al-ʿIraq.* 4 vols. Baghdad, 1947.

Baali, Fuad. "Agrarian Reform in Iraq: Some Socioeconomic Aspects." *American Journal of Economics and Sociology* 28, no. 1 (Jan. 1969): 61–76.

Baghdadi, Abbas. *Baghdad fi al-Ishrīnāt.* Baghdad: Dār al-Shuʾūn al-Thaqāfiyya al-ʿĀmma, 2000.

Bahādili, Muḥammad Bāqir al-. *Al-Sayyid Hibat al-Dīn al-Shahrastāni.* Beirut, 2002.

Baṣīr, Moḥammad Mahdi al-. *Tārīkh al-Qaḍiyya al-ʿIraqiyya.* Vols. 1 and 2. 1924. Reprint, London, 1990.

Baṣri, Mīr. *Aʿlām al-Siyāsa fi al-ʿIraq al-Ḥadīth.* Vols. 1 and 2. London: Dar al-Ḥikma, 2005.

Batatu, Hanna. *The Old Social Classes and the Revolutionary Movements of Iraq.* Princeton, N.J.: Princeton Univ. Press, 1978.

Bāzirgān, Ali al-. *Min Ahādith Baghdad wa Diyala.* Edited by Ḥassān al-Bāzirgān. Baghdad, 2000.

———. *Al-Waqāʾiʿ al-Ḥaqīqiyya fi al-Thawra al-ʿIraqiyya.* Baghdad, 1991.

Bell, Gertrude. *Review of the Civil Administration of Mesopotamia.* London: His Majesty's Stationery Office, 1920.

———. *The Letters of Gertrude Bell.* Vols. 1 and 2. New York: Boni and Liveright, 1927.

———. *The Letters of Gertrude Bell.* London: Penguin, 1953.

Bishr. *ʿUthman b. ʿAbdullah, ʿUnwan al-Majd fi Tarīkh Najd.* Riyadh, n.d.

Black Tab [pseud.]. *On the Road to Kut: A Soldier's Story of the Mesopotamian Campaign.* London: Hutchinson, 1917.

Buchanan, Zetton. *In the Hands of the Arabs.* London: Hodder and Stoughton, n.d. [c. 1921].

Burgoyne, Elizabeth. *Gertrude Bell from Her Personal Papers.* Vols. 1 and 2. London: Benn, 1958.

Buṭṭi, Fāʾiq. *Al-Mawsūʿa al-Ṣuḥufiyya al-ʿIrāqiyya.* Baghdad, 1976.

———. *Ṣaḥāfat al-Aḥzāb wa Tārīkh al-Ḥaraka al-Waṭaniyya.* Baghdad, 1969.

———. *Ṣaḥāfat al-ʿIrāq: Tārīkhuhā wa Kifāḥ Ajyāluhā.* Baghdad, 1968.

Buṭṭi, Rafāʾīl. *Al-Ṣaḥāfa fī al-ʿIrāq*. Cairo, 1955.

Buṭṭi, Sāmi Rafāʾīl, ed. *Ṣaḥāfat al-ʿIrāq*. Baghdad, 1985.

Callwell, C. E. *The Life of Sir Stanley Maude*. London: Constable, 1920.

Catherwood, Christopher. *Churchill's Folly: How Winston Churchill Created Modern Iraq*. New York: Basic Books, 2005.

Cleveland, William. *A History of the Modern Middle East*. 3rd ed. Boulder, Colo.: Westview, 2004.

Cohen, Stewart. *British Policy in Mesopotamia, 1903–1914*. London: Ithaca, 1976.

Darrāji, ʿAbd al-Razzāq al-. *Jaʿfar Abu al-Timman wa Dawruhu fi al-Ḥaraka al-Waṭaniyya fi al-ʿIraq, 1908–1945*. Baghdad, 1980.

Davis, Eric. *Memories of State: Politics, History, and Collective Identity in Modern Iraq*. Berkeley and Los Angeles: Univ. of California Press, 2005.

Dawisha, Adeed. *Arab Nationalism in the Twentieth Century: From Triumph to Despair*. Princeton, N.J.: Princeton Univ. Press, 2005.

Dodge, Toby. *Inventing Iraq: The Failure of Nation Building and a History Denied*. New York: Columbia Univ. Press, 2003.

Egan, Eleanor F. *The War in the Cradle of the World: Mesopotamia*. New York: Harper and Brothers, 1918.

Eppel, Michael. "The Elite, the Effendiyya, and the Growth of Nationalism and Pan-Arabism in Hashemite Iraq, 1921–1958." *International Journal of Middle East Studies 30, no. 2 (May 1998): 227–250.*

Erskine, Mrs. Steuart. *King Fayṣal of ʿIraq*. London: Hutchinson, 1933.

Ewing, William. *From Gallipoli to Baghdad*. London: Hodder and Stoughton, 1917.

Evans, Luther Harris. "The Emancipation of Iraq from the Mandate System." *American Political Science Review* 26, no. 6 (Dec. 1932): 1024–1049.

Farʿōn, Farīq Mizhir al-. *al-Ḥaqāʾiq al-Nāṣiʿa fi al-Thawra al-ʿIraqiyya Sanat 1920 wa Natāʾijuhā*. Baghdad, 1952.

Farouk-Sluglett, Marion, and Peter Sluglett. "The Historiography of Modern Iraq." *American Historical Review* 96, no. 5 (Dec. 1991): 1408–1421.

———. "The Transformation of Land Tenure and Rural Social Structure in Central and Southern Iraq, c. 1870–1958." *International Journal of Middle East Studies* 15, no. 4 (Nov. 1983): 491–505.

Fawzi, Ahmed. *12 Raʾīs Wizāraʾ fi al-ʿAhd al-Malaki*. Baghdad: Dar al-Jahiz, 1984.

Fayḍi, Sulaymān. *Mudhakkirāt Sulaymān Fayḍi*. Beirut, 1974.

Fayyad, ʿAbdullah. *Al-Thawra al-ʿIraqiyya al-Kubra Sanat 1920*. Baghdad: Dar Al-Irshad, 1963.

Fernea, Robert. *Shaykh and Effendi: Changing Patterns of Authority among the El Shabana of Southern Iraq*. Cambridge, Mass.: Harvard Univ. Press, 1970.

Foran, John. "The Strengths and Weaknesses of Iran's Populist Alliance: A Class Analysis of the Constitutional Revolution of 1905–1911." *Theory and Society 20, no. 6 (Dec. 1991): 795–823.*

Foster, Henry. *The Making of Modern Iraq.* 1935. Reprint, New York: Russell and Russell, 1972.

Fromkin, David. *A Peace to End All Peace: The Fall of the Ottoman Empire and the Creation of the Modern Middle East.* New York: Holt, 1989.

Ghareeb, Edmund. *Historical Dictionary of Iraq.* Lanham, Md.: Scarecrow, 2004.

Glubb, John. *Arabian Adventures: Ten Years of Joyful Service.* London: Cassell, 1978.

———. *Britain and the Arabs: A Study of Fifty Years, 1908–1958.* London: Hodder and Stoughton, 1959.

Haddad, Mahmoud. "Iraq before World War I: A Case of Anti-European Arab Ottomanism." In *The Origins of Arab Nationalism,* edited by Rashīd Khalidi, Lisa Anderson, Mohammad Muslih, and Reeva Simon, 120–150. New York: Columbia Univ. Press, 1991.

Haldane, Aylmer. *The Insurrection in Mesopotamia, 1920.* London: Blackwood, 1922.

Ḥamawi, Yaqūt al-. *Muʿjam al-Buldān.* Vols. 2, 3, and 4. Beirut: Dar Ṣadir, n.d.

Ḥasani, ʿAbd al-Razzāq al-. *Tarīkh al-ʿIraq al-Siyāsi al-Ḥadīth.* Beirut, 1975.

———. *Tārīkh al-Ṣaḥāfa al-ʿIraqiyya.* Sidon, Lebanon, 1971.

———. *Al-Thawra al-ʿIraqiyya al-Kubrā.* Sidon, Lebanon, 1952.

———. *Tarīkh al-Wazārāt al-ʿIraqiyya,* vols. 1–10. Sidon, Lebanon, 1935.

Ḥasani, Salim al-. *Dawr ʿUlemāʾ al-Shīʿa fi Muwājahat al-Istiʿmār, 1900–1920.* Beirut: al-Ghadīr, 1995.

Hashimi, Rasool, and Alfred Edwards. "Land Reform in Iraq: Economic and Social Implications." *Land Economics* 37, no. 1 (Feb. 1961): 66–81.

Hewett, John. *Some Impressions of Mesopotamia in 1919.* London: His Majesty's Stationery Office, 1920.

Ḥilli, Abd al-Ḥusayn al-. *Shaykh al-Sharīʿa: Qiyādatuhu fi Al-Thawra al-ʿIraqiyya al-Kubrā 1920 wa Wathāʾquhu al-Siyāsiyya.* Beirut, 2005.

Hurgronje, C. Snouck. *The Revolt in Arabia.* New York: Putnam's Sons, 1917.

Ḥusayn, ʿAbd al-Rasūl, and Ḥusayn, ʿAdnān. *Ṣaḥāfat Thawrat al-ʿIshrīn.* Baghdad, 1970.

Ḥusayn, Fāḍil. *Mushkilat al-Mosul.* Baghdad 1967.

Ḥusayn, Muḥammad Tawfiq. *ʿIndamā Yatūr al-ʿIraq.* Beirut, 1959.

Ḥusayn, Sharīf of Mecca. *The King of Hedjaz and Arab Independence.* London: Hayman, Christy and Lilly, 1917.

Ibrāhīm, Zāhida. *Kashshāf bi al-Jarāʾid wa al-Majallāt al-ʿIrāqiyya.* Baghdad, 1976.

Iraq. Ministry of Information. *Dirāsāt fi al-Ṣaḥāfa al-ʿIraqiyya*. Baghdad, 1972.

Ireland, Philip. *Iraq: A Study in Political Development*. London: Jonathan Cape, 1937.

Jabar, Faleh. *The Shʿite Movement in Iraq*. London: Saqi, 2003.

Jarman, Robert L., ed. *Political Diaries of the Arab World: Iraq*. Vol. 1: *1920–1921*. London: Archive Editions, 1998.

———. *Political Diaries of the Arab World: Iraq*. Vol. 2: *1922–1923*. London: Archive Editions, 1988.

Jubūri, Kāmil Salmān al-. *Al-Najaf al-Ashraf wa Maqtal al-Captain Marshall, 1336/1918*. Beirut, 2005.

———, ed. *Wathāʾiq al-Thawra al-ʿIrāqiyya al-Kubrā wa Muqaddimātihā wa Natāʾijihā, 1914–1923*. Vols. 1–4. Najaf: Dar al-Muʾarrikh al-ʿArabi, 2009.

Kadhim, Abbas. "Forging a Third Way: Sistani's *marjaʿiyya* between Quietism and *wilāyat al-faqīh*." In *Iraq, Democracy, and the Future of the Muslim World*, edited by Ali Paya and John Esposito, 66–80. New York: Routledge, 2010.

———. "The Politics and Theology of Imami Shīʿa in Baghdad in the 5th/11th Century." PhD diss., University of California, Berkeley, 2006.

Kamal al-Din, Muhammad Ali. *Al-Thawra al-ʿIraqiyya al-Kubrā of 1920*. Baghdad, 1971.

———. *Mudhakkirat al-Sayyid Muhammad Ali Kamāl al-Dīn*. Edited by Kāmil Salman al-Juburi. Baghdad, 1986.

———. *Thawrat al-ʿIshrīn fi Dhikrāhā al-Khamsīn*. Baghdad, 1970.

Karkūsh, Yūsuf. *Tarīkh al-Ḥilla*, Vol. 1. Najaf: al-Maṭbaʿa al-Ḥaydariyya, 1965.

Kelidar, Abbas, ed. *The Integration of Modern Iraq*. New York: St. Martin's, 1979.

Khadduri, Majid. *Independent Iraq, 1932–1958: A Study in Iraqi Politics*. Oxford: Oxford Univ. Press, 1960.

Khalidi, Rashīd, Lisa Anderson, Muhammad Muslih, and Reeva S. Simon, eds. *The Origins of Arab Nationalism*. New York: Columbia Univ. Press, 1991.

Khalīli, Jaʿfar al- [Furati, pseud.]. *ʿAlā Hāmish al-Thawra al-ʿIraqiyya al-Kubrā*. Baghdad, 1952.

Khaṭṭab, Rajaʾ Ḥusayn al-. *Taʾsīs al-Jaysh al-Iraqi wa Taṭawwuruhu al-Siyāsi min 1921–1941*. London and Baghdad: Dar Wasit, 1982.

Khuḍayyer, ʿAbd Al-Karīm. *Al-Shaykh Rāyiḥ al-ʿAṭiyya, 1891–1970*. Baghdad, 2005.

Kleine-Ahlbrandt, William L. *The Burden of Victory: France, Britain, and the Enforcement of the Versailles Peace, 1919–1925*. Lanham, Md.: Univ. Press of America, 1995.

Kubaysi, ʿInad Ismaʿīl al-. *Min Aʿlām al-Ḥadātha fi al-Adab wa al-Ṣaḥāfa.* Baghdad, 2007.

Lederer, Ivo. *The Versailles Settlement: Was It Foredoomed to Failure?* Lexington, Mass.: Heath, 1960.

Levin, N. Gordon Jr., ed. *Woodrow Wilson at the Paris Peace Conference.* Lexington, Mass.: Heath, 1972.

Litvak, Meir. *Shiʿi Scholars of Ninteenth-Century Iraq: The Ulama of Najaf and Karbala.* Cambridge: Cambridge Univ. Press, 1998.

Longrigg, Stephen Hemsley. *ʿIraq, 1900 to 1950.* London: Oxford Univ. Press, 1953.

Luizard, Pierre-Jean. *La Question Irakienne.* Paris: Fayard, 2002.

Lyell, Thomas. *The Ins and Outs of Mesopotamia.* London: Philpot, 1923.

Madani, ʿIzz al-Dīn al-. "Muhsin Abu-Ṭabīkh and His Role in the National Movement until 1958." MA thesis, University of Kūfa, Kūfa, Iraq, 1999.

Maḥbūba, Jaʿfar. *Māḍi al-Najaf wa Ḥāḍiruhā.* Vols. 1 and 2. Beirut: Dar al-Aḍwaʾ, 1986.

Main, Ernest. *Iraq: From Mandate to Independence.* London: Kegan Paul, 2004.

Mann, James S. *An Administrator in the Making.* London: Longmans, Green, and Co., 1921.

Marr, Phebe. *The Modern History of Iraq.* Boulder, Colo.: Westview, 1985.

Mathews, Basil. *The Liberator of Mesopotamia.* New York: Paget, 1918.

Muḍaffar, Kadhim al-. *Thawrat al-ʿIraq wa al-Taḥarruriyya.* Vols. 1 and 2. Najaf, 1972.

Nadhem, Hassan. "Sīmyaʾ al-Najaf" (The Semiology of Najaf). In *Al-Makān al-ʿIraqi: Jadal al-kitāba wa al-tajriba,* edited by Luʾay Ḥamza Abbas. Beirut: Dirasat ʿIraqiyya, 2009.

Nafisi, Abdullah al-. *Dawr al-Shīʿa fi taṭawwur al-ʿIraq al-Siyāsi al-Ḥadīth.* Beirut: Dar al-Nahar, 1973.

Nakash, Yitzhak. "The Conversion of Iraq's Tribes to Shiism." *International Journal of Middle East Studies* 26, no. 3 (Aug. 1994): 443–463.

———. *The Shīʿis of Iraq.* Princeton, N.J.: Princeton Univ. Press, 1994.

Nazmi [Nadhmi], Wamidh J. Omar. *Al-Judhūr al-Siyāsiyya wa al-Fikriyya wa al-Ijtimāʿiyya li al-Ḥaraka al-Qawmiyya al-ʿArabiyya (al-Istiqlāliyya) fi al-ʿIraq.* Beirut: Markaz Dirāsātal-Wiḥda al-ʿArabiyya, 1984.

———. "The Political, Intellectual and Social Roots of the Iraqi Independence Movement, 1920." PhD diss., Durham University, 1974.

Palmer, Robert. *Letters from Mesopotamia.* London: Women's Printing Society, n.d. The letters were written in 1915–1916.

Parfit, Joseph. *Marvellous Mesopotamia: The World's Wonderland.* London: Partridge, 1920.

Phillips, Percival. *Mesopotamia: The "Daily Mail" Inquiry at Baghdad*. London, n.d. (text written in 1922).

Pool, David. "From Elite to Class: The Transformation of Iraqi Leadership, 1920–1939." *International Journal of Middle East Studies 12, no. 3 (Nov. 1980)*: 331–350.

Qaṣṣāb, ʿAbd al-Azīz al-. *Mudhakkirāt ʿAbd al-Azīz al-Qaṣṣāb*. Beirut: Al-Muʾassasah al-Arabiyyah li al-Dirasat wa al-Nashr, 2007.

Qaysi, Sami al-. *Yāsīn al-Hāshimi wa Dauruhu fi al-Siyasah al-ʿIraqiyya*. Baghdad: University of Baghdad Press, 1975.

Rāfiʿi, ʿAbd al-Raḥmān al-. *Thawrat 1919*. 4th ed. Cairo, 1978.

Rasheed, Guzine. "Development of Agricultural Land Taxation in Modern Iraq." *Bulletin of the School of Oriental and African Studies* 25, no. 1 (1962): 262–274.

Rāwi, Khālid Ḥabīb al-. *Min Tārīkh al-Ṣaḥāfa al-ʿIrāqiyyah*. Baghdad, 1978.

Rayhani, Amin al-. *Fayṣal al-Awwal*. 1934. Reprint, Beirut, 1958.

Rothman, Stanley. "Barrington More and the Dialectics of Revolution: An Essay Review." *American Political Science Review* 64, no. 1 (Mar. 1970): 61–82.

Rothwell, V. H. "Mesopotamia in British War Aims, 1914–1918." *Historical Journal* 13, no. 2 (June 1970): 273–294.

Rufaiʿi, Muḥsin al-. *Dawr al-Nukhbah al-Qanuniyyah fi Taʾsīs al-Dawlah al-ʿIrāqiyyah, 1908–1932*. Beirut: Dar al-Rafidayn, 2005.

Safwat, Ahmad Zaki. *Jamharat Khuṭab al-ʿArab*. Vol. 2. Cairo, 1933.

Safwat, Najdat Fatḥi. *Khawaṭir wa Aḥadīth fi al-Tarikh*. Baghdad, 1983.

Sharp, Alan. *The Versailles Settlement: Peacemaking in Paris, 1919*. New York: St. Martin's, 1991.

Shiblak, Abbas. *Iraqi Jews: A History of Mass Exodus*. London: Saqi Books, 2005.

Simon, Reeva. *Iraq between the Two World Wars*. New York: Columbia Univ. Press, 1986.

Simon, Reeva, and Eleanor Tejirian, eds. *The Creation of Iraq, 1914–1921*. New York: Columbia Univ. Press, 2004.

Skocpol, Theda. *Social Revolutions in the Modern World*. Cambridge: Cambridge Univ. Press, 1994.

———. *States and Social Revolutions: A Comparative Analysis of France, Russia, and China*. Cambridge: Cambridge Univ. Press, 1979.

Sluglett, Peter. *Britain in Iraq: Contriving King and Country*. New York: Columbia Univ. Press, 2007.

Stansfield, Gareth. *Iraq: People, History, Politics*. Cambridge: Polity, 2007.

Swayne, Martin. *In Mesopotamia*. London: Hodder and Stoughton, 1917.

Ṭāha, Salīm. "Ṣaḥāfat Thawrat al-ʿIshrīn." *Al-Mawrid* 5, no. 4 (1976): pp. 7–16.
Tarbush, Mohammad. *The Role of the Military in Politics: A Case Study of Iraq to 1941*. London: Routledge, 1982.
Thomas, Bertram. *Alarms and Excursions in Arabia*. London: Allen and Unwin, 1931.
Tibi, Bassam. *Arab Nationalism: Between Islam and the Nation-State*. New York: Palgrave, 1997.
Tikrīti, Munīr Bakr al-. *Al-Ṣaḥāfa al-ʿIrāqiyya wa Ittijāhātuhā al-Siyāsiyya wa al-Ijtimāʿiyya wa al-Thaqāfiyya min 1869–1921*. Baghdad, 1969.
Tillman, Seth. *Anglo-American Relations at the Paris Peace Conference of 1919*. Princeton, N.J.: Princeton Univ. Press, 1961.
Townshend, Charles Vere Ferrers. *My Campaign*. Vol. 2. New York: McCann, 1920.
Tripp, Charles. *A History of Iraq*. Cambridge: Cambridge Univ. Press, 2000.
Ṭuʿma, Hādi. *Al-Iḥtilāl al-Birīṭāni wa al-Ṣaḥāfa al-ʿIrāqiyya: Dirāsa fī al-Ḥamla al-Diʿāʾiyya al-Birīṭāniyya*. Baghdad, 1984.
Ṭuʿma, Salman Hadi al-. *Turāth Karbalāʾ*. Beirūt: Muʾssasat al-Aʿlami, 1983.
———. *Karbalāʾ fī Thawrat al-ʿIshrīn*. Beirut, 2000.
United Kingdom. Parliament. *Draft Mandates for Mesopotamia and Palestine as Submitted for the Approval of the League of Nations*. London, 1921.
Vaughan, David. *Give Me Liberty: The Uncompromising Statesmanship of Patrick Henry*. Nashville: Cumberland House Publishing, 1997.
Wardi, Ali al-. *Lamaḥat Ijtimaʿiyya min Tarikh al-ʿIraq al-Ḥadīth*. 6 vols. Baghdad, 1976–1979.
Williamson, John Frederick. *The History of Shammar*. Arabic translation by Mīr Baṣri. London: Dar al-Hikma, 1999.
Wilson, Arnold. *Loyalties*. Vol. 1, *Mesopotamia, 1914–1917: From the Outbreak of War to the Death of General Maude; A Personal and Historical Record*. London: Oxford Univ. Press, 1930.
———. *Loyalties*. Vol. 2, *Mesopotamia, 1917–1920: A Clash of Loyalties; A Personal and Historical Record*. London: Oxford Univ. Press, 1931.
———. *Al-Thawra al- al-ʿIraqiyya*. Translation by Jaʿfar al-Khayyāṭ of chapters from Arnold Wilson, *Loyalties: Mesopotamia, 1917–1920*. Beirut, 1971.
Wright, Quincy. "The Proposed Termination of the Iraq Mandate." *American Journal of International Law* 25, no.3 (July 1931): 436–446.
Yaphe, Judith. "The Arab Revolt in Iraq of 1920." PhD diss., University of Illinois at Urbana-Champaign, 1973.
Yāsiri, ʿAbd al-Shahīd al-. *Al-Buṭūla fī Thawrat al-ʿIshrīn*. Najaf, 1966.
Zeine, Zeine N. *The Struggle for Arab Independence: Western Diplomacy and the Rise and Fall of Faiṣal's Kingdom in Syria*. 2nd ed. Delmar, N.Y.: Caravan, 1977.

Index

132, 136, 138, 140–142, 144, 146, 148–149, 155–157, 159–160, 163–166, 168–169, 171; administration, 5, 7, 10, 13, 15, 20, 26, 30, 50, 52, 66, 69, 80, 84, 87, 92, 99, 120, 131, 137, 161, 169; advisors to Iraqi ministries, 139–140, 147; anti-British Iraqis, 1, 4, 101, 114, 143, 148; bombardment, 6; commanders, 3; Empire, 5, 136; forces (troops), 2–3, 17, 23, 26, 45, 49, 53–54, 72–76, 79, 81, 84–85, 102, 114, 145, 171; government, 10, 30, 53, 61–62, 99–100, 108, 160; invasion, 5, 40, 161; media, 67, 136; occupation, 1, 4–5, 8, 11, 22–23, 25, 27, 29, 32, 34, 46, 54–55, 67, 87, 98–99, 103, 109, 116, 119, 136, 141, 152, 162–163, 169; office in Baghdad, 40; officers, 55–57, 70, 109, 140, 180; plebiscite in Iraq, 51; policy, 10, 28, 106; prisoners, 35, 102–103, 169; pro-British Iraqis, 5, 17, 33, 62, 114, 162, 170, 187. *See also* Great Britain
Buchanan, Captain, 84

Cairo, 47
Cairo Conference, 142–143
Chalabi Zādeh, Muḥammad ʿAli, 98
Christians (Iraqi), 5, 120–121
Churchill, Winston, 142
Clayton, Captain, 101, 139
Coalition Provisional Authority, 41
Committee of Union and Progress (CUP), 47
Coningham, General, 73, 78
Cornwallis, 157
Council of Ministers (Iraqi), 101, 146, 157
Cox, Sir Percy, 11, 45, 53, 85, 92–93, 101, 105, 108, 129, 135–136, 138–141, 146–147, 155–156, 159, 187, 192–194
Crawford, Captain, 82

Dabbūs, ʿAli al-, 81, 183
Daltāwa, 83–84
Daly, Major, 69–71, 77, 88
Damascus, 8, 48–49, 103, 114, 142
Ḍāri, Ḥārith al-, 42
Ḍāri, Muthannā Ḥārith al-, 42
Ḍāri, Shaykh, 21, 25, 31–32, 42, 56–57, 79–81, 104
Dāūd Pasha, 4
Davis, Eric, 1, 9, 30, 168
Dayr al-Zōr, 8, 49, 94, 114–115
Dhi Qar, 120
Ditchburn, Major, 82
Dīwāniyya, 6, 39, 69–71, 74, 76–77, 120–121, 124, 131–133, 172, 182, 189, 191
Diyālā, 42, 83–84, 116
Diyār Bakr, 8
Dobbs, Henry, 159–160
Dodge, Toby, 29–30, 40
Dulaym, 25, 80, 119–120
Ḍuwālim tribe, 70, 120

Egypt, 22, 26, 28, 49–50, 103, 162, 172
Egyptian Revolution of 1919, 49–50
Euphrates, 7–8, 62, 70, 77, 119–120, 182
Exchequer, Imperial, 1

Falāh, 103
Fallūja, 25, 31, 56, 120, 183
Fāo peninsula, 53
Fāṭima, daughter of the Prophet, 122, 126–127

CPSIA information can be obtained at www.ICGtesting.com
Printed in the USA
LVOW07s1201170715

446408LV00002B/145/P

9 780292 756892